Table of Contents

**Your League Receives 125
Free Background Checks Per Year**

Each year, Little League® International provides 125 free background checks.
Information on how to utilize this benefit, as well as how to conduct
background checks, can be found on the Little League website at:

LittleLeague.org/ChildProtectionProgram

Significant Changes for 2019

(NOTE: Unless noted otherwise, these apply to all baseball divisions.)

Significant changes will be identified by a shaded background.

REGULATIONS

Regulation I(c)(9) - Requires leagues to contact the Security Manager at Little League International if a potential volunteer appears on the National Sex Offender Registry prior to the volunteer being appointed. Pages 27-28 and 31-32.

Regulation VI(a), (c) NOTE, (k); 4.12; and Tournament Rule 4 - Provides a threshold for pitchers moving to the catcher position. Pages 44-46, 88, and 136-140.

PLAYING RULES

1.10 - Allows Tee Ball bats to be used in the Coach Pitch/Machine Pitch Divisions. Additionally allows bats meeting the BBCOR standard to be used in the Junior and Intermediate (50-70) Division. Pages 67-68.

2.00 - Defines Dead Ball Territory. Page 73.

3.11 - Intentionally deleted 3.11. Rule 4.13 remains and provides the same guidance concerning number of games per day for teams. Page 82.

8.02(a)(1) - Provides guidance on when the pitcher's hand may come in contact with the pitcher's mouth or lips. Page 113.

8.06 AR - Provides guidance on what is considered a visit to the pitcher. Page 117.

TOURNAMENT RULES AND GUIDELINES

Managers and Coaches - Restricts the number of adults in the dugout or on the field to one manager and one coach when a tournament team has eleven (11) or fewer eligible players are at the game site at the start of a game. Page 125.

Schedules - Revises the date for tournament schedule submission to be two (2) weeks prior to the start of tournament or June 15, whichever is earliest. Page 130.

Tournament Rule 14 - Added a rule concerning tie games after 6 innings for 8- to 10-, 9- to 11-, and Major Division, and 7 innings for Intermediate (50-70) Division, Junior, and Senior League Divisions. Page 145.

APPENDIX

Appendix C - Updates the Communicable Disease Policy to align with the National Federation of State High School Associations. Pages 161-162.

Appendix F - Updates to the Little League Privacy Policy. Pages 165-172.

OPERATING POLICIES

Little League Disability Policy - Little League policy and procedure for considering waivers of rules due to participant's disability. Pages 207-209.

Little League Gender Identity Policy - Little League policy and procedure for considering waivers of rules to accommodate gender identity. Pages 210-212.

A.R.—An Approved Ruling (A.R.) serves to illustrate the application of the regulations and rules. Approved Rulings follow the regulations and rules they amplify and are indicated by a box.

For rule, regulation, and policy updates throughout the year,
visit LittleLeague.org/Rules.

2019 Little League Age Chart

For Baseball Divisions Only

Jan	Feb	Mar	Apr	May	Jun	Jul	Aug	Sep	Oct	Nov	Dec	Age
2015	2015	2015	2015	2015	2015	2015	2015	2014	2014	2014	2014	4
2014	2014	2014	2014	2014	2014	2014	2014	2013	2013	2013	2013	5
2013	2013	2013	2013	2013	2013	2013	2013	2012	2012	2012	2012	6
2012	2012	2012	2012	2012	2012	2012	2012	2011	2011	2011	2011	7
2011	2011	2011	2011	2011	2011	2011	2011	2010	2010	2010	2010	8
2010	2010	2010	2010	2010	2010	2010	2010	2009	2009	2009	2009	9
2009	2009	2009	2009	2009	2009	2009	2009	2008	2008	2008	2008	10
2008	2008	2008	2008	2008	2008	2008	2008	2007	2007	2007	2007	11
2007	2007	2007	2007	2007	2007	2007	2007	2006	2006	2006	2006	12
2006	2006	2006	2006	2006	2006	2006	2006	2005	2005	2005	2005	13
2005	2005	2005	2005	2005	2005	2005	2005	2004	2004	2004	2004	14
2004	2004	2004	2004	2004	2004	2004	2004	2003	2003	2003	2003	15
2003	2003	2003	2003	2003	2003	2003	2003	2002	2002	2002	2002	16

Match month (top line) and box with year of birth. League age indicated at right.

Organizational Structure

LITTLE LEAGUE® BASEBALL Incorporated
P.O. Box 3485, Williamsport, PA 17701
(570) 326-1921

Board of Directors

Hugh E. Tanner, *Chairman*

Steven Johnson, *Chairman-Elect*

John Boyd

Pete Cacheiro

Corinne G.L. Chow

Janice Christensen

Jenice Condie

Chris Drury

Dr. Davie Jane Gilmour

Eng. Antonio J. Gonzalez

Tim Hughes

Sally John

Stephen D. Keener

Dennis Lewin

Ken Liesegang

Jon D. Litner

Dr. Daniel R. Lueders

Jonathan Mariner

Michael Mussina

JoJo Rinebold

Roy Romaya

Dwayne Tuggle

Shannon Walker

Travis Young, Sr.

Officers

Hugh E. Tanner
Chairman

David Houseknecht
*Senior Vice President Administration
and Chief Financial Officer*

Steven Johnson
Chairman-Elect

Patrick W. Wilson
*Senior Vice President and
Chief Program Operations Officer*

Stephen D. Keener
President and Chief Executive Officer

Dan Kirby
Vice President of Risk Management

Elizabeth DiLullo Brown
*Senior Vice President
and Chief Marketing Officer*

Melissa L. Singer
Vice President and Treasurer

Karl Eckweiler
*Senior Vice President
and Chief Legal Officer*

Lance Van Auken
*Vice President and Executive Director
of the Little League Museum*

Joseph W. Losch
Corporate Secretary

Rules Committee

Patrick W. Wilson, *Chairman*

Nicholas Caringi

Jenice Condie

Janice Christensen

Stephen D. Keener

Michael Mussina

Roy Romaya

Sara Thompson

Dwayne Tuggle

Daniel Velte

Charter Committee

Patrick W. Wilson, *Chairman and Secretary*

Nicholas L. Caringi

Demiko Ervin

Jamie Joy

Stephen D. Keener

Daniel P. Kirby

Sam Ranck

Brent Stahlnecker

Sara Thompson

Daniel Velte

Little League Regional Offices are fully staffed year-round to provide assistance and direction to Little League volunteers. All general questions, written suggestions for improving this Rulebook, tournament inquiries, rule interpretation requests, and supply orders should be directed to the appropriate office in your region as indicated.

UNITED STATES REGIONAL OFFICES

CENTRAL REGIONAL OFFICE

360 Ridge Point Drive | Carmel, IN 46032
Phone: (317) 897-6127 | Fax: (317) 897-6158
E-mail: CentralRegion@LittleLeague.org

EASTERN REGIONAL OFFICE

P.O. Box 2926 | Bristol, CT 06011-2926
Phone: (860) 585-4730 | Fax: (860) 585-4734
E-mail: EastRegion@LittleLeague.org

SOUTHWESTERN REGIONAL OFFICE

3700 S. University Parks Drive | Waco, TX 76706
Phone: (254) 756-1816 | Fax: (254) 757-0519
E-mail: SouthwestRegion@LittleLeague.org

WESTERN REGIONAL OFFICE

6707 Little League Drive | San Bernardino, CA 92407
Phone: (909) 887-6444 | Fax: (909) 887-6135
E-mail: WestRegion@LittleLeague.org

SOUTHEASTERN REGIONAL OFFICE

P.O. Box 7557 | Warner Robins, GA 31095
Phone: (478) 987-7227 | Fax: (478) 987-7232
E-mail: SoutheastRegion@LittleLeague.org

INTERNATIONAL REGIONAL OFFICES

CANADIAN REGIONAL OFFICE

#500-2210 Prince of Wales Drive | Ottawa, Ontario
Canada K2E 6Z9
Phone: (613) 731-3301 | Fax: (613) 731-2829
E-mail: Canada@LittleLeague.org

EUROPEAN AND AFRICAN REGIONAL OFFICE

Little League Europe | Al. Malej Ligi 1
Kunto, 99-300, Poland
Phone: 011-48-24-254-4569 | Fax: 011-48-24-254-4571
E-mail: Europe@LittleLeague.org

LATIN AMERICAN AND CARIBBEAN REGIONAL OFFICE

P.O. Box 10237 | Caparra Heights
Puerto Rico 00922-0237
Phone: (787) 982-3076 | Fax: (787) 728-8164
E-mail: LatinAmerica@LittleLeague.org

ASIA-PACIFIC REGIONAL OFFICE

c/o Hong Kong Little League | Room 1005
Sports House | 1 Stadium Path
Causeway Bay, Hong Kong
Phone: 011-852-2504-4007 | Fax: 011-852-2504-8629
E-mail: llbapr@hkbaseball.com.hk

General Information
Purpose of Little League Baseball and Softball

Better than any other youth sport activity, baseball and softball have become the thread that has sewn together a patchwork of nations and cultures around the world. Children in diverse nations such as Israel, Jordan, Ukraine, Germany, Japan, Canada, Hong Kong, Poland, Mexico, China, Venezuela, South Africa, and the U.S. have discovered baseball and softball — Little League Baseball and Softball – are ways to bring their people a sport that mirrors life itself.

Baseball and softball embody the discipline of teamwork. They challenge players towards perfection of physical skills and bring into play the excitement of tactics and strategy. The very nature of baseball and softball also teach that while every player eventually strikes out, or is on the losing team, there is always another chance for success in the next at-bat or game.

Millions of children on six continents and more than 80 countries can attest that baseball, softball, and Little League are synonymous. Little League is a heritage to be carried forward proudly in the future by ever increasing waves of those devoted to teaching children how to play and enjoy these great games.

Little League is a program of service to youth. It is geared to provide an outlet of healthful activity and training under good leadership in the atmosphere of wholesome community participation. The movement is dedicated to helping children become good and decent citizens. It inspires them with a goal and enriches their lives towards the day when they must take their places in the world. It establishes the values of teamwork, sportsmanship, and fair play.

Federal Charter

Little League operates under auspices of the highest recognition that may be accorded to any such organization by the government of the United States. By virtue of legislation approved unanimously by both the House of Representatives and the Senate and signed into law by President Lyndon B. Johnson on July 16, 1964, Little League has been granted a Congressional Charter of Federal Incorporation. No other youth sports organization has been so honored by the Federal government.

Structure

Basically, Little League has three structural components, each dependent upon the other and each vital to the success of the program.

The administrative and service core of the movement is Little League International, a non-profit membership organization that maintains the international program, with international headquarters in Williamsport, Pennsylvania. Part of the headquarters structure includes various Regional Headquarters in the U.S. and throughout the world.

The next component is the District. All the leagues within a District (a geographical area usually encompassing 10-20 leagues) elect a District Administrator (DA). The DA and his/her staff of Assistant District Administrators serve as liaisons between the various Regional Headquarters and the local Little Leagues. They are usually the most experienced Little League volunteers in the area, and are charged with helping to ensure that all the volunteers in their districts are well trained, and all the leagues are operating within the guidelines set by Little League. The District Administrator does not have the authority to suspend, limit, or revoke any rules, regulations, or privileges of charter by a local Little League, but may recommend such action to the Charter Committee in Williamsport.

The final, most important component is the local Little League. The league provides its services in the community. It furnishes physical facilities, volunteer services, and resources to provide a program for children. Through effective leadership and strong administrative policy at the top level, together with training extensions and adherence to rule and policy at District and local league level, Little League is able to provide liberal benefits to children who participate.

Administration

Little League affairs are administered by the Little League International Board of Directors. Policies, operating procedures, and controls of the program are carried out by Little League International staff, under the direction of the President and the Executive Committee.

The local league operates under a charter granted annually by Little League. The league is autonomous in the sense of having freedom to elect its own officers, finance its program, and carry on various other related functions, but it must adhere scrupulously to all rules and regulations established by Little League.

The charter privilege extends use of the name "Little League" and its official insignia to the local Little League. It can be suspended or revoked for violation of rules or regulations by action of the Charter Committee.

Charter Committee/Waivers of Rules and Regulations

The Charter Committee is a group of personnel at Little League International in Williamsport, Pennsylvania, in whom is placed (by the Little League International Board of Directors) the responsibility of reviewing, granting, suspending, or revoking the privileges and conditions of the local league's charter. When a local league wishes to request a waiver of a specific rule or regulation, it must submit the request in writing to the District Administrator, who will forward it with his/her recommendation to the Regional Director. The Regional Director or Assistant Regional Director will present the request to the Charter Committee for a final and binding decision. The league, as part of the chartering process, agreed to accept the decision of the Charter Committee as final and binding. Should any new or additional information become available after the Charter Committee's initial decision, which the league feels would alter the Committee's decision, the league may submit that information for reconsideration by the above outlined process. The league also agreed, as part of the chartering process, that all Charter Committee decisions will be made in Williamsport but understand that the league may request to personally present their position at a meeting with the Committee in Williamsport. No other person or group has the authority to approve waivers of ANY rules or regulations.

Player Eligibility

The player must qualify under Little League's definition of residence or school attendance as described within this rulebook, must be of the correct "league age" for the division, and must have parental consent. Little League offers baseball and softball programs for players league age 4 through 16. Local Little Leagues are encouraged to provide all programs, thus giving all the children in the area a chance to play Little League Baseball or Softball. League age is defined in Regulation IV(a).

Amateur Status

To be eligible in the Little League Baseball or Softball program, a participant must be an amateur in baseball or softball respectively. This requirement serves to increase interest and competitive balance in Little League Baseball and Softball. An amateur participant is one who engages in the Little League Baseball or Softball program solely for the educational, physical, mental, social, and recreational benefits derived thereof. The amateur status requirement enhances Little League's goals and values of character development, wholesome community participation, teamwork, sportsmanship, and fair play and, also, protects Little League athletes from being disqualified from high school and collegiate athletics.

NOTE: Loss of Amateur Status: A participant loses amateur status and therefore, the right to participate in the Little League program whenever:

- The participant, or the participant's parent(s) or guardian(s), receives compensation, in trust or otherwise, for or related to the participant's athletic ability, participation, or performance in baseball or softball.
- The participant plays on a professional team in baseball or softball.
- The participant signs a contract whereby the participant agrees to compete in any baseball or softball competition for compensation. It is not a violation to attend or participate in a professional try-out camp, provided that (1) no compensation or expenses are paid; (2) the try-out lasts no longer than forty-eight hours; and (3) if in the sport of baseball, the participation is otherwise in conformity with the National Federation Major - Minor League Agreement.

Divisions of Play

Most people know Little League through the Major Division for 9- to 12-year-olds. But today Little League provides organized youth sports programs for a wide range of ages. Charter fees are extremely reasonable, with Rulebooks and organizational materials provided free.

Tee Ball Baseball and Tee Ball Softball programs are for players 4-6 years old (with an option for 7-year-olds) who want to learn the fundamentals of hitting and fielding. In Tee Ball, players hit a ball off a batting tee. Rules of the game may be varied to accommodate the need for teaching. The primary goals of Tee Ball are to have fun, to instruct children in the fundamentals of baseball and softball, and to allow them to experience the value of teamwork.

Minor League Baseball and Minor League Softball programs may be operated within each division for younger players with less experience. The Minor League may be players ages 7-12. Divisions may be established within the Minor League for "Machine

Pitch," "Coach Pitch," or "Player Pitch." The goal of the Minor League is to prepare children for eventual selection to a Major Division team, and local leagues are encouraged to structure this division to provide flexibility, develop players, and, most importantly, have fun. Additional Coach Pitch resources, including a 12-week program for Coach Pitch baseball, are available at LittleLeagueU.org. Little League International requests leagues identify Coach Pitch/Machine Pitch and Player Pitch teams during the chartering process to help provide more details about these important levels of play in the Little League program.

Little League Baseball and Little League Softball (also known as the Major Division) are for players 9 to 12 years old. A league may choose to limit its Major Division to 10, 11, and 12-year-olds, or 11- and 12-year-olds. The 8- to 10- and 9- to 11-Year-Old Baseball and Softball Divisions were established as tournament programs to give children the opportunity to experience Tournament Play, up to State level. Leagues may also enter Tournament Play for 10- to 12-year-olds in the Little League Baseball and Little League Softball Divisions, each ending in World Series tournaments.

Little League Intermediate (50-70) Baseball Division is for players 11 to 13 years old. The program is a transitional program for 11- to 13-year-olds using 50-foot pitching distance and 70-foot base paths and offers a full range of tournament play, including a World Series.

Junior League Baseball and Junior League Softball are established as transitional programs for 12- to 14-year-olds. The programs link the Little League and Senior League divisions and offer a full range of Tournament Play, including World Series tournaments.

Senior League Baseball and Senior League Softball are for players 13 to 16 years old. Both divisions offer a full range of Tournament Play, including a World Series.

Little League Challenger Division is for players ages 4-18 with physical and/or intellectual disabilities. It incorporates other children in the league as "buddies" for the Challenger players.

Senior League Challenger Division is for players 15 years old and above with physical and/or intellectual disabilities. It incorporates other participants or volunteers in the league as "buddies" for the Challenger players.

Role of the Parent

The parents of millions of Little Leaguers combined with their children, league officials, umpires, managers, coaches, and countless volunteer agencies including sponsors, represent an imposing cross section of our world. Parents must take the initiative to make the local program successful and the experience meaningful for their children.

Practically speaking, Little League is an adult, volunteer work project constructed, supervised, and assisted by parents who want to extend this benefit to their children. Parents are essential to the local league by volunteering, raising funds, and supporting all operations within the community.

Little League continues to develop educational material for parents available through Little League University (LittleLeagueU.org) and that is also delivered via *The Parent Connection* (LittleLeague.org/Parents), which is a monthly e-newsletter designed to inform and engage Little League parents and families. Topics include the latest rules, registration information, fitness and safety tips, and equipment advice.

Volunteer Eligibility

As a condition of service to the league, all managers, coaches, Board of Directors members and any other persons, volunteers or hired workers, who provide regular service to the league and/or have repetitive access to, or contact with players or teams, must annually complete and submit a "Little League Official Volunteer Application" (LittleLeague.org/VolApp) to the local league president. Annual background screenings must be completed prior to the applicant assuming his/her duties for the current season. Refusal to annually submit a fully completed "Little League Official Volunteer Application" must result in the immediate dismissal of the individual from the local league. [See Regulation I(b) and I(c) 8 and 9.]

Leadership Programs

In the years ahead there will be millions of children playing Little League Baseball and Softball. Leadership training programs help to widen the scope and improve the standards of leadership at all levels.

Managers and Coaches

It cannot be stated too strongly that qualified adult volunteers must be enlisted as team managers and coaches. It is not enough that candidates for these important roles have previous experience in the game.

Managers and coaches must possess leadership ability and the know-how to work with young children. Training Little Leaguers in the fundamentals of teamwork, good sportsmanship, and discipline are attainable goals, and are readily available through publications, videos, seminars, and clinics produced for and by Little League.

Little League provides a variety of resources to train your league's managers and coaches, including Little League University (LittleLeagueU.org), and The Coach's Box newsletter (LittleLeague.org/Newsletters). Little League University is a free online resource that provides expert advice on coaching several different age groups of baseball and softball players, as well as drills that will help coaches better prepare their teams for games. The Coach's Box newsletter provides monthly tips and features on topics related to coaching baseball and softball. Little League International partners with organizations such as the Positive Coaching Alliance and ONE Softball for advice for parents and coaches to enhance the Little League experience.

Umpires

Often an overlooked aspect of the Little League program, umpiring is one of the most important. The volunteer umpire is as much a part of Little League as the volunteer manager, coach, or concession stand worker.

There is no sound reason for paying umpires, or any other person whose services should be provided on a volunteer basis. Many districts and leagues have found successful ways to operate volunteer umpiring programs, helping to defray the costs that might normally be passed on to the parents.

Little League also offers many training materials, clinics, and seminars on umpire education, as well as the Little League Umpire Registry. The registry allows volunteer umpires to receive regular mailings from Little League International on rule interpretations, updates, etc.

Little League is also pleased to offer Little League University, a free, online tool packed with educational content and video clips on plate and base mechanics and news articles, will provide an opportunity to build, recruit, train, and retain a program of volunteers. The resource center will also enable umpires to remain updated on the rules and regulations, exchange ideas, and offer suggestions that will continually improve their game. Learn more and register at LittleLeagueUmpire.org.

For more information on how to obtain these materials, how to sign up for the Umpire Registry, or on the clinics and seminars nearest you, contact your Regional Headquarters or visit LittleLeague.org/Umpires.

League Officers

Little League offers free training through Little League University (LittleLeagueU.org) as well as clinics, seminars, and materials for league officers in all duties. Leagues are strongly encouraged to utilize the League Resource Guide that is mailed annually to all U.S. league presidents listed on the Little League Data Center. The Resource Guide is also available at LittleLeagueU.org. Another resource is "A Year in the Life of Hometown Little League" (LittleLeague.org/Hometown) which follows a fictional league through a year of operation, showing the right way to solve the most common problems that arise. For information on attending a seminar, contact your Regional Office.

Initiatives

Little League is more than just bats and balls. It is also a part of life for millions of people every year, so it is important to educate children and adults in other aspects of life as well. Information on the following special projects and initiatives is available from your Regional Office.

ASAP (A Safety Awareness Program) — Designed to share the best safety ideas from around the world.

The Little League Challenger Program — Two divisions of play for individuals with intellectual and physical disabilities.

Little League Child Protection Program — A program to educate local Little League officials, parents, and children on ways to stay safe, and how to help ensure people with the proper motives are involved at the local level.

Little League Grow the Game Grant Program — A new $1.8 million grant program created to provide local leagues the resources needed for general improvement, to help recover from natural disaster, and to expand or establish Little League Softball, Little League Challenger Division, and Little League Urban Initiative programs and help strengthen the Little League opportunities in communities. Visit LittleLeague.org/GrowtheGame for more information.

Little League Urban Initiative — An initiative to bring baseball and softball to inner-city youths.

Frequently Asked Questions

Here are some answers to the most common questions we receive at Little League International each year.

Q: Can a local Little League or District program set-up a website in which any of the trademarks of Little League are used?

A: Local leagues and Districts are permitted to host websites that assist with communicating information about their activities in the local community. The local league name, affiliation with Little League, registration, facilities locations, board members, and other information for parents and volunteers should be clearly stated on the website.

Any league or district that wishes to host a website, which includes Little League Trademarks in any fashion, must submit its league website address (www.) or URL (Universal Resource Locator) into the Little League Data Center (LittleLeague.org/DataCenter) annually. This can be found under the "Review League Information" menu on the Little League Data Center. The web address or URL should be a combination of a league or district's name in conjunction with the words "Little League" or "LL." An example of how a URL should appear: www.HometownLittleLeague.org or www.PA50LittleLeague.org. Should a league elect not to re-charter or change its affiliation, the league is responsible for transferring any domain name containing Little League trademarks to Little League International at the local league's expense.

Use of the Little League Trademarks, logos, and links to LittleLeague.org are permitted on websites operated by local leagues or districts, however, permission must be granted in advance by contacting Marketing@LittleLeague.org. Under no circumstances may a league, district, or person register a website using the words Little League in a website address for any other purpose other than to represent their local league or district. This includes websites set-up for the purposes of raising funds such as crowdsourcing websites, as well as social media networks. If teams within local leagues also host websites, they are required to follow these guidelines and the guidelines for use of Little League Trademarks. At this time, team URLs are not required to be submitted to Little League International however leagues are responsible for educating the operators of team websites and/or social media accounts on Little League guidelines and trademark use. Leagues and teams should not use any commercial entity in their league URL. It is strongly encouraged that local league board members monitor the websites of their associated teams to ensure appropriate content is being provided.

Leagues are also encouraged to secure model releases as part of the player and volunteer registration process. This allows leagues to display and distribute images or video of players participating in league activities.

Little League reserves the right to review any league or district website that uses Little League trademarks and logos to ensure appropriate permissions from those individuals is granted. It is recommended that you incorporate the Little League model release (LittleLeague.org/ModelRelease) as part of the player registration process. Little League reserves the right to require a league or district to remove content on its websites, including social media sites, if content is deemed inappropriate.

Local leagues or districts are encouraged to establish a website using the DICK'S Team Sports HQ powered by Blue Sombrero, which is free to Little League districts and local leagues. Information is available at LittleLeague.org/TSHQ. Additional information can be found in the section title: Websites in the Operating Policies of this book.

Q: If a manager, coach, or umpire is returning from previous years, do they automatically get the same position in the next year?

A: Volunteers in the local Little League program DO NOT HAVE TENURE, regardless of the years of service. In order to serve, a manager, coach, or umpire must be appointed by the league president and approved by the local league Board of Directors annually. Prior service does NOT guarantee re-appointment.

Q: Can a local Little League waive its rights to a player who qualifies within its boundaries, allowing that player to participate in another Little League program?

A: A local Little League does not have the authority to waive such rights. ONLY THE CHARTER COMMITTEE IN WILLIAMSPORT HAS THIS AUTHORITY. (See "CHARTER COMMITTEE/WAIVERS OF RULES AND REGULATIONS"in the previous section). If the Charter Committee votes to grant a waiver, the District Administrator will be informed in writing. Waivers, if granted, are for the current season only.

Q: Can a child who does not qualify within a league's boundaries play in that league for the regular season only, provided he/she is not eligible for Tournament Play (all stars)?

A: No. However, the local league may request a waiver, listing all circumstances that warrant such a waiver. Only the Charter Committee in Williamsport can make the final decision. (See "CHARTER COMMITTEE/WAIVERS OF RULES AND REGULATIONS" in the previous section). If the Charter Committee votes to grant a waiver, the District Administrator will be informed in writing. Waivers, if granted, are for the current season only.

Q: If a parent signs a notarized statement granting temporary custody of a child to a friend or other family member, can that friend or family member's residence be used for registering a child to play in Little League?

A: The ONLY acceptable documentation regarding a change of custody is COURT-ORDERED CUSTODY, a decree issued by a judge who has jurisdiction in the matter.

Q: Does the District Administrator have the authority to grant a waiver of a rule or regulation? Example: Could the District Administrator give permission for a local league to register players whose residence is outside the league's boundaries? Could a District Administrator waive ANY rule or regulation?

A: NO. ANY waiver of a rule or regulation can only be made by the Charter Committee in Williamsport. No other person or group has this authority. If the Charter Committee votes to grant a waiver, the District Administrator will be informed in writing. Waivers, if granted, are for the current season only.

Q: What is the required method for selecting Tournament (all-star) teams?

A: There is no required method. The local league Board of Directors decides annually on the selection method. However, a suggested method is included in the Tournament Rules and Guidelines section of this book.

Q: How much does it cost to belong to Little League?

A: The charter fee paid once per year to Little League Baseball, Incorporated, by the local Little League, is $10 per team. One Rulebook for each team chartered is provided free, although the local league president or designated officer may order additional Rulebooks at $2 each. Each league must also provide adequate accident and liability insurance coverage. If the league purchases the insurance through the Little League group insurance program underwritten by an AIG member company, the cost is between $23 and $31 per team, per season, depending upon the location and division of play. Detailed information on the accident and liability insurance offered through Little League's Risk Management department is available at (570) 326-1921.

Q: What is the difference between Regular Season and Tournament Play (all-stars)?

A: During the Regular Season, every eligible child in the league's boundaries is given the opportunity to tryout and participate on a team. Generally, the Regular Season begins in the spring and can last until September, but the start/end dates for the Regular Season vary. In Tournament Play, a league holding charters in the proper divisions may enter teams in up to six baseball and five softball divisions in the International Tournament. Tournament Play begins around July 1 and ends in late August with World Series tournaments in seven divisions of baseball and softball. Many of the rules and regulations are the same for Regular Season and Tournament Play. However, there are some exceptions, detailed in the Tournament Rules and Guidelines section of this book. Little League also offers a "Second Season" program, sometimes called "Fall Ball" or "Winter League," with details available at your Regional Office.

Q: Can our league or district (or any other level) allow a television station or website to broadcast, web-cast, or stream regular season games, Special Games, or International Tournament games?

A: No. The only authority that can permit this is Little League International. More information on broadcasting, webcasting, and streaming Little League games can be found at LittleLeague.org.

Residency and School Attendance Eligibility Requirements

Each local Little League determines the actual geographic boundaries of the area from within which it shall select players. These boundaries must be described in detail and shown on a map and dated when making application for a Little League charter. Players will be eligible to play with that league only if they reside or the physical location of the school where they attend classes is within the boundaries provided to and approved by Little League Baseball, Incorporated. NOTE: Players who established "residence" or "school attendance" for regular season and/or tournament in a prior season using the Tournament Player Verification form, and can produce the form with proper proofs and signatures, will NOT need to complete a new Tournament Player Verification form.

I. A player will be deemed to reside within the league boundaries if:

    A. His/her parents are living together and are residing within such league boundaries, OR;

    B. Either of the player's parents (or his/her court-appointed legal guardian) reside within such boundaries. It is unacceptable if a parent moves into a league's boundaries for the purpose of qualifying for tournament play. As detailed later in these rules, the penalty for violation of this rule may, in Little League Baseball, Incorporated's discretion, result in the disqualification of a player, team or entire league from regular season and/or tournament play.

"Residence," "reside," and "residing" refers to a place of bona fide continuous habitation. A place of residence once established shall not be considered changed unless the parents, parent, or guardian makes a bona fide change of residence.

Residence shall be established and supported by documents containing the full residence which includes parent(s) or guardian(s) name, street address, city, state, and zip code information, dated or in force between February 1, 2018 (previous year) and February 1, 2019 (current year), from one or more documents from each of the three Groups outlined below:

Group I

1. Driver's License
2. School records
3. Vehicle records (i.e., registration, lease, etc.)
4. Employment records
5. Insurance documents

Group II

1. Welfare/child care records
2. Federal records (i.e., Federal Tax, Social Security, etc.)
3. State records
4. Local (municipal) records
5. Support payment records

6. Homeowner or tenant records
7. Military records

Group III
1. Voter's Registration
2. Utility bills (i.e., gas, electric, water/sewer, phone, mobile phone, heating, waste disposal)
3. Financial (loan, credit, investments, etc.) records
4. Medical records
5. Internet, cable, or satellite records

NOTE: Example – Three documents from the same Group (utility bill, cable bill, and bank statement) constitute only ONE document.

Any documents submitted as proof of residence must demonstrate bona fide continuous habitation as determined by Little League Baseball, Incorporated in its sole discretion.

II. A player will be deemed to attend school in the boundaries if:

A. The physical location of the school where he/she attends classes is within the boundaries established by the local league. NOTE: This excludes home schools, cyber schools, sports-related schools, sports academies, preschools, or after school where a student participates outside of the primary school the player is enrolled.

"School attendance" refers to the (place) physical location the player in question attends school during the traditional academic year. Once established, a location of school attendance shall not be considered changed unless the child is enrolled and attends another school or is no longer enrolled in or attending the previous school.

School attendance shall be established and supported by a document indicating enrollment for the current academic year, dated prior to October 1, 2018, and with the physical location of the school, from ONE of the following categories to determine school attendance by such player:

1. Official/Certified School enrollment record dated prior to October 1, 2018
2. A Little League-issued school attendance form completed by the principal, assistant principal, or administrator authorized to sign on behalf of the school

It is recommended that the league require some proof of residence or school attendance within the league's boundaries at the time the player registers. Players and their parents/guardians are advised that a false statement of residence or school attendance may lead to ineligibility to play Little League Baseball or Softball. Under NO circumstances does ANY person have the authority to grant a waiver that allows a child to play in a local Little League program IN ANY DIVISION, when that child does not qualify under these eligibility requirements. Any league who accepts any player outside of its boundaries and fails to properly document compliance with the "Residence and/or School Attendance Player Eligibility Requirement" or obtain a waiver through the Charter Committee may result in the disqualification of a player, team, or entire league from regular season and/or tournament play.

If the claim for residency or school attendance is challenged, the above materials must be submitted to Little League Baseball, Incorporated, with an affidavit of residency or school attendance from the parent(s) or guardian(s). Little League Baseball, Incorporated shall have the right to request additional documentation in support of the claim of residency or school attendance. The parent(s) or legal guardian(s) will be required to provide said documentation to obtain eligibility. Little League Baseball, Incorporated shall decide the issue in its sole discretion, and that decision will be final and binding. Residency or school documents must illustrate that the residence or school attendance (as defined above) was inside the league's boundaries throughout the regular season (as of June 15 of the year in question).

In the case of a Regulation II(d) Waiver Form, or a Regulation IV(h) Waiver Form, the proof of residence for the FORMER residence of the parent(s)/guardian(s) or former school that was within the current league's boundaries must be obtained. This proof of residence for the former residence or former school attendance must be supported by the same documentation as noted above.

Tournament Requirement for Non-Citizens: *A participant who is not a citizen of the country in which he/she wishes to play, but meets residency requirements as defined by Little League, may participate in that country if:*

1. his/her visa allows that participant to remain in that country for a period of at least one year, or;

2. the prevailing laws allow that participant to remain in that country for at least one year, or;

3. the participant has an established bona fide residence in that country for at least two years prior to the start of the regular season.

Exceptions can only be made by action of the Charter Committee in Williamsport. Any request for a waiver pertaining to the eligibility of a player must be submitted in writing, by the president of the local Little League through the District Administrator, to the respective Regional Director not later than the date prescribed in Regulation IV(j). Requests submitted after that date will not be considered.

Proof-of-Age Requirements

Acceptable Forms of Proof of Birth Date

1. Original proof of age document, if issued by federal, state, or provincial registrars of vital statistics in the country in which the Little Leaguer is participating.

2. If country of participation differs from the country of proof of age document, original proof-of-age document issued by federal, state, or provincial registrars of vital statistics, or local offices thereof, are acceptable proof of age, provided the document was filed, recorded, registered, or issued within one (1) year of the birth of the child.

3. An original document issued by federal, state, or provincial registrars of vital statistics, or local offices thereof, listing the date of birth, with reference to the location and issue date of the original birth certificate, is acceptable. (The original birth certificate referenced must have been filed, recorded, registered, or issued within one (1) year of the birth of the child.) Also issued by these agencies are photocopies of the certificate of live birth with the certification also photocopied, including the signature, and include the seal impressed thereon. Such documents are acceptable without "live" signatures, provided the original filed, recorded, registered, or issued date of the birth certificate was within one (1) year of the date of birth.

4. For children born abroad of a parent or parents who are U.S. citizens, any official government document issued by a U. S. federal agency or service, is acceptable. For military dependents, Department of Defense identification cards and military hospital certificates are acceptable. These must be originals, not copies, and must refer to a filing, recording, registration, or issue date that is within one (1) year of the birth of the child.

5. A "Statement in Lieu of Acceptable Proof of Birth" issued by a District Administrator is acceptable.

NOT ACCEPTABLE AS SOLE PROOF OF BIRTH: Baptismal Certificate; Certificate of Blessing; Certificate of Dedication; Certificate of Circumcision, etc.; Hospital Certificate; photocopied records; passports.

NOTE: Little League International has authorized the Regional Directors for Latin America and Caribbean, Europe and Africa, and Asia-Pacific, to adopt a policy that excludes No. 1 above. Local Little Leagues and districts in those regions will be informed of the regional policy.

How to Obtain Acceptable Documents Proving Date of Birth

Certified copy-of-birth records may be obtained from the Registrar of Vital Statistics of each state, province, or local office where the child was born. For U.S.-born persons, addresses of these offices or bureaus, fees required, and other pertinent information are supplied by the United States Department of Health and Human Services (National Center for Health Statistics). A database listing the method for obtaining birth records from any U.S. state or territory is available at the following Internet address:

cdc.gov/nchs/w2w.htm

Individual states may also have online instructions on how to obtain "rush" birth records. To find out a state's latest policies regarding birth records, go to the Internet site listed below and type "birth records" into the search field, designate the appropriate state, then click on "SUBMIT."

USA.gov

Persons in the U.S. who need a copy of a non-U.S. birth record should contact the Embassy or the nearest Consulate of the country in which the birth occurred. Addresses and telephone numbers for these offices are listed in the U.S. Department of State Publication 7846, "Foreign Consular Offices in the United States," which is available in many local libraries. This information may also be located at the following Internet address: https://2009-2017.state.gov/documents/organization/64190.pdf. Such proof-of-birth records must meet the criteria for acceptable proof listed above.

How to Obtain a "Statement in Lieu of Acceptable Proof of Birth"

When an "Acceptable Proof of Birth" as described previously is not available, then the appropriate number of items in EACH of these FOUR groups are required so that the participant may obtain a "Statement in Lieu of Acceptable Proof of Birth," which is required for such a participant to be eligible for regular season or tournament play:

Group 1 – Any one (1) of the following, provided the date of birth is listed: a naturalization document issued by the United States Department of Justice; photocopy of birth certificate; original birth certificate or government record of birth if not containing a filing, recording, registration, or issue date within one (1) year of the date of birth; passport; *PLUS...*

Group 2 – Any two (2) of the following, provided the date of birth is listed: Baptismal Certificate; Certificate of Blessing; Certificate of Dedication; Certificate of Circumcision; or any other religious-related certificate; Hospital Certificate; School Record (must be dated, and date of issue must be at least two years prior to current season); Social Security document; Welfare Department document; adoption record. Any item in this group must be an original document, not a copy; *PLUS...*

Group 3 – Any two (2) of the following: A written, signed, and notarized statement from...
    ... the doctor who delivered the child;
    ... a hospital administrator where the child was delivered;
    ... the principal or headmaster of the school the child attends;
    ... a Social Worker with personal knowledge of the child's date of birth;
    ... a Priest, Rabbi, Minister, Mullah, or other titled religious figure with personal knowledge of the child's date of birth;
    ... the child's pediatrician or family doctor.

NOTE: In each statement in Group 3, the writer must describe his/her responsibilities or his/her relationship to the child, and must attest to his/her personal knowledge that the child was born on the date claimed; *PLUS...*

Group 4 – A written, signed, and notarized statement from one or both parents, or the legal guardian (as appointed by a court of jurisdiction), attesting to the date of birth claimed.

The league president will forward the above documentation to the District Administrator (or, if the team is traveling, the Tournament Director). If in the opinion of the District Administrator, such evidence is satisfactory, a "Statement In Lieu of Acceptable Proof of Birth" will be issued. This statement will be considered to be acceptable proof of age from that point forward, throughout the child's Little League experience, provided all the information submitted is accurate. (**NOTE:** If the District Administrator is unable to review the documents, they may be submitted to the appropriate Regional Headquarters.)

NOTE: Situations where players use the name of an adopting family or the name of the family with whom they live, but whose births are recorded under the surname of the natural father or mother, will be handled as follows: The president of the league will obtain from the parents or guardian a document that qualifies under Proof-of-Age Requirements, as well as a copy of the adoption papers (if the player has been legally adopted). If the player was not adopted, a notarized statement from the mother and/or father or legal guardian (as appointed by a court of jurisdiction), saying that the player living under one or the other of their surnames is the same player (for whom the birth certificate was issued) is also required.

These documents will be submitted to the District Administrator. If the documents are found to be acceptable, a "Statement in Lieu of Acceptable Proof of Birth" will be issued and all original documents returned. The information submitted will be kept confidential.

Official Regulations
LITTLE LEAGUE BASEBALL® (MAJOR) DIVISION, MINOR LEAGUE BASEBALL, TEE BALL BASEBALL, INTERMEDIATE (50-70) BASEBALL DIVISION, JUNIOR LEAGUE BASEBALL, AND SENIOR LEAGUE BASEBALL

These regulations govern the conduct and operation of chartered Little League Baseball programs.

An Approved Ruling (A.R.) serves to illustrate the application of the regulations and rules. Approved Rulings follow the regulations and rules they amplify and are indicated by a box.

Regulation I
The League

(a) The league is the only unit of organization.

1. The Little League (Major) Division is to accommodate participants league ages 9-12.

2. The Minor League Division is an extension of the local Little League to accommodate participants league ages 7-12.

3. The Tee Ball Division is an extension of the local Little League to accommodate participants league ages 4-7 and may utilize the batting tee or the pitched ball (by a coach). The league may opt to deliver a designated number of pitches to all batters and then utilize the tee if necessary.

   NOTE 1: 7 year-olds may play in Tee Ball or Minor League depending on the local structure and ability of the players.

   NOTE 2: Major/Intermediate (50-70) Division/Junior/Senior League: A local league may allow players to participate in two divisions. **Tee Ball/Minor Division:** Players shall not participate in more than one division.

   NOTE 3: Participants league age 5 and 6 are permitted to advance to Minor League Coach Pitch or Machine Pitch after participation in Tee Ball for one year.

(b) **The league shall be governed by a Board of Directors elected from and by the membership, consisting of volunteer personnel. As a condition of service to the league, all managers; coaches; Board of Directors members; and any other persons, volunteers or hired workers, who provide regular service to the league and/or have repetitive access to, or contact with players or teams, must complete and submit a "Little League Official Volunteer Application" to the local league president. Annual background screenings must be completed prior to the applicant assuming his/her duties for the current season. Refusal to annually submit a fully completed "Little League Official Volunteer Application" must result in the immediate dismissal of the individual from the local league. [See also Regulation I(c) 8 and 9.]**

Officers shall be elected by the Board (i.e. president, one or more vice presidents, secretary, treasurer, safety officer, coaching coordinator, and player agent or agents). The president may manage, coach, or umpire provided he/she does not serve on the Protest Committee. The president of record or anyone who assumes the position or duties of president, on or after January 1 of the current year, may be eligible for selection by the local league Board of Directors as tournament team manager or coach with approval from their respective District Administrator. The president will not serve in the capacity of District Administrator. Player Agents shall not manage, coach, or umpire in their respective divisions. Vice presidents may manage, coach, or umpire provided they do not serve on the Protest Committee.

The president, with approval of Board of Directors, shall appoint managers, coaches, and umpires annually. Manager/coach representation on the Board shall not exceed a minority. **NOTE:** All members of the local league Board of Directors, as well as managers and coaches, whose activities in another youth baseball/softball program are deemed detrimental to the operation of the local league, can be removed by a majority vote of the Board of Directors. **Additionally, the local league's Board of Directors has the right to NOT approve that individual as tournament team manager/coach.**

(c) Each league shall:

1. prepare, adopt, and submit to Little League International, a constitution consistent with all rules, regulations, and policies of Little League Baseball, Incorporated.

2. be considered as a separate and not as a division of the same league.

3. apply for and, if approved, be issued a separate charter certificate.

4. have separate boundaries as provided for in Regulation II.

5. adopt and play a separate schedule of games as provided for in Regulation VII. Interleague play and practice with other league(s) may be permitted during the regular season with the **approval of the District Administrator. The District Administrator must verify that all leagues involved in the interleague combination are properly chartered and insured. Interleague play during the regular season between leagues from two districts must be approved by the regional office. Leagues involved in interleague play will field separate tournament teams. Players shall not be transferred from one league to another. Requests to combine for tournament play must be submitted through the district to the regional offices for approval per guidelines established by Little League. Districts will be required to submit interleague play forms with all insurance claims that result from interleague play.**

6. provide all players with conventional uniforms. **Tee Ball and Minor League:** T-shirts and caps are recommended, but hand-me-down type uniforms may be worn if so approved by the local Board. (The Little League Official Shoulder Patch must be affixed to the upper left sleeve of the uniform shirt in all divisions of play, and may not be sublimated or screen-printed.)

7. obtain Accident and General Liability insurance.

    A. Accident Insurance coverage is mandatory for all players on all rosters as well as managers, coaches, and umpires. The policy must have a minimum coverage of $100,000 per person per accident.

B. General Liability insurance is mandatory for the league including its volunteers. The policy must have a minimum coverage of $1,000,000 single limit bodily injury and property damage. **The policy must include coverage for claims involving each of the following: 1. athletic participants, and, 2. sexual abuse and molestation.**

If insurance is purchased locally, a copy of the policy naming Little League Baseball, Incorporated as an additional insured must be submitted to Little League International with your "Charter Application and Insurance Enrollment" form.

8. **require that all of the following persons have annually submitted a fully completed "Little League Official Volunteer Application" to the local league president, prior to the applicant assuming his/her duties for the current season: managers; coaches; Board of Directors members; and any other persons, volunteers or hired workers, who provide regular service to the league and/or have repetitive access to, or contact with, players or teams. The "Little League Official Volunteer Application" must be maintained by the president of the local league Board of Directors for all persons named above, for a minimum of at least two years after the volunteer is no longer in the league. When it comes time to dispose of these records, they should be destroyed as they contain sensitive information. Failure to comply with this regulation may result in the suspension or revocation of tournament privileges and/or the local league's charter by action of the Charter or Tournament committees in Williamsport.**

9. **conduct an annual background check on all persons that are required to complete a "Little League Official Volunteer Application" prior to the applicant assuming his/her duties for the current season. A local league within the United States must conduct a nationwide background check utilizing J.D. Palatine (JDP) or another provider that is comparable to JDP in accessing background check records for sex offender registry data and other criminal records. Each year, Little League International provides each local league located within the United States one hundred twenty-five (125) free criminal background checks administered through JDP. JDP can be accessed at LittleLeague.org/Background. Further information on how to utilize JDP, as well as how to conduct background checks, can be found at LittleLeague.org/ChildProtectionProgram. Local leagues located outside the United States must conduct a comprehensive criminal background check, including checks in the relevant country, as well as that country's provinces/ states and municipalities unless otherwise prohibited by the laws of the country of which the local league is located.**

No local league shall permit any person to participate in any manner whose background check reveals a conviction, guilty plea, no contest plea, or admission to any crime involving or against a minor or minors. If a potential volunteer appears on the National Sex Offender Registry, the league must contact the Security Manager at Little League International prior to appointing the volunteer to participate in any capacity in the league. All

local leagues must take into consideration criminal records when making the determination whether the individual is unfit to participate in any manner in the league.

Local leagues shall be required to determine the applicability of, and comply with, all state, local, and municipal laws; administrative rules and regulations; and municipal ordinances regarding background checks including, but not limited to, sex offender registry checks, criminal history records or reports, fingerprinting, certifications, or other requirements associated with volunteers, coaches, participants, and/or employees. Failure to comply with this regulation may result in the suspension or revocation of tournament privileges and/or the local league's charter by action of the Charter or Tournament Committees in Williamsport.

Several states have enacted laws that require additional background check requirements that are separate and additional to those mandated by Little League. For more information to assist you regarding state law requirements go to our website at LittleLeague.org/StateLaws.

As of January 15, 2018, those states with additional background check requirements either enacted or pending are: Alabama, California, Florida, Massachusetts, Mississippi, New Hampshire, Oklahoma, Oregon, and Pennsylvania.

*Occasionally Sex Offender Registry data may be unavailable for an individual state(s) when you run your background checks. If this occurs, you have the option of going immediately to the individual state(s) SOR website or going back and re-running the Sex Offender Registry data on the National Sex Offender Registry until the data becomes available. Information on accessing individual State Sex Offender Registry data can be found on the Little League website at LittleLeague.org/ChildProtectionProgram.

If a local league becomes aware of information, by any means whatsoever, that an individual, including, but not limited to, volunteers, players, or hired workers, has been convicted of, pled guilty, pled no contest, or admitted to any crime involving or against a minor or minors, the local league must contact the applicable government agency to confirm the accuracy of the information. If a potential volunteer appears on the National Sex Offender Registry, the league must contact the Security Manager at Little League International prior to appointing the volunteer to participate in any capacity in the league. Upon confirmation of a conviction for, guilty plea, no contest plea, or admission to a crime against or involving a minor or minors, the local league shall not permit the individual to participate in any manner.

NOTE: Information regarding background checks is available at LittleLeague. org/Background. Information gathered for background checks and results should be considered confidential, protected from public disclosure, and not used for any purpose beyond determining volunteer eligibility.

(d)   The Little League (Major) Division may be composed of not more than ten (10) teams. If more than 10 teams are requested, application for a divisional format must be made to the Charter Committee through the District Administrator. If approved, each division must field a separate tournament team.

(e) Not more than one league will be permitted to operate under the same management without expressed recommendation of the District Administrator to Little League International and subject to final approval by the Charter Committee.

(f) Mergers where there is sufficient enrollment to maintain separate charters shall require the recommendation of the District Administrator to Little League International and be subject to final approval by the Charter Committee.

(g) A local Little League is not permitted to sponsor, administer, underwrite, advertise, pay any fees, or otherwise support in any manner, any team or teams, any individual or group of individuals, for the purpose of participating in a non-Little League Baseball or Softball program, event, or game. Any violation of this regulation by the local Little League may result in revocation of charter and/or suspension of tournament privileges. While Little League does not recommend or endorse participation in more than one baseball program, this does not prohibit an individual who plays in a chartered Little League, or a group of such individuals, from participation in a non-Little League program, event, or game, subject to the provisions of this Regulation, Regulation IV(a) Note 2, and the provisions of the Tournament Rules and Guidelines regarding "Player Participation in Other Programs;" however, such participation may not take place in uniforms by the local Little League, with equipment provided by the local Little League, or as a representative of the local Little League.

Regulation I
The League: Intermediate (50-70) Division/Junior/Senior League

(a) The Intermediate (50-70) Division is an extension of the local Little League to accommodate participants league ages 11 through 13. Junior League is an extension of the local Little League to accommodate participants league ages 13 and 14 with an exception for 12-year-old players as noted in Regulation IV(a); Senior League is an extension of the local Little League to accommodate participants league ages 13-16. **NOTE 1: Intermediate (50-70) Division/Junior/Senior League:** A local league may allow players to participate in two divisions. This allows the local league Board of Directors to place some or all 13 and 14 year olds in the Junior League Division AND/OR Senior League Division. **NOTE 2:** Intermediate (50-70) Division/Junior/Senior League players may participate in other baseball programs during the regular season and tournament subject to the provisions of Regulation IV.

(b) The Intermediate (50-70) Division, Junior League, and Senior League Divisions shall be governed by the Board of Directors of the local Little League. The Board of Directors of the local Little League shall elect a player agent and vice president for each division and shall approve the appointment of its managers and coaches annually. The president may manage, coach, or umpire provided he/she does not serve on the Protest Committee. The president of record or anyone who assumes the position or duties of president, on or after January 1 of the current year, may be eligible for selection by the local league Board of Directors as tournament team manager or coach with approval from their respective District Administrator. The player agent shall not manage, coach, or umpire in his/her respective division. Vice president may manage, coach, or umpire provided they do not serve on the Protest Committee.

As a condition of service to the league, all managers, coaches, Board of Directors, members, and any other persons, volunteers or hired workers, who provide regular service to the league and/or have repetitive access to, or contact with players or teams, must complete and submit a "Little League Official Volunteer Application" to the local league president. Annual background screenings must be completed prior to the applicant assuming his/her duties for the current season. Refusal to annually submit a fully completed "Little League Official Volunteer Application" must result in the immediate dismissal of the individual from the local league.

(c) Each division shall operate under the constitution of the local Little League, which is the only unit of organization.

Each participating local Little League will:

1. select managers and coaches for its teams;

2. select its players from within the boundaries of the local Little League;

3. obtain Accident and General Liability insurance.

   A. Accident Insurance coverage is mandatory for all players on all rosters as well as managers, coaches, and umpires. The policy must have a minimum coverage of $100,000 per person per accident.

   B. General Liability insurance is mandatory for the league including its volunteers. The policy must have a minimum coverage of $1,000,000 single limit bodily injury and property damage. The policy must include coverage for claims arising out of athletic participants.

   If insurance is purchased locally, a copy of the policy naming Little League Baseball, Incorporated as an additional insured must be submitted to Little League International with your "Charter Application and Insurance Enrollment" form.

4. supply uniforms, bats, and equipment for its team(s) and contribute proportional costs of baseballs, supplies, and operation of program.

5. require that all of the following persons have annually submitted a fully completed "Little League Official Volunteer Application" to the local league president, prior to the applicant assuming his/her duties for the current season: managers, coaches, Board of Directors, members, and any other persons, volunteers or hired workers, who provide regular service to the league and/or have repetitive access to, or contact with, players or teams. The "Little League Official Volunteer Application" must be maintained by the president of the local league Board of Directors for all persons named above, for at least two years after the volunteer is no longer in the league. When it comes time to dispose of these records, they should be destroyed as they contain sensitive information. Failure to comply with this regulation may result in the suspension or revocation of tournament privileges and/or the local league's charter by action of the Charter or Tournament Committee in Williamsport.

6. conduct an annual background check on all persons that are required to complete a "Little League Official Volunteer Application" prior to the applicant assuming his/her duties for the current season. A local league within the United States must conduct a nationwide background check

utilizing JDP or another provider that is comparable to JDP in accessing background check records for sex offender registry data and other criminal records. Each year, Little League International provides each local league located within the United States one hundred twenty-five (125) free criminal background checks administered through JDP. JDP can be accessed at LittleLeague.org/Background. Further information on how to utilize JDP, as well as how to conduct background checks, can be found at LittleLeague. org/ChildProtectionProgram. Local leagues located outside the United States must conduct a comprehensive criminal background check, including checks in the relevant country, as well as that country's provinces/states and municipalities unless otherwise prohibited by the laws of the country of which the local league is located.

No local league shall permit any person to participate in any manner whose background check reveals a conviction, guilty plea, no contest plea, or admission to any crime involving or against a minor or minors. If a potential volunteer appears on the National Sex Offender Registry, the league must contact the Security Manager at Little League International prior to appointing the volunteer to participate in any capacity in the league. All local leagues must take into consideration criminal records when making the determination whether the individual is unfit to participate in any manner in the league.

Local leagues shall be required to determine the applicability of, and comply with, all state, local, and municipal laws; administrative rules and regulations; and municipal ordinances regarding background checks including, but not limited to, sex offender registry checks, criminal history records or reports, fingerprinting, certifications, or other requirements associated with volunteers, coaches, participants, and/or employees. Failure to comply with this regulation may result in the suspension or revocation of tournament privileges and/or the local league's charter by action of the Charter or Tournament committees in Williamsport.

Several states have enacted laws that require additional background check requirements that are separate and additional to those mandated by Little League. For more information to assist you regarding state law requirements go to our website at LittleLeague.org/StateLaws.

As of January 15, 2018, those states with additional background check requirements either enacted or pending are: Alabama, California, Florida, Massachusetts, Mississippi, New Hampshire, Oklahoma, Oregon, and Pennsylvania.

*Occasionally Sex Offender Registry data may be unavailable for an individual state(s) when you run your background checks. If this occurs, you have the option of going immediately to the individual state(s) SOR website or going back and re-running the Sex Offender Registry data on the National Sex Offender Registry until the data becomes available. Information on accessing individual State Sex Offender Registry data can be found on the Little League website at LittleLeague.org/ChildProtectionProgram.

If a local league becomes aware of information, by any means whatsoever, that an individual, including, but not limited to, volunteers, players, or hired workers, has been convicted of, pled guilty, pled no contest, or admitted to any crime involving or against a minor or minors, the local league must contact the applicable government agency to confirm the accuracy of the information. If a potential volunteer appears on the National Sex Offender Registry, the league must contact the Security Manager at Little League International prior to appointing the volunteer to participate in any capacity in the league. Upon confirmation of a conviction for, guilty plea, no contest plea, or admission to a crime against or involving a minor or minors, the local league shall not permit the individual to participate in any manner.

NOTE: Information regarding background checks is available at LittleLeague. org/Background. Information gathered for background checks and results should be considered confidential, protected from public disclosure, and not used for any purpose beyond determining volunteer eligibility.

(d) Each division shall be composed of no more than 10 teams.

(e) On or before April 15, the chartered Little League shall apply for and, if approved, be granted permission to operate an Intermediate (50-70) Division, Junior League, and/ or Senior League program for the year.

(f) Boundaries for selection of players shall conform to those of the local Little League.

(g) Each division shall adopt and play a separate schedule of games as provided for in Regulation VII. Interleague play or practice shall not be permitted, nor shall players be transferred from one league to another except as provided for in Regulation VII.

(h) Not more than one Intermediate (50-70) Division, Junior League, or Senior League program will be permitted to operate under the same local Little League. However, where a lack of enough player personnel exists and with the recommendation of the District Administrator and approval of the Charter Committee, two or more adjacent chartered Little Leagues comprising not more than 40,000 population of the same district may combine to form one Junior League and/or Senior League. Where two or more leagues have combined to form one Junior League and/or Senior League, a tournament team must be selected from each league, unless an exception is approved by the Charter Committee.

(i) Where two or more Intermediate (50-70) Division, Junior, and/or Senior Leagues combine, each will make application for charter indicating thereon the number of teams each will field and the need for joint operation. Players from more than one league may be pooled for the purpose of organizing teams, with Charter Committee approval.

(j) Where two or more Intermediate (50-70) Division, Junior Leagues, and/or Senior Leagues combine, the operation shall be governed jointly by the Board of Directors of the local leagues. They shall each elect a vice president and player agent to be in charge of the league(s).

(k) The vice presidents will administer the joint Intermediate (50-70) Division. Junior League, and/or Senior League program subject to the agreement of their Board of Directors.

(l)   Each Intermediate (50-70) Division, Junior League, and Senior League will select managers and coaches for its teams.

(m) Each Intermediate (50-70) Division, Junior League, and Senior League will supply a proportionate number of adult personnel including volunteer umpires.

(n)   Each Intermediate (50-70) Division, Junior League, and Senior League will supply uniforms, bats, and playing equipment for its teams and contribute proportionate costs for baseballs, supplies, and maintenance of playing field(s). When each league has a field, each will maintain its own.

(o)   Each Intermediate (50-70) Division. Junior League, and Senior League will pay its proportionate share for player accident, liability, and volunteer insurance.

Regulation II
League Boundaries

(a) Each league shall determine actual boundaries of the area from WITHIN which it shall select players. Only those participants whose residence or the physical location of the school where they attend classes is within the boundaries of the league shall be eligible to participate. "Residence" and "school attendance," for the purposes of this regulation, are defined in "Residence and School Attendance Eligibility Requirements." **NOTE: Any player who does not reside in or the school where they attend classes is not WITHIN the league's boundaries must have an approved waiver issued by the Charter Committee at Little League International. All waiver requests to the Charter Committee must be submitted and approved in writing by the league president before the start of the league's regular season or June 1, whichever occurs first. Requests must be submitted to the regional office through the District Administrator. Failure to properly document compliance with the "Residence and School Attendance Player Eligibility Requirement" or obtain a waiver through the Charter Committee may result in the disqualification of a player, team, or entire league from regular season and/or tournament play.** These boundaries MUST be described in detail AND shown on a map when making application for the charter. The league boundaries as detailed on the boundary map must be a physical structure (such as a road), or a geographic feature (such as a river). The boundary line will be considered to be in the center of such structures or features, unless noted otherwise. The boundaries must not encroach on the territory of any other chartered Little League's boundaries. The local Little League boundaries shall be the boundaries of the Intermediate (50-70) Division/Junior/Senior League.

(b) When there are two (2) or more leagues within a locale, each must have separate boundaries, detailed by a map. No exception to this provision will be made without written approval of Little League International.

(c) Team boundaries may be permitted where communities making up a league are widely separated, upon application to and approval by Little League International.

(d) **The Board of Directors of the local league, with the approval of the player involved, reserves the right to continue as a player, any individual (1) whose residence or school enrollment/attendance changes from within the boundary to outside the league's boundary or (2) who lives or school enrollment/attendance is outside the league's boundaries because of a revision of such boundaries even if the child then resides in the territory of another league. Current players, or any sibling of a current player whose brother or sister met the criteria under II(d) at one time may be retained. Any player meeting (1) or (2) above may be retained for the remainder of his/her career, including Little League, Intermediate (50-70) Division, Junior, and Senior League competition. NOTE: A player who qualifies under this regulation and elects not to participate for a playing season is not eligible to be retained for the subsequent season.**

Regulations II (d) - Processing Procedure
> *The league president will process a II(d) form. Once the president completes the form, he/she must compile "Residency or School Attendance Eligibility Requirement"*

verification that each player meets the conditions of II(d) as outlined above. The league president will present this information to the District Administrator for review. Once the District Administrator reviews the documentation in an effort to determine if it meets the regulations, the District Administrator will sign the II(d) form. The league and the district will maintain the form and documentation in their files. This review process is only required once during a participant's career. The league must maintain this form and documentation for this player for the duration of his/her career until the player graduates from the program or breaks service with the league. Tournament team players will be required to carry a copy of this form and documentation with them throughout the tournament. If contested during tournament play, the league will be required to produce the documentation. Additionally, if it is determined at a later date that the player does not meet the conditions of II(d), the player is ineligible for further participation. Situations in which documentation is not available must be referred to the Charter Committee through the regional office for a decision. The decision of the Charter Committee is final and binding.

(f) Boundaries approved by Little League International for a chartered league shall be protected. No other league will be chartered to accept player candidates from all or any part of the same territory for that calendar year. When necessary the District Administrator shall have the authority to recommend adjusting the league boundaries and be subject to review and approval of the Charter Committee.

(g) **Upon approval of the Little League International Board of Directors, each local Little League's boundaries was "frozen" at the status as of April 23, 2007. "Frozen" means, each league will continue to operate under that boundary. The league shall limit its boundary to and draw its players from an area approved by the District Administrator and Regional Director. Boundary maps for leagues (and any changes made after April 23, 2007, to the approved map on file at the Regional Office) must be signed and dated by the league president and District Administrator with a copy to be sent to the Regional Office. The approved map on file at the Regional Office is the "official" map, provided it does not encroach on any other chartered Little League's boundary. The Charter Committee reserves the right to grant waivers and adjust boundaries where needed. All requests for mergers and to expand league boundaries by adding additional territory must be provided to the Charter Committee through the District Administrator and Regional Director. The decision of the Charter Committee on these requests is final and binding.** ·

NOTE 1: Each league will be required to have a current boundary map, approved by the District Administrator, in the regional office files. This will be required for tournament privileges for the current season.

NOTE 2: All leagues currently operating under a divisional format must continue to operate under this method. *Exceptions to the divisional format can only be granted by the Charter Committee in Williamsport.*

NOTE 3: Any request for newly chartered leagues will be reviewed by the Charter Committee under this regulation before a charter is granted. The decision of the Charter Committee is final and binding.

Regulation III
The Teams

(a)   The league shall, at least 10 days prior to the first regular game, establish the number of players on each team. No team may have more than 15 players nor less than 12. **Tee Ball and Minor League:** There will be no minimum or maximum established at the Tee Ball and Minor League levels. Roster size of 8-10 players is recommended. **NOTE:** If a local league elects to roster less than nine (9) players at the Tee Ball and/or Minor League levels, rules 3.03 Note 3, 4.16, and 4.17 do not apply.

The manager of a team must, at least five days prior to the first regularly scheduled game, register the Regular Season team roster. All teams in a particular division must carry the same number of players on their rosters.

(b)   No more than the number of players established by the league under Regulation III(a) may be in uniform during any game. Batboys and/or batgirls are not permitted.

(c)   **Little League (Major) Division:** Local league must establish the age structure for the Little League (Major) Division. It is recommended that the local Little League set a maximum and/or minimum number of participants of a particular league age per team. For **Intermediate (50-70) Division/Junior/Senior League,** it is recommended that the local Little League set a maximum and/or minimum number of participants of a particular league age. (**Example:** If the league has all 15 and 16 year olds in its Senior League Division, it may have a local rule that states that each team must carry between four and eight players of league age 16.)

Minor League: Local league must establish the age structure for the Minor League Division. The Minor League may be sub-divided into Minor League Coach Pitch, Minor League Machine Pitch, and/or Minor League Player Pitch divisions, with the method for division determined by the local Little League Board of Directors. A player listed on a Little League (Major) Division roster shall not be permitted to play with a Minor League team.

Tee Ball: Local league must establish the age structure for the Tee Ball Division. Players league age 4 are eligible ONLY for Tee Ball, unless otherwise approved by the Charter Committee. **EXCEPTION:** Participants league age 5 and 6 are permitted to advance to Minor League Coach Pitch or Machine Pitch after participation in Tee Ball for one year. A player listed on a Tee Ball roster shall not be permitted to play with a Minor League team.

(d)   If a team loses any player(s) on the roster during the current season through illness, injury, change of address, or other justifiable reasons (subject to Board approval), another player shall be obtained through the player agent, to replace the one lost. The playing ability of the participant shall not be considered a justifiable reason for replacement. Such replacement must be of such league age as to comply with Regulation III(c), and must be eligible under all sections of Regulation IV. The local league should specify in its local rules the number of days allowed for a manager to comply with selection of a replacement. When changes are desired, the following procedures must be followed:

1.   Manager shall acquaint the Board of Directors of the local league with the conditions which necessitate the request for a replacement.

2. If the majority of the Board of Directors agrees that the reasons are justifiable, the manager may call up a replacement who is eligible under Regulation III(c) and all sections of Regulation IV.

NOTE 1: A league may adopt a local rule prohibiting replacements from the Minor League program onto a Little League (Major) Division team during the last two weeks of the regular season schedule.

NOTE 2: When a player misses more than seven (7) continuous days (**EX:** Monday through Sunday) of participation for an illness or injury, a physician or other accredited medical provider must give written permission for a return to full baseball activity.

NOTE 3: If a medical professional, Umpire in Chief, the player's coach, the player's manager, or the player's parent has determined a player sustains a possible concussion, the player must be, at a minimum, removed from the game and/or practice for the remainder of that day. The league must also be aware of its respective state/provincial/municipal laws with regards to concussions and impose any additional requirements as necessary. His/her return to full participation is subject to 1) the league's adherence to its respective state/provincial/municipal laws, 2) an evaluation and a written clearance from a physician or other accredited medical provider, and 3) written acknowledgment of the parents.

Little League International strongly encourages all leagues and teams to not only comply with any applicable state/provincial/municipal laws, but also, to review the information and training materials on concussions that are available free of charge on the Centers For Disease Control website, accessible at LittleLeague.org/Concussions. This link also provides concussion information from all 50 states.

(e) Managers may request to release players for any justifiable reason [as in (d) above, subject to Board approval] between the conclusion of one season and seven (7) days prior to the tryout session, but not later than the players selection or draft meeting of the subsequent season. In the event that a player is released, the president of the league shall notify the player agent, and the player in writing. Such written notice of release shall be given in sufficient time for the player to qualify for tryouts and selection to another team.

Tee Ball and Minor League: If a team manager loses any players on the roster during the current season through illness, injury, change of address, or other justifiable reasons (subject to Board approval), another player could be transferred within that Division, through the player agent, to replace the one lost, or a player may be obtained, through the player agent, from a list of participants who registered after the teams were formed.

NOTE 1: Tee Ball and Minor League players may be reassigned at the discretion of the local league Board of Directors and player agent in order to provide a balanced training program.

NOTE 2: Tee Ball and Minor League teams must be dissolved at the end of the current season, with all players being returned to a player pool.

Regulation IV
The Players

(a) **Tee Ball Division:** Any candidate with amateur status who will attain the age of 4 years before September 1, 2019, and who will not attain the age of 8 on or before August 31, 2019, shall be eligible to compete in the Tee Ball Baseball Division (subject to the local league Board of Directors alignment of this division). This means that a participant who will be 8 years old on September 1 or later is eligible to play that year; a participant who will be 8·years old on August 31 or earlier will not be eligible at any time during the calendar year in question.

NOTE: If a league elects to operate a Tee Ball baseball program only, it must use the league age determination date noted above.

Minor League Division: Any candidate with amateur status who will attain the age of 7 years before September 1, 2019, and who will not attain the age of 13 before August 31, 2019, shall be eligible to compete in the Minor League Baseball Division (subject to the local league Board of Directors alignment of this division). This means that a participant who will be 13 years old on September 1 or later is eligible to play that year; a participant who will be 13 years old on August 31 or earlier will not be eligible for either local league play or tournament play at any time during the calendar year in question.

NOTE: Tee Ball/Minor Divisions: Players shall not be rostered on more than one team nor in more than one division.

Little League (Major) Division: Any candidate with amateur status who will attain the age of 9 years before September 1, 2019, and who will not attain the age of 13 before August 31, 2019, shall be eligible to compete in Little League Baseball (subject to the local league Board of Directors alignment of this division). This means that a participant who will be 13 years old on September 1 or later is eligible to play that year; a participant who will be 13 years old on August 31 or earlier will not be eligible for either local league play or tournament play at any time during the calendar year in question. **NOTE:** League age 12-year-olds may participate in Minor Division under certain circumstances.

Intermediate (50-70) Division: Any participant with amateur status who will attain the age of 11 years before September 1, 2019, and who will not attain the age of 14 years on or before August 31, 2019, shall be eligible to compete in the Intermediate (50-70) Division. This means a participant who will be 14 years old on September 1 or later is eligible to play that year; a participant who will be 14 years old on August 31 or earlier will not be eligible for either local league or tournament play in the Intermediate (50-70) Division at any time during the calendar year in question.

Junior League: Any player with amateur status who will attain the age of 12 years before September 1, 2019, and who will not attain the age of 15 years on or before August 31, 2019, shall be eligible to compete. This means that a player who will be 15 years old on September 1 or later is eligible to play that year; a player who will be 15 years old on August 31 or earlier will not be eligible for either local league or tournament play in the Junior League at any time during the calendar year in question.

Senior League: Any player with amateur status who will attain the age of 13 years before September 1, 2019, and who will not attain the age of 17 years on or before August 31, 2019, shall be eligible to compete. This means that a player who will be 17 years old on September 1 or later is eligible to play that year; a player who will be 17 years old on August 31 or earlier will not be eligible for either local league or tournament play in the Senior League at any time during the calendar year in question.

Major/Intermediate (50-70) Division/Junior/Senior League: An age appropriate player, in the Major Division and above, AND who is otherwise eligible under all conditions, would be eligible for selection to a team in two regular season divisions in the same league. A local Little League's Board of Directors determines age structure and may limit player selection and participation to one regular season team/division.

A player who is otherwise eligible under all conditions could be eligible for selection to multiple tournament teams; however, a player may only be selected to and participate on one (1) tournament team. Player tournament eligibility is governed by Player Eligibility in the Tournament Rules and Guidelines.

Any player who is league age 12 must be permitted to play in the Major Division. The local league cannot force any player who is league age 12 to play in the Intermediate (50-70) Division or Junior Division if the league offers the Major Division.

NOTE: All Divisions: The Little League group accident insurance program underwritten by an AIG member company covers only those activities approved or sanctioned by Little League Baseball, Incorporated. A unit Tee Ball, Minor League, Little League (Majors), Intermediate (50-70) Division, Junior, or Senior League team shall not participate as a Tee Ball, Minor League, Little League (Majors), Intermediate (50-70) Division, Junior, or Senior League team in games with other teams of other programs or in tournaments except those authorized by Little League International.

Tee Ball, Minor League, Little League (Majors), Intermediate (50-70) Division, Junior, and Senior League participants may participate in other programs during the Tee Ball, Minor League, Little League (Majors), Intermediate (50-70) Division, Junior, and Senior League regular season provided such participation does not disrupt the Tee Ball, Minor League, Little League (Majors), Intermediate (50-70) Division, Junior, or Senior League season.

NOTE 1: See Tournament Rules, ("Player Participation in Other Programs"), regarding participation in non-Little League programs during the International Tournament ("All-Stars").

NOTE 2: Consistent with a manager's ability to conduct the affairs of his or her team, a manager may remove a player from the team, subject to Board of Directors approval, for the current regular season or tournament season if the player repeatedly misses practice or games. If a player is repeatedly missing practices or games, the manager must make the local league Board of Directors aware of the situation immediately.

(b) Each candidate must present acceptable proof of age to the league president at least 48 hours before the player selection plan is put into operation. When and if such formal proof of age is not available, the league president shall gather as much documentary evidence as possible and promptly forward it to the District Administrator. If, in the opinion of the District Administrator, such evidence is satisfactory, a statement to that effect will be sent to the league president, which shall be acceptable in lieu of a birth certificate. Such statement will be held in the local Little League files as acceptable proof-of-age.

(c) The president of the local league MUST certify and be responsible for the eligibility of each candidate prior to player selection. **NOTE 1:** At the time of registration, a player must designate whether he or she will tryout for baseball, softball, or both, if program option permits. A player may be on two rosters in a local Little League program; however, a player shall not register and participate in more than one local Little League program.

(d) The "League Age" of each candidate shall be recorded and announced at the player selection to guide the managers in making their selections.

(e) "League Age" is that age attained before September 1 in any given year. Thus a participant whose 12th birthday is on September 1 or later has a League Age of 11; a participant whose 12th birthday is on August 31 or earlier (of that year), has a League Age of 12. This principle applies regardless of age.

(f) **Majors/Intermediate (50-70) Division/Junior/Senior League:** Any candidate failing to attend at least 50 percent of the spring tryout sessions, shall forfeit league eligibility unless an excuse is presented which is accepted by a majority of the Board of Directors.

Tee Ball and Minor League: Any eligible player who qualifies and becomes available after player assignment should be assigned to a team or placed on a waiting list created by the local league.

NOTE: A local league should accept registrations until the time of player selections. Thereafter, registration may be closed.

(g) Player, manager, and coach data must be supplied to Little League International annually. Leagues may submit information from registration by April 1, 2019. Players claimed under Regulation II(d) and/or IV(h) must be declared on appropriate forms available from Little League International annually. It is highly recommended that data be supplied electronically in approved formats to Little League International via the Little League Data Center. Look for related information online at LittleLeague. org/DataCenter.

> Leagues using DICK'S Team Sports HQ for online registration will have their registration and volunteer information sent automatically and directly to Little League International, helping to fulfill Regulation IV(g) and ASAP Requirement 14.

(h) **If a person had previously resided within the league boundaries for two or more years while serving that league as a dedicated manager, coach, or member of the local league Board of Directors for two or more years, his or her sons and/or daughters are eligible to tryout and be selected by teams in that league (1) provided such service to the league from which the person has moved has continued, (2) subject to written agreement from the league within whose boundaries they currently reside, and (3) approved by the District Administrator.**

Regulation IV(h) – Processing Procedure

The league president will process a IV(h) form. Once the president completes the form, he/she must compile "residency requirement" verification that each player meets the conditions of IV(h) as outlined above. The league president will present this information to the District Administrator for review. Once the District Administrator reviews the documentation in an effort to determine if it meets the regulations, the District Administrator will sign the IV(h) form. The league and the district will maintain the form and documentation in their files. This review process is only required once during a participant's career. The league must maintain this form and documentation for this player for the duration of his/her career until the player graduates from the program or breaks service with the league. Tournament team players will be required to carry a copy of this form and documentation with them throughout the tournament. If contested during tournament play, the league will be required to produce the documentation. Additionally, if it is determined at a later date that the player does not meet the conditions of IV(h), the player is ineligible for further participation. Situations in which documentation is not available must be referred to the Charter Committee through the regional office for a decision. The decision of the Charter Committee is final and binding.

(i) Mandatory Play: Every rostered player present at the start of a game will participate in each game for a minimum of six (6) defensive outs and bat at least one (1) time. For the purposes of this rule, "six (6) defensive outs" is defined as: A player enters the field in one of the nine defensive positions when his/her team is on defense and occupies such position while six outs are made; "bat at least one (1) time" is defined as: A player enters the batter's box with no count and completes that time at bat by being retired or by reaching base safely.

PENALTY: The player(s) involved shall start the next scheduled game, play any previous requirement not completed for Section (i), and the requirement for this game before being removed.

The manager shall for the:

    A.   First Offense - receive a written warning.

    B.   Second Offense - a suspension for the next scheduled game.

    C.   Third Offense - a suspension for remainder of the season.

NOTE 1: If the violation is determined to have been intentional, a more severe penalty may be assessed by the Board of Directors. However, forfeiture of a game may not be invoked.

NOTE 2: There is no exception to this rule unless the game is shortened for any reason, at which time the local league may elect not to impose a penalty on the manager/coach. However, the penalty in this regulation regarding the player who did not meet mandatory play cannot be reduced or waived in a shortened game.

NOTE 3: In Minor League, if a half-inning ends because of the imposition of the five-run limit in "Rule 2.00 - Inning," and a player on the defense has played for the entire half-inning, that player will be considered to have participated for three consecutive outs for the purposes of this rule. However, if the player has not played on defense for the entire inning, that player will be credited only as having played for the number of outs that occurred while the player was used defensively.

Tee Ball and Minor League: If a league uses 15 to 20 player rosters they may reduce the Mandatory Play Rule to three (3) defensive outs and one (1) at bat per game.

> A.R. - If a player/batter is called out by an umpire for using an illegal bat or for Rule 6.07 violation, this will qualify as an at bat for the purpose of this rule.

(j)　Any request for a waiver pertaining to the eligibility of a player, team, manager, or coach must be submitted in writing, by the president of the local Little League through the District Administrator, to their respective Regional Director not later than June 1 of the current year. Requests submitted after that date will not be considered.

Age Alignment For Intermediate (50-70) Division, Junior League, and Senior League

The table below outlines methods of operation for Intermediate (50-70) Division, Junior, and Senior League.

However, if a local league wishes to operate the Junior Division for 13- to 15-year-olds in Regular Season play, it must request permission in writing from the respective regional office. This division may be subject to Senior League rules.

	Intermediate (50-70) Division	Junior League	Senior League
League A	11, 12	13, 14	15, 16
League B	11, 12, 13	13, 14	14, 15, 16
League C	12, 13	13, 14	14, 15, 16
League D	11, 12	13, 14	14, 15
League E	12, 13	13, 14	15, 16
League F	11, 12, 13	13	14, 15, 16
League G	11, 12	13	14, 15, 16
League H	12, 13	13	14, 15
League I	11, 12, 13	13	13, 14, 15, 16

NOTE 1: The structure for Tournament Play is: 8- to 10-Year-Old Division (8, 9, and 10); 9- to 11-Year-Old Division (9, 10, and 11); Little League (Major) Division (10, 11, and 12); Intermediate (50-70) Division (11, 12, and 13); Junior League Division (12, 13, and 14); Senior League Division (13, 14, 15, and 16).

NOTE 2: Little League International requires each local league to assess and evaluate the participants in its player pool prior to structuring its Intermediate (50-70) Division, Junior, and Senior League programs.

Regulation V
Selection of Players

(a) The selection of players for the various teams within a league shall be in compliance with the Little League Draft Methods as detailed in the Operating Policies section in the back of this book. **NOTE:** All candidates who are league age twelve (12) must be drafted to a Major Division team and/or an Intermediate (50-70) Division team. Exceptions can only be made with written approval from the ***District Administrator***, and only if approved at the local league level by the Board of Directors and the parent of the candidate.

(b) When a league decides to substitute a selection system for the ones outlined in the Little League Operating Policies section, a complete description of such substituted system MUST BE PRESENTED in writing FOR APPROVAL to the Charter Committee prior to the player selection process.

(c) **Alternate method of operation**
To aid leagues that are having a difficult time getting enough players for their regular season teams the following option is available: A pool of players from existing regular season teams can be created with players that are willing to participate in extra games during the regular season when teams face a shortage of rostered players for a regular season game within their respective division.

NOTE: Players may not be "borrowed" from an opponent. They must be assigned by the player agent.

Guidelines:
1. The league's player agent will create and run the pool. The league's player agent will use the pool to assign players within their respective division to teams that are short of players on a rotating basis.
2. Managers and/or coaches will not have the right to randomly pick and choose players from the pool within their respective division.
3. Under this option, when a player participates in a game on a team other than his/her own team, such player will not be permitted to pitch in that game.
4. Pool players that are called and show up at the game site must play at least nine (9) consecutive defensive outs and bat once.

(d) Teams are not permitted to enter the Little League program intact, or nearly intact, from non-Little League programs. Under no circumstances will any team or group of players, which did not play on the same team for the previous regular season in the same division of a chartered local Little League, be placed together onto a regular season team in that local Little League. Such players must be processed through the Little League Draft Methods as noted in this regulation.

Regulation VI
Pitchers

(a) Any player on a regular season team may pitch. ***Exception:*** *Any player who has played the position of catcher in four (4) or more innings in a game is not eligible to pitch on that calendar day.*

A player who played the position of catcher for three (3) innings or less, moves to the pitcher position, and delivers 21 pitches or more (**15- and 16-year-olds:** 31 pitches or more) in the same day, may not return to the catcher position on that calendar day. **EXCEPTION:** If the pitcher reaches the 20-pitch limit (**15- and 16-year-olds:** 30-pitch limit) while facing a batter, the pitcher may continue to pitch, and maintain their eligibility to return to the catcher position, until any one of the following conditions occur: (1) that batter reaches base; (2) that batter is retired; or (3) the third out is made to complete the half-inning or the game.

A.R. - The catcher receiving one pitch to a batter in the fourth inning constitutes having caught four (4) innings. Warm-up pitches do not count, only when the ball is live will the pitches count toward innings caught.

(b) A pitcher once removed from the mound cannot return as a pitcher. **Intermediate (50-70) Division, Junior League, and Senior League only:** A pitcher remaining on defense in the game, but moving to a different position, can return as a pitcher anytime in the remainder of the game, but only once per game.

(c) The manager must remove the pitcher when said pitcher reaches the limit for his/her age group as noted below, but the pitcher may remain in the game at another position:
League Age

13 -16	95 pitches per day
11-12	85 pitches per day
9-10	75 pitches per day
7-8	50 pitches per day

EXCEPTION: If a pitcher reaches the limit imposed in Regulation VI(c) for his/her league age while facing a batter, the pitcher may continue to pitch until any one of the following conditions occurs:
1. That batter reaches base;
2. That batter is put out;
3. The third out is made to complete the half-inning or the game.

NOTE: If a pitcher reaches 40 pitches while facing a batter, the pitcher may continue to pitch, and maintain their eligibility to play the position of catcher for the remainder of that day, until any one of the following conditions occurs: (1) that batter reaches base; (2) that batter is retired; or (3) the third out is made to complete the half-inning or the game. The pitcher would be allowed to play the catcher position provided that pitcher is moved, removed, or the game is completed before delivering a pitch to another batter. If a player delivers 41 or more pitches, and is not covered under the threshold exception, the player may not play the position of catcher for the remainder of that day.

(d) Pitchers league age 14 and under must adhere to the following rest requirements:

- If a player pitches 66 or more pitches in a day, four (4) calendar days of rest must be observed.
- If a player pitches 51-65 pitches in a day, three (3) calendar days of rest must be observed.
- If a player pitches 36-50 pitches in a day, two (2) calendar days of rest must be observed.
- If a player pitches 21-35 pitches in a day, one (1) calendar day of rest must be observed.
- If a player pitches 1-20 pitches in a day, no (0) calendar day of rest is required.

NOTE: Under no circumstance shall a player pitch in three (3) consecutive days.

EXCEPTION: If a pitcher reaches a day(s) of rest threshold while facing a batter, the pitcher may continue to pitch until any one of the following conditions occurs: (1) that batter reaches base; (2) that batter is retired; or (3) the third out is made to complete the half-inning or the game. The pitcher will only be required to observe the calendar day(s) of rest for the threshold he/she reached during that at-bat, provided that pitcher is removed or the game is completed before delivering a pitch to another batter.

Pitchers league age 15-16 must adhere to the following rest requirements:

- If a player pitches 76 or more pitches in a day, four (4) calendar days of rest must be observed.
- If a player pitches 61-75 pitches in a day, three (3) calendar days of rest must be observed.
- If a player pitches 46-60 pitches in a day, two (2) calendar days of rest must be observed.
- If a player pitches 31-45 pitches in a day, one (1) calendar day of rest must be observed.
- If a player pitches 1-30 pitches in a day, no (0) calendar day of rest is required.

NOTE: Under no circumstance shall a player pitch in three (3) consecutive days.

EXCEPTION: If a pitcher reaches a day(s) of rest threshold while facing a batter, the pitcher may continue to pitch until any one of the following conditions occurs: (1) that batter reaches base; (2) that batter is retired; or (3) the third out is made to complete the half-inning or the game. The pitcher will only be required to observe the calendar day(s) of rest for the threshold he/she reached during that at-bat, provided that pitcher is removed or the game is completed before delivering a pitch to another batter.

(e) Each league must designate the scorekeeper or another game official as the official pitch count recorder.

(f) The pitch count recorder must provide the current pitch count for any pitcher when requested by either manager or any umpire. However, the manager is responsible for knowing when his/her pitcher must be removed.

(g) The official pitch count recorder should inform the Umpire-in-Chief when a pitcher has delivered his/her maximum limit of pitches for the game, as noted in Regulation VI(c). The Umpire-in-Chief will inform the pitcher's manager that the pitcher must be removed in accordance with Regulation VI(c). However, the failure by the pitch count recorder to notify the Umpire-in-Chief, and/or the failure of the Umpire-in-Chief to notify the manager, does not relieve the manager of his/her responsibility to remove a pitcher when that pitcher is no longer eligible.

(h) Violation of any section of this regulation can result in protest of the game in which it occurs. Protest shall be made in accordance with Playing Rule 4.19.

(j) A player who has attained the league age of twelve (12) is not eligible to pitch in the Minor League. (See Regulation V – Selection of Players)

(k) Pitching in more than one game in a day:

Minor League, Little League (Majors), and Intermediate (50-70) Division — A player may not pitch in more than one game in a day;

Junior League and Senior League — A player may be used as a pitcher in up to two games in a day. **NOTE:** If a pitcher reaches 30 pitches while facing a batter in the first game, the pitcher may continue to pitch, and maintain their eligibility to pitch in the second game on that day, until any one of the following conditions occurs: (1) that batter reaches base; (2) that batter is retired; or (3) the third out is made to complete the half-inning or the game. The pitcher would be allowed to pitch in a second game provided that pitcher is moved, removed, or the game is completed before delivering a pitch to another batter. If a player delivers 31 or more pitches in the first game, and is not covered under the threshold exception, the player may not pitch in the second game that day);

> A.R. - If a **Junior or Senior League** pitcher pitches in more than one game in a day, and has not pitched 31 or more pitches in the first game except as noted under the threshold, the total number of pitches that pitcher may pitch in both games combined is the daily maximum of 95.

NOTES:

1. The withdrawal of an ineligible pitcher after that pitcher is announced, or after a warm-up pitch is delivered, but before that player has pitched a ball to a batter, shall not be considered a violation. Little League officials are urged to take precautions to prevent protests. When a protest situation is imminent, the potential offender should be notified immediately.

> A.R. - **Minor League and Little League (Majors)**: When warming up, if a pitcher is discovered to be ineligible, he/she must be removed and the previous pitcher of record may not return.

2. Pitches delivered in games declared "Regulation Tie Games" or "Suspended Games" shall be charged against pitcher's eligibility.

3. In suspended games resumed on another day, the pitchers of record at the time the game was halted may continue to pitch to the extent of their eligibility for that day, provided said pitcher has observed the required days of rest.

Example 1: A league age 12 pitcher delivers 70 pitches in a game on Monday when the game is suspended. The game resumes on the following Thursday. The pitcher is not eligible to pitch in the resumption of the game because he/she has not observed the required days of rest.

Example 2: A league age 12 pitcher delivers 70 pitches in a game on Monday when the game is suspended. The game resumes on Saturday. The pitcher is eligible to pitch up to 85 more pitches in the resumption of the game because he/she has observed the required days of rest.

Example 3: A league age 12 pitcher delivers 70 pitches in a game on Monday when the game is suspended. The game resumes two weeks later. The pitcher is eligible to pitch up to 85 more pitches in the resumption of the game, provided he/she is eligible based on his/her pitching record during the previous four days.

Regulation VII
Schedules

(a)   The schedule of games for the regular season shall be prepared by the Board of Directors of the league and must provide for not less than twelve (12) games [**Senior Division: Ten (10) games**] per team per regular season against other Little League teams within their respective division, exclusive of playoff and tournament games. **Tee Ball:** It is recommended that no more than twelve (12) games be scheduled per team per season.

(b)   The schedule should provide for not less than two (2) games per week per team. Any facility used for practices and/or games must be approved by the local league Board of Directors. **Intermediate (50-70) Division, Junior League, and Senior League:** Interleague play is permitted provided the proper form is submitted to the District Administrator for approval.

(c)   Where there are two (2) or more leagues in one locality, teams of one league shall not play teams of another league, without approval of the District Administrator, and Regional Director, when necessary as noted in Regulation I(c)(5).

(d)   **Little League (Major) Division:** A team may play one (1) doubleheader in a calendar week. No team shall play three games in a day. (Exception under condition of Rule 4.12.)

   Tee Ball and Minor League: No team shall be scheduled to play two games in one day. (See Rule 4.12).

   Intermediate (50-70) Division/Junior/Senior League: Doubleheaders are permitted.

   If two games involving four teams are played on the same day and on the same field, the first game must be completed before the second game starts. (Exception under condition of Rule 4.12.)

   When league size and limited field availability require leagues to schedule more than one game on the same night and on the same field, the league may be permitted to impose time limits on the games. However, the game must meet the requirements of Rule 4.10 or 4.11 to be official.

(e)   The schedule should be arranged so that at least one-half of the games are scheduled prior to June 15.

(f)   **Majors/Intermediate (50-70) Division/Junior/Senior League:** It is recommended that a split season schedule be arranged with a playoff between the winners of the first and second halves to determine the league champion. **Intermediate (50-70) Division/Junior/Senior:** When approval is granted for two or more leagues – comprising not more than 40,000 population - to form one Intermediate (50-70) Division, Junior League, or Senior League, as provided for in Regulation I(h), one regular season schedule will be prepared by a joint committee from the two or more leagues.

(g)   All play must be terminated by the opening date of school for the fall term but no later than September 1st unless participating in the Training and Development Program.

(h)   **Little League (Major) Division:** There should be no time limits on games unless necessary, based on field limitations. [See Regulation X(c)].

Tee Ball and Minor League: A local league may impose a time limit on games regardless of the number of innings played. It is recommended that no league standings be kept, and no championship games be played.

Regulation VIII
Minor Leagues

(Does not apply to Intermediate (50-70) Division/Junior/Senior League.)

(a)   The purpose of the Minor League program is to provide training and instruction for those candidates who by reason of age and other factors do not qualify for selection in the regular Little League. **NOTE: League age 12-year-olds may only participate under certain circumstances.**

(b)   The Minor League program is the responsibility and is an integral part of the chartered Little League. It is not and may not be operated as a separate entity. It must be restricted to the boundaries of the local league and its players are subject to selection by draft by any Little League (Major) Team of the local league. Refusal of a player to comply shall result in forfeiture of further eligibility in the Little League (Major) Division for the current season.

NOTE: The local league should establish a policy, approved by the Board of Directors, regarding players who decline to move up to a Major League team. Such policy should be distributed at the time of registration and/or tryouts.

(c)   No player or team may be deemed to be the property of, or under the jurisdiction or control of, a particular team in the local league.

(d)   A local league may elect to utilize adult pitch ("Minor League Coach Pitch") or machine pitch ("Minor League Machine Pitch") in Minor League games involving players league ages 7-12. Pitching machines, if used, must be in good working order and must be operated by adult managers, coaches, umpires, or any adult approved by the local league.

NOTE: Participants league age 5 and 6 are permitted to advance to Minor League Coach Pitch or Machine Pitch after participation in Tee Ball for one year.

Regulation IX
Special Games

(a) Special Games are defined as games that:
1. are non-regular season games, and,
2. are not Little League International Tournament games, and,
3. involve only teams from chartered Little League programs, and,
4. have been approved in writing by the Regional Office.

Exception: Intermediate (50-70) Division/Junior League: Up to six (6) games played under Special Games against Little League teams may count towards players' Regular Season schedule. **Senior League:** Up to ten (10) games played under Special Games against Little League teams may count towards players' Regular Season schedule.

(b) Unless expressly authorized under conditions of this Regulation, games played for any purpose other than to establish a league champion or as part of the International Tournament are prohibited. Violation may result in revocation of charter and/or suspension of tournament privileges.

(c) With the approval of the Charter Committee of Little League International, and on recommendation of the Regional Director and District Administrator, chartered leagues may engage in Special Games during and after the regular season but prior to the opening of the school term or September 1st, whichever comes sooner.

(d) Special Games may be played between:
1. Regular season teams or;
2. Tournament teams using either regular season or tournament rules, but not in combination.

(e) Teams participating in Special Games during the regular season shall be regular season teams only. Tournament teams, regular season teams, and Minor League teams involving players below league age 11 may use 8- to 10-Year-Old Division Tournament rules.

(f) **Tournament teams may participate in Special Games after June 1.**

(g) The league president will be charged with responsibility for conducting special games under all rules, regulations, and policies of Little League Baseball.

(h) This rule does not prohibit pre-season practice games between teams in the same division in the same league or the practicing of the league's tournament team against other players in the same division in the same league, provided such practice is done out of uniform.

(i) **Tee Ball:** Special Games are permissible only with regular season teams. However, they are not recommended by Little League International. "All Stars" are not authorized.

Regulation X
Night Games

(a) **Tee Ball, Minor League, Little League (Majors) Division, Intermediate (50-70) Division, Junior, and Senior League** games may be played after sundown under artificial lights. This responsibility shall rest with the local leagues. In any event, no inning shall start after 10:00 p.m. prevailing time (9:00 p.m. for **Tee Ball**). **Intermediate (50-70) Division, Junior, and Senior:** No inning shall start after 10:30 p.m. prevailing time. It will be held that an inning starts the moment that the third out is made, completing the preceding inning.

(b) Artificial lights for Little League games must meet the minimum standards approved by Little League International. (See LittleLeague.org/LightingStandards for more information and standards.)

(c) When league size and limited field availability require leagues to schedule more than one game on the same day or night and on the same field, the league may be permitted to impose time limits on the games. However, the game must meet requirements of Rule 4.10 or 4.11 to be official.

Regulation XI
Admission to Games

No admission shall be charged to any Tee Ball, Minor League, or Little League (Major) Division game. Voluntary contributions are permitted. **Intermediate (50-70) Division/ Junior/Senior League:** Admission charge is permitted.

Regulation XII
Awards

(a) Value of awards and material gifts to individual players must be in accordance with the prevailing rules of the High School Athletic Association of the state in which the player participates.

(b) No awards shall be made to players on the basis of comparable skills or accomplishments. **NOTE:** Honor certificates, team pictures, inexpensive medals, or pins give adequate recognition and provide lasting mementos from Little League.

Regulation XIII
Commercialization

(a) Exploitation of Little League in any form or for any purpose is prohibited.

(b) Solicitation for fundraising by Tee Ball, Minor League, Little League (Major) Division, Intermediate (50-70) Division, Junior, or Senior League players in or out of uniform is prohibited, except for one fundraising project annually under adult supervision. **NOTE:** Reference fundraising guidelines in the Operating Policies section.

(c) A reasonable Little League participation fee may be assessed as a parent's obligation to assure the operational continuity of the local Little League. *AT NO TIME SHOULD PAYMENT OF ANY FEE BE A PREREQUISITE FOR PARTICIPATION IN THE LITTLE LEAGUE PROGRAM.* It is recommended that no fee be collected. It is recommended that parents who are unable to pay a participation fee be encouraged to contribute volunteer time to the league.

(d) No Little League volunteer, employee, or participant, while acting in such capacity, shall execute a contract for or otherwise agree to, accept compensation, personal or otherwise, or remuneration for the use of, or for promoting the use of, any product, service, or organization.

(e) A local Little League or District shall not require any player to use any specific brand/manufacturer of equipment, for the purpose of the league receiving compensation (including deferred compensation) for such a requirement. **NOTE:** Little League's policy on amateurism can be found on page 12.

(f) A local Little League may permit a Regular Season Team and/or Tournament Team to include the name of a team sponsor on the uniform, and the local league may receive a fee for such sponsorships, provided the sponsorship does not conflict with any Little League Rule, Regulation, and/or Policy. Such sponsor shall have no authority with regard to the composition or operation of the league, the team, or its manager and/or coaches. A district, league, or team may not permit a local sponsor of a district, league, or team to use any trademarks of the Little League International at any time. For the sake of clarity, the words Little League in any form or combination, including in a league's name, and the Little League uniform patch are trademarks of Little League International. Please refer to the Little League Operating Policies for detailed guidelines including information on solicitation of funds, such as local league sponsorship, as a charitable organization. **NOTE:** Once a Tournament Team plays its first game in the International Tournament, a reference to a company, product, service, or organization (including, but not limited to, a slogan or logo) may not be added to, included on, or appear on any Tournament Team uniform, apparel, or equipment.

(g) Violation of any part of this regulation shall result in penalties up to and including removal from the Little League program and/or revocation of the league's charter and/or forfeiture of International Tournament game(s).

Regulation XIV
Field Decorum

(a) The actions, on or off the field, of players, managers, coaches, umpires, and league officials must be above reproach. Any player, manager, coach, umpire, or league representative who is involved in a verbal or physical altercation, or an incident of unsportsmanlike conduct, at the game site or any other Little League activity including through online or social media, is subject to disciplinary action by the local league Board of Directors.

(b) Uniformed players, news photographers, managers, coaches, and umpires only shall be permitted within the confines of the playing field just prior to and during games. Batboys and/or batgirls are not permitted at any level of play. Except for the batter, base-runners, and base coaches at first and third bases, all players shall be on their benches in their dugouts or in the bullpen when the team is at bat. When the team is on defense, all reserve players shall be on their benches or in the bullpen. **EXCEPTION:** The on-deck position is permitted in **Intermediate (50-70) Division, Junior, and Senior League.**

(c) Two adult base coaches are permitted.

(d) A manager or coach shall not leave the bench or dugout except to confer with a player or an umpire and only after receiving permission from an umpire. (**EXCEPTION:** In Tee Ball and Minor League, managers and coaches may be on the field for instructional purposes, but shall not assist runners or touch a live ball. At least one adult manager or coach must be in the dugout at all times.)

(e) The possession and/or use of firearms, tobacco products, cigarettes (including e-cigarettes and vapors), controlled substances, and alcoholic beverages in any form is prohibited on the playing field, benches, or dugouts. Alcohol is prohibited at the game site.

(f) Managers and coaches shall not warm up pitchers.

Regulation XV
Appearance of Little Leaguers in the Media

(a) The appearance of Little League players in uniform in advertisements of any kind, or on commercial television programs, or in motion pictures, without the written approval of Little League International, is forbidden.

(b) Brief, televised reports of games and activities on news programs are permitted. Online and traditional print outlets are also permitted to photograph or otherwise record games and activities, solely for news/editorial purposes.

(c) The televising of regular season games, special games, or International Tournament games on a local or regional basis is permitted, provided a contract (available at LittleLeague.org/GameContracts) is in place, and provided written permission from Little League Baseball, Incorporated has been received to televise the specific game(s) or tournament(s).

(d) Radio broadcasts of regular season games and special games are permitted, provided a "Little League Regular Season Radio Contract" (available at LittleLeague.org/GameContracts) for the specific game(s) is properly completed and on file with the local league.

(e) Radio broadcasts of International Tournament games are permitted, provided a "Little League International Tournament Radio Contract" (available at LittleLeague.org/GameContracts) for the specific game(s) or tournament is properly completed and on file with the district.

(f) Internet web-casts of regular season games and special games are permitted, provided a "Little League Regular Season Internet Web-Cast Contract" (available at LittleLeague.org/GameContracts) for the specific game(s) is properly completed and on file with the local league.

(g) Internet web-casts of International Tournament games are permitted, provided a "Little League International Tournament Internet Web-Cast Contract" (available at LittleLeague.org/GameContracts) for the specific game(s) or tournament is properly completed and on file with the district.

(h) Local leagues wishing to initiate a broadcast, web-cast, or live stream of their games on a league-owned and/or operated website, social network, or other digital platform may do so, and must follow Little League's trademark and commercialization policies.

Regulation XVI
Use of Little League Name and Emblem

Use of the Official Emblem "LL," "LLB" and/or words "Little League," "Little League Baseball," "Little Leaguer," "Senior League Little League, "Big League Little League," "Senior League Little League Baseball," "Big League Little League Baseball," "Little League Softball," "Little League Challenger Division," related International Tournament trademarks, etc., (registered under Federal Certificate in U.S. Patent Office), is granted to chartered leagues and cannot be extended by local leagues to any other organization for any purpose whatsoever. These marks are protected both by a special Act of Congress and registrations with the United States Patent and Trademark Office. All rights in and to any and all marks of Little League Baseball, Incorporated are reserved.

Regulation XVII
Tournament Play

This regulation applies to the International Tournament, which includes the 8- to 10-Year-Old Division, the 9- to 11-Year-Old Division, Little League (Major) Division, Intermediate (50-70) Division, Junior League, and Senior League tournaments.

(a) Tournament team practice or tryouts shall be specified by the Tournament Committee.

(b) The practicing of the league's tournament team against other players in the same division in the same league is permitted providing such practice is done out of uniform.

(c) Tournament rules are published herein.

(d) Unless officially notified to the contrary, each league shall assume full responsibility for expenses incurred in tournament competition.

(e) The structure for tournament play in baseball will be: 8- to 10-Year-Old Division; 9- to 11-Year-Old Division; Major Division (10- to 12-); Intermediate (50-70) Division (11, 12, and 13); Junior Division (12, 13, and 14); and Senior Division (13, 14, 15, and 16).

Official Playing Rules
LITTLE LEAGUE BASEBALL® (MAJOR) DIVISION, MINOR LEAGUE BASEBALL, TEE BALL BASEBALL, INTERMEDIATE (50-70) DIVISION BASEBALL, JUNIOR LEAGUE BASEBALL, AND SENIOR LEAGUE BASEBALL

An Approved Ruling (A.R.) serves to illustrate the application of the regulations and rules. Approved Rulings follow the regulations and rules they amplify and are indicated by a box.

Rule 1.00
Objectives of the Game

1.01 - Little League Baseball in all divisions is a game between two teams of nine players each, under the direction of a manager and not more than two rostered coaches, played on a regulation Little League field in accordance with these rules, under the jurisdiction of one or more umpires. **Tee Ball/Minor League Instructional Division** is a game between two teams, under the direction of a manager and not more than two coaches, played on a regulation Little League field in accordance with these rules, under the jurisdiction of one or more umpires. **NOTE: Competitive Minor Leagues and above may only use nine players on defense. See Rules 4.16 and 4.17.**

1.02 - The objective of each team is to win by scoring more runs than the opponent. **Tee Ball:** It is recommended that no score be kept.

1.03 - The winner of the game shall be that team which shall have scored, in accordance with these rules, the greater number of runs at the conclusion of a regulation game.

1.04 - THE PLAYING FIELD. The field shall be laid out according to the instructions, supplemented by Diagrams No. 1 and No. 2. Diagrams No. 3, No. 4, and No. 5 for **Intermediate (50-70) Division/Junior/Senior League**.

The infield shall be a 60-foot square for Little League (Major) division and below. For **Intermediate (50-70) Division**, the infield shall be a 70-foot square. For **Junior/Senior League,** the infield shall be a 90-foot square. **Tee Ball option:** The infield may be a 50-foot square.

The outfield shall be the area between two foul lines formed by extending two sides of the square, as in Diagram 1. The distance from home base to the nearest fence, stand, or other obstruction on fair territory should be 200 feet or more [200 feet or more for **Intermediate (50-70) Division** and 300 feet or more for **Junior/Senior League**]. A distance of 200 feet or more [200 feet or more for **Intermediate (50-70) Division** and 300 feet or more for **Junior/Senior League**] along the foul lines and to center field is recommended. The infield shall be graded so that the base lines and home plate are level.

The pitcher's plate shall be six inches [eight inches for **Intermediate (50-70) Division** and 10 inches for **Junior/Senior League**] above the level of home plate. The infield and outfield, including the boundary lines, are fair territory and all other area is foul territory.

It is desirable that the line from home base through the pitcher's plate to second base shall run east-northeast.

It is recommended that the distance from home base to the backstop, and from the base lines to the nearest fence, stand, or other obstruction on foul territory should be 25 feet or more [45 feet or more for **Intermediate (50-70) Division/Junior/Senior**]. See Diagrams.

Diagram No. 1

Diagram showing Tee Ball/Coach Pitch/Machine Pitch/Minor League/Little League (Major) field layout. All dimensions are compulsory unless marked "optional" or "recommended."

NOTE: Tee Ball base paths may be 50 feet.

Diagram No. 2

Diagram showing layout of Tee Ball/Coach Pitch/Machine Pitch/Minor League/Little League (Major) batter's box and compulsory dimensions.

Diagram No. 3

Diagram showing Intermediate (50-70) Division field layout. All dimensions are compulsory unless marked "optional" or "recommended."

FENCE LIMITS 60'-0" FROM FOUL LINES OR BASE LINES

Diagram No. 4

Diagram showing Junior/Senior League field layout. All dimensions are compulsory unless marked "optional" or "recommended."

NOTE: Junior base paths may be 80 feet.

FENCE LIMITS 60'-0" FROM FOUL LINES OR BASE LINES

Diagram No. 5

Diagram showing layout of Intermediate (50-70) Division/Junior/Senior League batter's box and compulsory dimensions.

Diagram No. 6

See Rule 1.13 and Rule 1.14

When the location of home base is determined, with a steel tape measure 84 feet, 10 inches (99 feet for **Intermediate (50-70) Division** and 127 feet, 3⅜ inches for **Junior/Senior League**) in the desired direction to establish second base. From home base, measure 60 feet (70 feet for **Intermediate (50-70) Division** and 90 feet for **Junior/Senior League**) towards first base; from second base, measure 60 feet (70 feet for **Intermediate (50-70) Division** and 90 feet for **Junior/Senior League**) towards first base, the intersection of these lines establishes first base. From home base, measure 60 feet (70 feet for **Intermediate (50-70) Division** and 90 feet for **Junior/Senior League**) towards third base; from second base, measure 60 feet (70 feet for **Intermediate (50-70) Division** and 90 feet for **Junior/Senior League**) towards third base, the intersection of these lines establishes third base. The distance between first base and third base is 84 feet, 10 inches (99 feet for **Intermediate (50-70) Division** and 127 feet, 3⅜ inches for **Junior/Senior League**). All measurements from home base shall be taken from the point where the first and third base lines intersect. (Base paths of 80 feet are optional for **Junior League** regular season play only.)

The catcher's box, the batter's box, the base coaches boxes, and the three-foot runner's lane shall be laid out as shown in Diagrams.

The catcher's box extends approximately 6 feet 4¾ inches to the rear of home plate. It is determined by extending each foul line 9 feet beyond the back point of home plate. **Intermediate (50-70) Division/Junior/Senior League**: The rear line of the catcher's box is 8 feet directly back from the point of home plate. It extends forward to the rear line of the batter's box. It is 3 feet 7 Inches wide.

The batter's box shall be rectangular, 6 feet by 3 feet [6 feet by 4 feet for **Intermediate (50-70) Division/Junior/Senior League**]. The inside line, if used, shall be parallel to and 4 inches [6 inches for **Intermediate (50-70) Division/Junior/Senior League**] away from the side of home plate. It shall extend forward from the center of home plate 3 feet and to the rear 3 feet.

The base coaches boxes shall be 4 feet by 8 feet (10 feet by 20 feet for **Intermediate (50-70) Division/Junior/Senior League**) and shall not be closer than 6 feet [10 feet for **Intermediate (50-70) Division/Junior/Senior League**] from the foul lines.

The foul lines and all other playing lines indicated in the diagrams by solid black lines shall be marked with chalk or other white material. Caustic lime must not be used.

The grass lines and dimensions shown on the diagrams are those used in many fields, but they are not mandatory. Each league shall determine the size and shape of the grassed and bare areas of its playing field.

1.05 - Home base shall be marked by a five-sided slab of whitened rubber. It shall be a 17-inch square with two of the corners filled in so that one edge is 17 inches long, two 8½ inches, and two are 12 inches. It shall be set in the ground with the point at the intersection of the lines extending from home base to first base and to third base; with the 17-inch edge facing the pitcher's plate and the two 12-inch edges coinciding with the first and third base lines. The top edges of home base shall be beveled and the base shall be fixed in the ground level with the ground surface. The black beveled edge is not considered part of home plate.

1.06 - First, second, and third bases shall be marked by white canvas or rubber covered bags, securely attached to the ground. The first and third base bags shall be entirely within the infield. The second base bag shall be centered on second base. The base bags shall not be less than fourteen (14) nor more than fifteen (15) inches square and the outer edges shall not be more than two and one-fourth (2¼) inches thick and filled with a soft material. **Leagues are required to ensure that first, second, and third bases will disengage their anchor.** A list of licensed, disengageable bases can be found at LittleLeague.org/FieldSupplies.

NOTE 1: If a base is dislodged from its position during a play, any following runner on the same play shall be considered as touching or occupying the base if, in the umpire's judgment, that runner touches or occupies the dislodged bag or the point marked by the original location of the dislodged bag.

NOTE 2: Use of the "Double First Base" is permissible at all levels of play. See Rule 7.15.

1.07 - The pitcher's plate shall be a rectangular slab of whitened rubber 18 inches by 4 inches [24 inches by 6 inches for **Intermediate (50-70) Division/Junior/Senior League**]. It shall be set in the ground as shown in the Diagrams, so that the distance between the front side of the pitcher's plate and home base (the rear point of home plate) shall be 46 feet [50 feet for **Intermediate (50-70) Division** and 60 feet, 6 inches for **Junior/Senior League**]. (Detailed diagrams may be downloaded at LittleLeague.org/FieldLayout.);

NOTE: 54 feet pitching distance is optional for Junior League regular season only.

1.08 - The league shall furnish players' benches, one each for the home and visiting teams. Such benches should not be less than 25 feet from the base lines. They shall be protected by wire fencing.

NOTE 1: The on-deck position is not permitted in **Little League (Major) Division and below**.

A.R. - Fenced-in areas MAY NOT be used for an on-deck batter.

NOTE 2: Only the first batter of each half-inning will be permitted outside the dugout between half-innings in **Little League (Major) Division and below**.

A.R. - The next batter should be ready with a helmet on, but may not pick up a bat until it is his/her turn at bat.

1.09 - The ball used must meet Little League specifications and standards. It shall weigh not less than five (5) nor more than five and one-fourth (5¼) ounces, and measure not less than nine (9) nor more than nine and one-fourth (9¼) inches in circumference. (**Tee Ball:** The ball may carry the words "Little League Tee Ball.")

NOTE: Baseballs licensed by Little League will be printed with one of two designations: "RS" (for regular season play) or "RS-T" (for regular season and tournament play).

1.10 - The bat must be a baseball bat which meets the USA Baseball Bat standard (USABat) as adopted by Little League. It shall be a smooth, rounded stick, and made of wood or of material and color tested and proved acceptable to the USA Baseball Bat standard (USABat).

Non-wood and laminated bats used in the Little League (Majors) and below, Intermediate (50-70) Division, and Junior League divisions shall bear the USA Baseball logo signifying that the bat meets the USABat - USA Baseball's Youth Bat Performance Standard. All BPF – 1.15 bats are prohibited. The bat diameter shall not exceed 2⅝ inches for these divisions of play. Bats meeting the Batted Ball Coefficient of

Restitution (BBCOR) standard may also be used in the Intermediate (50-70) Division and Junior League Division. Additional information is available at LittleLeague.org/BatInfo.

Tee Ball: Under the USABat standard, certified Tee Ball bats (26" and shorter) will feature the USA Baseball mark and text which reads ONLY FOR USE WITH APPROVED TEE BALLS. All Tee Ball bats must feature the USA Baseball mark and accompanying text. Tee Ball bats that were produced and/or purchased prior to the implementation of the new standard can be certified using an Approved Tee Ball Sticker via the USA Baseball Tee Ball Sticker Program (USABaseballShop.com). **NOTE 1:** Approved Tee Ball bats may also be used for Coach Pitch/Machine Pitch Minor Divisions only with the use of approved Tee Balls.

Minor/Major Divisions: It shall not be more than 33 inches in length; nor more than 2⅝ inches in diameter, and if wood, not less than fifteen-sixteenths ($^{15}/_{16}$) inches in diameter (⅞ inch for bats less than 30") at its smallest part. Wood bats taped or fitted with a sleeve may not exceed sixteen (16) inches from the small end. **NOTE 1:** Solid one-piece wood barrel bats do not require a USA Baseball logo. **NOTE 2:** Approved Tee Ball bats may also be used for Coach Pitch/Machine Pitch Minor Divisions only with the use of approved Tee Balls.

Intermediate (50-70) Division and Junior League: It shall not be more than 34" inches in length; nor more than 2⅝ inches in diameter, and if wood, not less than fifteen-sixteenths ($^{15}/_{16}$) inches in diameter (⅞ inch for bats less than 30") at its smallest part. Wood bats taped or fitted with a sleeve may not exceed eighteen (18) inches from the small end. **NOTE 1:** Solid one-piece wood barrel bats do not require a USA Baseball logo. **NOTE 2:** Also, permitted for the Intermediate (50-70) Division and Junior League Division are bats meeting the BBCOR performance standard, and so labeled with a silkscreen or other permanent certification mark. The certification mark shall be rectangular, a minimum of a half-inch on each side and located on the barrel of the bat in any contrasting color. Aluminum/alloy and composite bats shall be marked as to their material makeup being aluminum/alloy or composite. This marking shall be silkscreen or other permanent certification mark, a minimum of one-half-inch on each side, and located on the barrel of the bat in any contrasting color.

Senior League: It shall not be more than 36 inches in length, nor more than 2⅝ inches in diameter, and if wood, not less than fifteen-sixteenths ($^{15}/_{16}$) inches in diameter (⅞ inch for bats less than 30") at its smallest part. Wood bats taped or fitted with a sleeve may not exceed eighteen (18) inches from the small end. The bat shall not weigh, numerically, more than three ounces less than the length of the bat (e.g., a 33-inch-long bat cannot weigh less than 30 ounces). All bats not made of a single piece of wood shall meet the Batted Ball Coefficient of Restitution (BBCOR) performance standard, and such bats shall be so labeled with a silkscreen or other permanent certification mark. The certification mark shall be rectangular, a minimum of a half-inch on each side and located on the barrel of the bat in any contrasting color. Aluminum/alloy and composite bats shall be marked as to their material makeup being aluminum/alloy or composite. This marking shall be silkscreen or other permanent certification mark, a minimum of one-half-inch on each side, and located on the barrel of the bat in any contrasting color.

In all divisions, non-wood bat must have a grip of cork, tape, or composition material, and must extend a minimum of 10 inches from the small end. Slippery tape or similar material is prohibited.

NOTE 1: The traditional batting donut is not permissible.

NOTE 2: The use of pine tar or any other similar adhesive substance is prohibited at all levels of Little League Baseball. Use of these substances will result in the bat being declared illegal and removed from play.

NOTE 3: Non-wood bats may develop dents from time to time. Bats that have cracks or sharp edges, or that cannot pass through the approved Little League bat ring for the appropriate division must be removed from play. The 2¼-inch bat ring must be used for bats labeled 2¼. The 2⅝-inch bat ring must be used for bats labeled for 2⅝.

NOTE 4: An illegal bat must be removed. Any bat that has been altered shall be removed from play. **PENALTY** – See Rule – 6.06(d).

> A.R. - If the certification mark/s on a bat are not legible, that bat cannot be used and shall be removed from the game.

1.11 -

(a) (1) All players on a team shall wear numbered uniforms identical in color, trim, and style.

(2) The Little League Official Shoulder Patch must be affixed to the upper left sleeve or left chest of the uniform shirt. Patches shall be placed centered on the left shoulder sleeve; or, centered on the left chest for sleeveless style. The patch may not be screen-printed or sublimated.

 Worn centered on the left shoulder sleeve;

 Patches centered over left chest on sleeveless style.

(3) Any part of the pitcher's undershirt or T-shirt exposed to view shall be of a solid color. The pitcher's undershirt sleeves, if exposed, shall not be white or gray. Neoprene sleeves, if worn by a pitcher, must be covered by an undershirt. **NOTE:** A pitcher shall not wear any items on his/her hands, wrists, or arms which may be distracting to the batter, e.g. sweat bands.

(b) A league must provide each team with a distinctive uniform. Uniforms are the property of the league. **Tee Ball and Minor League:** T-shirts and caps are recommended, but hand-me-down uniforms may be worn.

(c) Sleeve lengths may vary for individual players, but the sleeves of each individual shall be approximately the same length. No player shall wear ragged, frayed, or slit sleeves.

(d) No players shall attach to a uniform tape or other material of a different color than the uniform.

(e) No part of the uniform shall include a pattern that imitates or suggests the shape of a baseball.

(f) Glass buttons and polished metal shall not be used on a uniform.

(g) No player shall attach anything to the heel or toe of the shoe other than a toe plate.

(h) Shoes with metal spikes or cleats are not permitted. Shoes with molded cleats are permissible. [**Intermediate (50-70) Division/Junior/Senior League**: shoes with metal spikes or cleats are permitted.]

> A.R. - **Little League (Majors) and below**: Removable spikes or cleats are permitted if, when removed, no metal remains exposed.

(i) Managers and coaches must not wear conventional baseball uniforms or shoes with metal spikes but may wear cap, slacks, and shirt. [**Intermediate (50-70) Division/Junior/Senior League:** Managers and coaches may wear conventional baseball uniforms or cap, slacks, and shirts. They may not wear shoes with metal spikes.]

(j) Players must not wear jewelry such as, but not limited to, rings, watches, earrings, bracelets, necklaces, nor any hard cosmetic/decorative items. This rule applies regardless of the composition of such jewelry, hard cosmetic item, or hard decorative item. **EXCEPTION**: Jewelry that alerts medical personnel to a specific condition is permissible.

(k) Casts may not be worn during the game by players and umpires.

NOTE: Persons wearing casts, including managers and coaches, must remain in the dugout during the game.

1.12 - The catcher must wear a catcher's mitt (not a first baseman's mitt or fielder's glove) of any shape, size, or weight consistent with protecting the hand.

1.13 - The first baseman must wear a glove or mitt of any weight with the following maximum specifications:

(a) not more than 14 inches long (measured from the bottom edge or heel straight up across the center of the palm to a line even with the highest point of the glove or mitt), and;

(b) not more than eight inches wide across the palm (measured from the bottom edge of the webbing farthest from the thumb in a horizontal line to the outside of the little finger edge of the glove or mitt), and;

(c) webbing not more than 5¾ inches wide (measured across the top end or along any line parallel to the top). See Diagram No. 6.

1.14 - Each defensive player (other than the first baseman and catcher) must wear a glove of any weight, with the same maximum specifications as noted in Rule 1.13.

1.15 -

(a) The pitcher's glove may not, exclusive of the piping, be white or light gray, nor, in the judgment of an umpire, distracting in any manner.

(b) No pitcher shall attach to the glove any foreign material of a color different from the glove. The pitcher may wear a batting glove on the non-pitching hand under the pitcher's glove provided the batting glove is not white, gray, or optic yellow.

1.16 - Each league shall provide in the dugout or bench of the offensive team six (6) [seven (7) for **Intermediate (50-70) Division/Junior/Senior League**] protective helmets which must meet NOCSAE (National Operating Committee on Standards for Athletic Equipment) specifications and standards. Use of the helmet by the batter, all base runners, and base coaches is mandatory. Use of a helmet by an adult base coach or any defensive player is optional. Each helmet shall have an exterior warning label. Helmets must have a non-glare surface and cannot be mirror-like in nature. Each helmet must meet NOCSAE specifications and bear the NOCSAE stamp as well as an exterior warning label as noted above. **Warning!** Manufacturers have advised that altering helmets in any way can be dangerous. Altering the helmet in any form, including painting or adding decals (by anyone other than the manufacturer or authorized dealer) may void the helmet warranty. Helmets may not be re-painted and may not contain tape or re-applied decals unless approved in writing by the helmet manufacturer or authorized dealer.

A.R. - If a player, during play, removes his/her helmet or causes his/her helmet to come off, he/she shall NOT be called out, but shall be warned not to intentionally remove his/her helmet and, if it continues, the player may be removed for unsportsmanlike conduct, as this can cause an unsafe condition.

1.17 - All male players must wear athletic supporters. Male catchers must wear the metal, fibre, or plastic type cup, and approved long or short-model chest protector. Female catchers must wear long or short model chest protectors. All catchers must wear chest protectors with neck collar, throat guard, shin guards, and catcher's helmet, all of which must meet Little League specifications and standards. The catcher's helmet must meet NOCSAE specifications and standards, and bear the NOCSAE stamp. All catchers must wear a mask, "dangling" type throat protector, and catcher's helmet during infield/outfield practice, pitcher warm-up, and games. **NOTE:** Skull caps are not permitted. **Warning!** Manufacturers have advised that altering helmets in any way can be dangerous. Altering the helmet in any form, including painting or adding decals (by anyone other than the manufacturer or authorized dealer) may void the helmet warranty. Helmets may not be re-painted and may not contain tape or re-applied decals unless approved in writing by the helmet manufacturer or authorized dealer.

A.R. - Wearing of a catcher's helmet with mask and dangling throat guard (even if the mask has a wire extension) is required during games, pitcher warm-up, and any form of infield or infield/outfield practice. The "Hockey Style" helmet is authorized for use at all levels of play. The "dangling" throat guard still must be attached properly.

Rule 2.00
Definition of Terms

(All definitions in Rule 2.00 are listed alphabetically)

ADJUDGED is a judgment decision by an umpire.

An **APPEAL** is an act of a fielder in claiming a violation of the rules by the offensive team.

An **AT-BAT**, for the purposes of meeting the requirements of Mandatory Play (if applicable), is when a batter assumes the position of a batter with no count and is retired or reaches base. An at-bat for scorekeeping/statistical purposes is defined in the publication, "What's the Score?"

A **BACKSTOP** is the barrier erected behind the catcher in order to allow the catcher to retrieve passed balls easily.

A **BALK** is an illegal act by the pitcher with a runner or runners on base entitling all runners to advance one base [**Intermediate (50-70) Division/Junior/Senior League**]. A balk is not called in the **Little League (Major) Division and below**. (See Rule 8.05 - Illegal Pitch.)

A **BALL** is a pitch which does not enter the strike zone in flight and is not struck at by the batter. **NOTE:** If the pitch touches the ground and bounces through the strike zone it is a "ball." If such a pitch touches the batter, the batter shall be awarded first base. If the batter swings at such a pitch and misses, it is a strike. **Majors/Intermediate (50-70) Division/Junior/Senior League:** If the batter swings at such a pitch after two strikes, the ball cannot be caught for the purposes of Rule 6.05(b)(2) and 6.09(b). If the batter hits such a pitch, the ensuing action shall be the same as if the batter hit the ball in flight.

A **BASE** is one of four points which must be touched by a runner in order to score a run; more usually applied to the canvas bags and the rubber plate which mark the base points.

A **BASE COACH** is a team member in uniform or an adult manager and/or coach who is stationed in the base coach's box at first and/or third base to direct the batter and the runners. **NOTE:** Two (2) adult base coaches are permitted at all levels. The second coach may be 16 years or older. See Rule 4.05 for restrictions.

A **BASE ON BALLS** is an award of first base granted to batters who, during their time at bat, receive four pitches outside the strike zone. See Rule 6.08(a).

A **BATTER** is an offensive player who takes a position in the batter's box.

BATTER-RUNNER is a term that identifies the offensive player who has just finished a time at bat until that player is retired or until the play on which that player becomes a runner ends.

The **BATTER'S BOX** is the area within which the batter must stand during a time at bat.

The **BATTERY** is the pitcher and catcher.

The **BATTING ORDER** is the list of current defensive players (and the designated hitter in **Senior League**) in the order in which they are to bat. **Exceptions:** In all divisions, the batting order may contain the entire roster of players. In **Tee Ball and Minor League**, the batting order shall contain the entire roster of players.

BENCH or **DUGOUT** is the seating facilities reserved for players, substitutes, one manager, and not more than two coaches when they are not actively engaged on the playing field. Batboys and/or batgirls are not permitted.

A.R. - Bench or dugout is not for additional coaches or scorekeepers.

A **BUNT** is a batted ball not swung at, but intentionally met with the bat and tapped slowly. The mere holding of the bat in the strike zone is not an attempted bunt. (**Tee Ball:** Bunts are not permitted. Batters are not permitted to take a half-swing. If the umpire feels the batter is taking a half-swing, the batter may be called back to swing again.)

A.R. - If no attempt is made to make contact with a ball outside the strike zone while in the bunting stance, it shall be called a ball. The batter must offer at the pitch for it to be a strike.

A **CALLED GAME** is one in which, for any reason, the Umpire-in-Chief terminates play.

A **CATCH** is the act of a fielder in getting secure possession in the hand or glove of a ball in flight and firmly holding it before it touches the ground providing such fielder does not use cap, protector, pocket, or any other part of the uniform in getting possession. It is not a catch, however, if simultaneously or immediately following contact with the ball, the fielder collides with a player, or with a wall, or if that fielder falls down, and as a result of such collision or falling, drops the ball. It is not a catch if a fielder touches a fly ball which then hits a member of the offensive team or an umpire and then is caught by another defensive player. If the fielder has made the catch and drops the ball while in the act of making a throw following the catch, the ball shall be adjudged to have been caught. In establishing the validity of the catch, the fielder shall hold the ball long enough to prove complete control of the ball and that release of the ball is voluntary and intentional. A catch is legal if the ball is finally held by any fielder, even though juggled, or held by another fielder before it touches the ground. Runners may leave their bases the instant the first fielder touches the ball.

The **CATCHER** is the fielder who takes the position back of the home base.

The **CATCHER'S BOX** is that area within which the catcher shall stand until the pitcher delivers the ball. (See Rule 4.03)

A **COACH** is an adult appointed to perform such duties as the manager may designate. **NOTE**: If two (2) coaches are appointed, the second coach may be age 16 or older.

A **DEAD BALL** is a ball out of play because of a legally created temporary suspension of play.

DEAD BALL AREA is the area beyond any intended physical boundary, such as a fence, rope, chalk line, any stands, bleachers, dugouts, player's benches, or designated media areas, or any other boundary line as determined in the pregame conference. If a ball becomes lodged in a fence, backstop, umpire's equipment, or catcher's equipment, it is considered to be in a dead ball area.

The **DEFENSE** (or **DEFENSIVE**) is the team, or any player of the team, in the field.

A **DOUBLE HEADER** is two regularly scheduled or rescheduled games, played by the same team(s) on the same day.

A **DOUBLE PLAY** is a play by the defense in which two offensive players are retired as a result of continuous action, providing there is no error between putouts.

(a) A force double play is one in which both putouts are force plays.

(b) A reverse force double play is one in which the first out is made at any base and the second out is made by tagging a runner who originally was forced, before the runner touches the base to which that runner was forced.

DUGOUT (see definition of "BENCH")

A **FAIR BALL** is a batted ball that settles on fair ground between home and first base, or between home and third base, or that is on or over fair territory when bounding to the outfield past first or third base, or that touches first, second, or third base, or that first falls on fair territory on or beyond first base or third base, or that, while on or over fair territory touches the person of an umpire or player, or that, while over fair territory, passes out of the playing field in flight.

NOTE: A fair fly shall be adjudged according to the relative position of the ball and the foul line, including the foul pole, and not as to whether the fielder is on fair or foul territory at the time such fielder touches the ball.

FAIR TERRITORY is that part of the playing field within, and including the first base and third base lines, from home base to the bottom of the playing field fence and perpendicularly upwards. Home plate, first base and third base and all foul lines are in fair territory.

A **FIELDER** is any defensive player.

FIELDER'S CHOICE is the act of a fielder who handles a fair grounder and, instead of throwing it to first base to put out the batter-runner, throws to another base in an attempt to put out a preceding runner. The term is also used by scorers (a) to account for the advance of the batter-runner who takes one or more extra bases when the fielder who handles the safe hit attempts to put out a preceding runner; (b) to account for the advance of a runner (other than by stolen base or error) while a fielder is attempting to put out another runner; and (c) to account for the advance of a runner made solely because of the defensive team's indifference. (Undefended steal).

A **FLY BALL** is a batted ball that goes high in the air in flight.

A **FORCE PLAY** is a play in which a runner legally loses the right to occupy a base by reason of the batter becoming a runner. (**NOTE:** Confusion regarding this play is removed by remembering that frequently the "force" situation is removed during the play. **Example:** Runner on first, one out, ground ball hit sharply to first baseman, who touches the base and the batter-runner is out. The force is removed at that moment and the runner advancing to second must be tagged. If there had been a runner at second or third, and either of these runners scored before the tag-out at second, the run(s) would count. Had the first baseman thrown to second and the ball had been returned to first, the play at second would have been a force-out, making two outs, and the return throw to first would have made the third out. In that case, no run would score.)

A.R. - Runners forced to advance as a result of the batter-runner being awarded first base.

A **FORFEITED GAME** is a game declared ended by the Umpire-in-Chief in favor of the offended team by the score of 6 to 0 [7-0 for **Intermediate (50-70) Division/Junior/ Senior League**], for violation of the rules. **Tee Ball:** There shall be no forfeits in Tee Ball.

A **FOUL BALL** is a batted ball that settles on foul territory between home and first base, or between home and third base, or that bounds past first or third base on or over foul territory, or that first falls on foul territory beyond first or third base, or that while on or over foul territory, touches the person of an umpire or player, or any object foreign to the natural ground.

NOTE 1: A foul fly shall be judged according to the relative position of the ball and the foul line, including the foul pole, and not as to whether the fielder is on foul or fair territory at the time that fielder touches the ball.

NOTE 2: In Tee Ball, the ball is foul if it travels less than 15 feet in fair territory from home plate. The ball is also foul if the batter hits the tee with the bat.

FOUL TERRITORY is that part of the playing field outside the first and third base lines extended to the fence and perpendicularly upwards.

A **FOUL TIP** is a batted ball that goes sharp and direct from the bat to the catcher's hands and is legally caught. It is not a foul tip unless caught and any foul tip that is caught is a strike, and the ball is in play. It is not a catch if it is a rebound, unless the ball has first touched the catcher's glove or hand. A foul tip can only be caught by the catcher.

A **GROUND BALL** is a batted ball that rolls or bounces close to the ground.

The **HOME TEAM** is the team which takes the field first at the start of the game. Adopted schedules will determine which team this will be.

ILLEGAL (or **ILLEGALLY**) is contrary to these rules.

An **ILLEGAL BAT** is a bat that has been altered or a bat that is not approved for play because it does not meet specifications with regard to length, weight, barrel diameter, labeling, or performance standard for the division in which it is used. **PENALTY** – See Rule 6.06(d).

An **ILLEGAL PITCH** is (1) a pitch delivered to the batter when the pitcher does not have the pivot foot in contact with the pitcher's plate; or (2) a quick return pitch. **Intermediate (50-70) Division/Junior/Senior League:** An illegal pitch with runners on base is a balk. (See also definition of "Pitch.")

A.R. - This would apply to rule 8.05(e) and 8.05(g). In all other instances of Rule 8.05 with no runners on base, no penalty is enforced. In such cases, the umpire shall call "Time" and the pitcher and batter will resume the count without reference to the pitch.

An **ILLEGALLY BATTED BALL** is one hit by the batter with one or both feet on the ground entirely outside the batter's box.

INELIGIBLE PITCHER - Applies to regular season violations of Regulation VI. (See also Rule 4.19.)

INELIGIBLE PLAYER - Applies to regular season violations of regulations regarding league age, residence or school attendance (as defined by Little League International), and participation on the proper team within the local league. (See also Rule 4.19.)

The **INFIELD** is that portion of the field in fair territory, which includes areas normally covered by infielders.

An **INFIELDER** is a fielder who occupies a position in the infield.

An **INFIELD FLY** is a fair fly ball (not including a line drive nor an attempted bunt) which can be caught by an infielder with ordinary effort, when first and second, or first, second and third bases are occupied, before two are out. The pitcher, catcher, and any outfielder stationed in the infield on the play shall be considered infielders for the purpose of this rule.

When it seems apparent that a batted ball will be an Infield Fly, the umpire shall immediately declare "Infield Fly" for the benefit of the runners. If the ball is near the baseline, the umpire shall declare "Infield Fly, if fair."

The ball is alive and runners may advance at the risk of that ball being caught, or retouch and advance after the ball is touched, the same as on any fly ball. If the hit becomes a foul ball, it is treated the same as any foul.

NOTE 1: If a declared Infield Fly is allowed to fall untouched to the ground, and bounces foul and remains foul before passing first or third base, it is a foul ball. If a declared Infield Fly falls untouched to the ground outside the baseline, and bounces fair before passing first or third base, it is an Infield Fly.

NOTE 2: The Infield Fly Rule does not apply in **Tee Ball**.

A.R. - The infield dirt and the outfield grass do not form a boundary line for infield fly purposes.

IN FLIGHT describes a batted, thrown, or pitched ball which has not yet touched the ground or some object other than a fielder. If the pitch touches the ground and bounces through the strike zone, without being struck at by the batter, it is a "ball." If such a pitch touches the batter, that batter shall be awarded first base. **Majors/Intermediate (50-70) Division/Junior/Senior League:** If the batter swings at such a pitch after two strikes, the ball cannot be caught for the purpose of Rule 6.05(b). If the batter hits such a pitch, the ensuing action shall be the same as if the ball was hit in flight.

IN JEOPARDY is a term indicating that the ball is in play and an offensive player may be put out.

An **INNING** is that portion of a game within which the teams alternate on offense and defense and in which there are three putouts for each team. Each team's time at bat is a half-inning. It will be held that an inning starts the moment the third out is made completing the preceding inning. **(Minor League Only – A five-run limit is to be imposed which would complete the half inning.)**

INTERFERENCE

(a) Offensive interference is an act by a member of the team at bat which interferes with, obstructs, impedes, hinders, or confuses any fielder attempting to make a play. If the umpire declares the batter, batter-runner, or a runner out for interference, all other runners shall return to the last base that was, in the judgment of the umpire, legally touched at the time of the interference, unless otherwise provided by these rules.

> A.R. - Interference does not have to be intentional for it to be called.

(b) Defensive interference is an act by a fielder which hinders or prevents a batter from hitting a pitch.

(c) Umpire's interference occurs (1) when an umpire hinders, impedes, or prevents a catcher's throw attempting to retire a runner, or (2) when a fair ball touches an umpire in fair territory before passing a fielder.

> A.R. - Only the plate umpire may interfere with the catcher and only on a cleanly caught ball or a pitched ball that doesn't cause the catcher to move from his/her position. If the catcher errs on the ball, the umpire will be considered part of the field, and no interference results.

(d) Spectator interference occurs when a spectator reaches out of the stands or goes on the playing field, and touches a live ball.

(e) On any interference the ball is dead.

The **LEAGUE** is a group of teams who play each other in a pre-arranged schedule under these rules for the league championship.

LEGAL (or **LEGALLY**) is in accordance with these rules.

A **LINE DRIVE** is a batted ball that goes sharp and direct from the bat to a fielder without touching the ground.

A **LIVE BALL** is a ball which is in play.

The **MANAGER** is an adult appointed by the president to be responsible for the team's actions on the field, and to represent the team in communications with the umpire and the opposing team.

(a) The manager shall always be responsible for the team's conduct, observance of the official rules, and deference to the umpires.

(b) If a manager leaves the field, that manager shall designate an adult coach as a substitute, and such substitute manager shall have the duties, rights, and responsibilities of the manager. If no adult coach is available, the Umpire-in-Chief shall designate a temporary adult manager. If no adult is available, the game or team activities shall be terminated. (See Rule 4.16.)

OBSTRUCTION is the act of a fielder who, while not in possession of the ball, impedes the progress of any runner. A fake tag is considered obstruction. (**NOTE:** Obstruction shall be called on a defensive player who blocks off a base, base line, or home plate from a base runner while not in possession of the ball.)

OFFENSE is the team, or any player of the team, at bat.

OFFICIAL RULES - The rules contained in this book.

OFFICIAL SCORER - See Rule 10.00 in "What's the Score" publication.

An **OUT** is one of the three required retirements of an offensive team during its time at bat.

The **OUTFIELD** is that portion of the field in fair territory which is normally covered by outfielders.

An **OUTFIELDER** is a fielder who occupies a position in the outfield, which is the area of the playing field most distant from home base.

OVERSLIDE (or **OVERSLIDING**) is the act of an offensive player when the slide to a base, other than when advancing from home to first base, is with such momentum that the player loses contact with the base.

A **PENALTY** is the application of these rules following an illegal act.

The **PERSON** of a player or an umpire is any part of the body, clothing, or equipment.

A **PITCH** is a ball delivered to the batter by the pitcher. **Little League (Major)/ Minor League Exception:** For the purpose of maintaining a pitch count, an illegal pitch shall count as one pitch; even if a pitch is not actually thrown.

A **PITCHER** is the fielder designated to deliver the pitch to the batter.

The pitcher's **PIVOT FOOT** is that foot which is in contact with the pitcher's plate as the pitch is delivered.

"PLAY" is the umpire's order to start the game or to resume action following any dead ball.

A **QUICK RETURN** is a pitch made with obvious intent to catch a batter off balance. It is an illegal pitch. (See Penalty – 8.05)

REGULATION GAME - See Rules 4.10 and 4.11.

A **RETOUCH** is the act of a runner returning to a base as legally required.

A **RUN** (or **SCORE**) is the score made by an offensive player who advances from batter to runner and touches first, second, third, and home bases in that order.

A **RUNDOWN** is the act of the defense in an attempt to retire a runner between bases.

A **RUNNER** is an offensive player who is advancing toward, touching, or returning to any base.

"SAFE" is a declaration by the umpire that a runner is entitled to the base for which that runner was trying.

SET POSITION is one of the two legal pitching positions.

A **STRIKE** is a legal pitch which meets any of these conditions -
(a) Is struck at by the batter and is missed;
(b) Is not struck at, if any part of the ball passes through any part of the strike zone;
(c) Is fouled by the batter when there is less than two strikes;
(d) Is bunted foul (batter is out and ball is dead, if the batter bunts foul on the third strike);
(e) Touches the batter's person as the batter strikes at it (dead ball);
(f) Touches the batter in flight in the strike zone; or
(g) Becomes a foul tip (ball is live and in play).

NOTE: In **Tee Ball**, the local league will determine whether or not strikeouts will be permitted.

The **STRIKE ZONE** is that space over home plate which is between the batter's armpits and the top of the knees when the batter assumes a natural stance. The umpire shall determine the strike zone according to the batter's usual stance when that batter swings at a pitch.

A **SUSPENDED GAME** is a called game which is to be completed at a later date.

A **TAG** is the action of a fielder in touching a base with the body while holding the ball securely and firmly in the hand or glove; or touching a runner with the ball, or with the hand or glove holding the ball, while holding the ball securely and firmly in the hand or glove.

A **THROW** is the act of propelling the ball with the hand and arm to a given objective and is to be always distinguished from the pitch.

A **TIE GAME** is a regulation game which is called when each team has the same number of runs.

"TIME" is the announcement by the umpire of a legal interruption of play, during which the ball is dead.

To **TOUCH** a player or umpire is to touch any part of the player or umpire's body, clothing, or equipment.

A **TRIPLE PLAY** is a play by the defense in which three offensive players are retired as a result of continuous action, providing there is no error between putouts.

A **WILD PITCH** is one so high, so low, or so wide of the plate that it cannot be handled with ordinary effort by the catcher.

WIND-UP POSITION is one of the two legal pitching positions.

Rule 3.00
Game Preliminaries

3.01 - Before the game begins the umpires shall-

(a)   require strict observance of all rules governing team personnel, implements of play, and equipment of players;

(b)   be sure that all playing lines (heavy lines on Diagrams No. 1 and No. 2) are marked with non-caustic lime, chalk, or other white material easily distinguishable from the ground or grass;

(c)   receive from the league a supply of baseballs which meet Little League specifications and standards. The umpire shall be the sole judge of the fitness of the balls to be used in the game;

(d)   be assured by the league that additional balls are immediately available for use if required;

(e)   have possession of at least two alternate balls and shall require replenishment of such supply of alternate balls as needed throughout the game. Such alternate balls shall be put in play when -

(1)   a ball has been batted out of the playing field or into the spectator area;

(2)   a ball has become discolored or unfit for further use;

(3)   the pitcher requests such alternate ball.

3.02 - No player shall intentionally discolor or damage the ball by rubbing it with soil, rosin, paraffin, licorice, sand-paper, emery-paper, or other foreign substance.

PENALTY: The umpire shall demand the ball and remove the offender from the pitching position. In case the umpire cannot locate the offender, and if the pitcher delivers such discolored or damaged ball to the batter, the pitcher shall be removed from the pitching position at once.

3.03 - A player in the starting line-up who has been removed for a substitute may re-enter the game, in the SAME position in the batting order, provided:

(a)   his or her substitute has completed one time at bat and;

(b)   has played defensively for a minimum of six (6) consecutive outs;

(c)   pitchers once removed from the mound may not return as pitchers; **Intermediate (50-70) Division/Junior/Senior:** A pitcher remaining in the game, but moving to a different position, can return as a pitcher any time in the remainder of the game, but only once per game.

NOTE: A player who has met the mandatory play requirements, and is a pitcher at the time he/she is removed, may be removed for a substitute batter and re-enter the game as pitcher once, provided the pitcher was not physically replaced on the mound.

EXAMPLE: Player A is a starter and not a pitcher. Player B substitutes into the game for Player A. Both players have met mandatory play by completing one (1) at-bat and six (6) defensive outs and both occupy the same spot in the batting order. In the fifth inning, Player A becomes a pitcher and is scheduled to bat in the sixth inning, but Player B bats for Player A. Both players have met mandatory play requirements and Player A was not physically replaced on the mound as a pitcher, therefore, Player A can return to pitch in the sixth.

(d) a starter and his/her substitute must not be in the line-up at the same time, except as provided in 3.03 NOTE 3. Once mandatory play is met, a starter and substitute(s) can enter/re-enter for each other as desired, but must re-enter in the SAME position in the batting order.

(e) Defensive substitutions must be made while the team is on defense. Offensive substitutions must be made at the time the offensive player has her/his turn at bat or is on base.

NOTE 1: A substitute may not be removed from the game prior to completion of his/her mandatory play requirements.

NOTE 2: When two or more substitute players of the defensive team enter the game at the same time, the manager shall, immediately before they take their positions as fielders, designate to the Umpire-in-Chief such players' positions in the team's batting order and the Umpire-in-Chief shall notify the official scorer. The Umpire-in-Chief shall have authority to designate the substitutes' places in the batting order, if this information is not immediately provided.

NOTE 3: If during a game either team is unable to place nine (9) players on the field due to illness, injury, ejection, or inability to make a legal substitution, the opposing manager shall select a player previously used in the line-up to re-enter the game, but only if use of all eligible players has exhausted the roster. A player ejected from the game is not eligible for re-entry.

Senior League Designated Hitter Rule:

(a) At the beginning of a game, each manager may list on the lineup card a designated hitter to bat throughout the game for a designated player in the regular lineup. A designated hitter, who has been removed for a substitute may re-enter the game once, provided such player occupies the same batting position.

(b) Only a player not in the regular batting order may be used as a designated hitter.

(c) In the event a manager decides to use the designated hitter as a defensive player, the player must remain in the same position in the batting order, unless otherwise replaced by a substitute. If so, the player for whom the designated hitter was batting must be removed from the game. Such player may re-enter the game once, but only in the batting order position of the former designated hitter, who must be removed.

NOTE: If during a game either team is unable to place nine (9) players on the field due to illness, injury, or ejection, the opposing manager shall select a player previously used in the line-up to re-enter the game, but only if the use of all other eligible players has exhausted the roster. A player ejected from the game is not eligible for re-entry. This provision does not apply to injury, illness, or ejection of the designated hitter or the player for whom he or she is batting, in which case the role of the designated hitter must be terminated

3.04 - A player whose name is on the team's batting order may not become a substitute runner for another member of the team. "Courtesy runner" not permitted.

3.05 -

(a) The pitcher named in the batting order handed to the Umpire-in-Chief, as provided in Rules 4.01(a) and 4.01(b) shall pitch to the first batter or any substitute batter until such batter or any substitute batter is retired or reaches first base, unless the pitcher sustains an injury or illness which, in the judgment of the Umpire-in-Chief, incapacitates the pitcher from further play as a pitcher.

(b) If the pitcher is replaced, the substitute pitcher shall pitch to the batter then at bat, or any substitute batter, until such batter is retired or reaches first base, or until the offensive team is put out, unless the substitute pitcher sustains an injury or illness, which in the Umpire-in-Chief's judgment, incapacitates the pitcher from further play as a pitcher.

3.06 - The manager shall immediately notify the Umpire-in-Chief of any substitution and shall state to the Umpire-in-Chief the substitute's place in the batting order.

3.07 - The Umpire-in-Chief, after having been notified, shall immediately announce, or cause to be announced, each substitution.

3.08 -

(a) If no announcement of a substitution is made, the substitute shall be considered to have entered the game when -

    (1) if a pitcher, the substitute takes a position on the pitcher's plate and throws one warm-up pitch to the catcher;

    (2) if a batter, the substitute takes a position in the batter's box;

    (3) if a fielder, the substitute reaches the position usually occupied by the fielder being replaced and play commences;

    (4) if a runner, the substitute takes the place of the runner being replaced.

(b) Any play made by, or on, any of the above mentioned unannounced substitutes shall be legal.

3.09 - Players, managers, and coaches of the participating teams shall not address, or mingle with spectators, nor sit in the stands during a game in which they are engaged. Managers or coaches must not warm up a pitcher at home plate or in the bull pen or elsewhere at any time. They may, however, stand by to observe a pitcher during warm-up in the bullpen.

3.10 -

(a) The managers of both teams shall agree on the fitness of the playing field before the game starts. In the event that the two managers cannot agree, the president or a duly delegated representative shall make the determination.

(b) The Umpire-in-Chief shall be the sole judge as to whether and when play shall be suspended during a game because of unsuitable weather conditions or the unfit condition of the playing field; as to whether and when play shall be resumed after such suspension; and as to whether and when a game shall be terminated after such suspension. Said umpire shall not call the game until at least thirty minutes after play has been suspended. The umpire may continue suspension as long as there is any chance to resume play.

3.12 - When the umpire suspends play, "Time" shall be called. At the umpire's call of "Play" the suspension is lifted and play resumes. Between the call of "Time" and the call of "Play" the ball is dead.

3.13 - The local league will establish ground rules to be followed by all teams in the league.

> A.R. - Local ground rules should pertain to particular situations or field conditions that are not specifically covered in the rulebook, but at no time should they supersede or change the rulebook.

3.14 - Members of the offensive team shall carry all gloves and other equipment off the field and to the dugout while their team is at bat. No equipment shall be left lying on the field, either in fair or foul territory.

3.15 - No person shall be allowed on the playing field during a game except uniformed players, managers, and coaches, umpires and news photographers authorized by the league. In case of intentional interference with play by any person authorized to be on the playing field, the ball is dead at the moment of the interference and no runners on base may advance. Should an overthrown ball accidentally touch an authorized person, it will not be considered interference and the ball will remain live.

3.16 - When there is spectator interference with any thrown or batted ball, the ball shall be dead at the moment of interference and the umpire shall impose such penalties as in the umpire's opinion will nullify the act of interference.

> A.R. - If spectator interference clearly prevents a fielder from catching a fly ball, the umpire shall declare the batter out.

3.17 - Players and substitutes shall sit on their team's bench or in the dugout unless participating in the game or preparing to enter the game. No one except eligible players in uniform, a manager, and not more than two coaches shall occupy the bench or dugout. When batters or base runners are retired, they must return to the bench or dugout at once. Batboys and/or batgirls are not permitted. The use of electronic communication equipment during the game is restricted. No team shall use electronic communication equipment, including walkie-talkies, cellular telephones, etc., for any communication with on-field personnel including those in the dugout, bullpen, or field.

PENALTY: If, in the umpire's judgment, any player, manager, or coach uses an electronic communications device during the game, the penalty is ejection from the game.

NOTE: A manager or coach is permitted to use a scorekeeping and/or pitch-counting application on an electronic device without penalty, provided such device is not used to receive messages of any sort.

3.18 - The local league shall provide proper protection sufficient to preserve order and to prevent spectators from entering the field. Either team may refuse to play until the field is cleared.

Rule 4.00
Starting and Ending the Game

4.01 - The umpires shall proceed directly to home plate where they shall be met by the managers of the opposing teams, just preceding the established time to begin the game. In sequence-

(a) The home team manager shall give the batting order in duplicate to the Umpire-in-Chief;

(b) Next, the visiting manager shall give the batting order in duplicate to the Umpire-in-Chief;

(c) The Umpire-in-Chief shall make certain that the original and duplicate copies are the same, then provide a copy of each batting order to the opposing manager. The original copy retained by the umpire shall be the official batting order;

(d) As soon as the home team's batting order is handed to the Umpire-in-Chief, the umpires are in charge of the playing field and from that moment shall have sole authority to determine when a game shall be called, halted, or resumed on account of weather or the conditions of the playing field.

NOTE 1: In Tee Ball and non-competitive Minor Leagues, all players on the roster may be given a defensive position. Only one player may occupy the catcher's position.

NOTE 2: Rostered players who arrive at the game site after a game begins may be inserted in the lineup, if the manager so chooses. This applies even when a suspended game is resumed at a later date.

4.02 - The players of the home team shall take their defensive positions, the first batter of the visiting team shall take a position in the batter's box, the umpire shall call "Play" and the game shall start.

4.03 - When the ball is put in play at the start of, or during a game, all fielders other than the catcher shall be in fair territory.

(a) The catcher shall be stationed in the catcher's box. The catcher may leave that position at any time to catch a pitch or make a play except that when the batter is being given an intentional base on balls, the catcher must stand with both feet within the lines of the catcher's box until the ball leaves the pitcher's hand.

PENALTY: Illegal pitch - ball called on the batter (see Rule 8.05).

[Intermediate (50-70) Division/Junior/Senior League PENALTY: Balk with runner or runners on base.]

(b) The pitcher, while in the act of delivering the ball to the batter, shall take the legal position.

(c) Except the pitcher and the catcher, any fielder may be stationed anywhere in fair territory.

4.04 - The batting order shall be followed throughout the game unless a player is substituted for another. Substitutes must take the place of the replaced player's position in the batting order except as covered by Rule 3.03. A league may adopt a policy of a continuous batting order that will include all players on the team roster present for the game batting in order. If this option is adopted, each player would be required to bat in his/her respective spot in the batting order. However, a player may be entered and/or re-entered defensively in the game anytime provided he/she meets the requirements of mandatory play. **NOTE 1:** The continuous batting order is mandatory for all Tee Ball and Minor League Divisions. **NOTE 2:** For the Tee Ball and Minor League Divisions (and when the continuous batting order is adopted for other divisions), when a player is injured, becomes ill, or must leave the game site after the start of the game, the team will skip over him/her when his/her time at bat comes up without penalty. If the injured, ill, or absent player returns he/she is merely inserted into their original spot in the batting order and the game continues. Also, if a player arrives late to a game site, if the manager chooses to enter him/her in the lineup (see Rule 4.01 NOTE 2), he/she would be added to the end of the current lineup.

> A.R. - For the purpose of continuous batting order, all players listed in the batting order shall be considered starters.

4.05 - The offensive team shall station two base coaches on the field during its time at bat, one near first base and one near third base. The coaches shall not leave their respective dugouts until the pitcher has completed his/her preparatory pitches to the catcher. Base coaches shall-

(a) be eligible players in the uniform of their team; a manager and/or coach. Both base coaches may be managers or coaches.

(b) be a manager or coach only if there is at least one other adult manager or coach in the dugout.

(c) remain within the base coaches boxes at all times, except as provided in Rule 7.11;

> A.R. - Once an inning starts, coaches shall not alternate between the first and third base coaches boxes.

(d) talk to members of their own team only.

An offending base coach shall be removed from the base coach's box.

4.06 - No manager, coach, or player, shall at any time, whether from the bench or the playing field or elsewhere -

(a) incite, or try to incite, by word or sign, a demonstration by spectators;

(b) use language which will in any manner refer to or reflect upon opposing players, manager, coach, an umpire, or spectators;

(c) make any move calculated to cause the pitcher to commit an illegal pitch [a balk in **Intermediate (50-70) Division/Junior/Senior League**];

(d) take a position in the batter's line of vision, with the deliberate intent to distract the batter.

The umpire may first warn the player, coach, and/or manager. If continued, remove the player, coach, and/or manager from the game or bench. If such action causes an illegal pitch [a balk in **Intermediate (50-70) Division/Junior/Senior League**], it shall be nullified.

4.07 - When a manager, coach, or player is ejected from a game, they shall leave the field immediately and take no further part in that game. They may not sit in the stands and may not be recalled. **A manager or coach ejected from a game must not be present at the game site for the remainder of that game.** Any manager, coach, or player ejected from a game is suspended for his or her team's next physically played game and may not be in attendance at the game site. This includes pregame and postgame activities.

4.08 - When the occupants of a player's bench show violent disapproval of an umpire's decision, the umpire shall first give warning that such disapproval shall cease. If such action continues -

PENALTY: The umpire shall order the offender out of the game and away from the spectators' area. If the umpire is unable to detect the offender or offenders, the bench may be cleared of all players. The manager of the offending team shall have the privilege of recalling to the playing field only those players needed for substitution in the game.

4.09 - HOW A TEAM SCORES

(a) One run shall be scored each time a runner legally advances to and touches first, second, third, and home base before three players are retired to end the inning.

EXCEPTIONS: A run is not scored if the runner advances to home base during a play in which the third out is made (1) by the batter-runner before touching first base; (2) by any runner being forced out; or (3) by a preceding runner who is declared out because that runner failed to touch one of the bases (appeal play).

> A.R. - One out, Jones on third, Smith on first and Brown flies out to right field for the second out. Jones tags up and scores after the catch. Smith attempted to return to first but the right fielder's throw beat Smith to the base for the third out. But Jones scored before the throw to catch Smith reached first base. Hence, Jones' run counts. It was not a force play.

(b) When the winning run is scored in the last half-inning of a regulation game, or in the last half of an extra inning, as the result of a base on balls, hit batter, or any other play with the bases full which forces the runner on third to advance, the umpire shall not declare the game ended until the runner forced to advance from third has touched home base and the batter-runner has touched first base.

4.10 -

(a) A regulation game consists of six innings [**Intermediate (50-70) Division/ Junior/Senior League:** seven innings], unless extended because of a tie score, or shortened (1) because the home team needs none of its half of the sixth inning [**Intermediate (50-70) Division/Junior/Senior League:** seventh] or only a fraction of it; or (2) because the umpire calls the game.

(b) If the score is tied after six completed innings (**Intermediate (50-70) Division/ Junior/Senior League:** seven innings), play shall continue until (1) the visiting team has scored more total runs than the home team at the end of a completed inning; or (2) the home team scores the winning run in an uncompleted inning.

(c) If a game is called, it is a regulation game:
  (1) If four innings [**Intermediate (50-70) Division/Junior/Senior League:** five innings] have been completed;
  (2) If the home team has scored more runs in three and one-half innings [**Intermediate (50-70) Division/Junior/Senior League:** four and one-half innings] than the visiting team has scored in four completed half-innings;
  (3) if the home team scores one or more runs in its half of the fourth inning [**Intermediate (50-70) Division/Junior/Senior League:** fifth inning] to tie the score.

(d) If a game is called before it has become a regulation game, it shall be resumed exactly where it left off.

(e) If after three (3) innings [**Intermediate (50-70) Division/Junior/Senior League:** four innings], two and one-half innings [**Intermediate (50-70) Division/ Junior/Senior League:** three and one-half innings] if the home team is ahead, one team has a lead of fifteen (15) runs or more, the manager of the team with the least runs shall concede the victory to the opponent. If after four (4) innings [**Intermediate (50-70) Division/Junior/Senior League:** five innings], three and one-half innings [**Intermediate (50-70) Division/Junior/Senior League:** four and one-half innings] if the home team is ahead, one team has a lead of ten (10) runs or more, the manager of the team with the least runs shall concede the victory to the opponent. **NOTE:** (1) If the visiting team has a lead of fifteen (15) or ten (10) runs or more respectively, the home team must bat in its half of the inning. (2) The local league may adopt the option of not utilizing this rule. A game determined by the 15-run rule, shall be considered a regulation game.

(f) **Tee Ball:** The local league may determine appropriate game length but shall not exceed 6 innings. It is recommended that Tee Ball games be 4 innings or 1½ hour time limit or less.

4.11 - The score of a regulation game is the total number of runs scored by each team at the moment the game ends.

(a) The game ends when the visiting team completes its half of the sixth inning [**Intermediate (50-70) Division/Junior/Senior League:** seventh inning] if the home team is ahead.

(b) The game ends when the sixth inning [**Intermediate (50-70) Division/Junior/ Senior League:** seventh inning] is completed, if the visiting team is ahead.

(c) If the home team scores the winning run in its half of the sixth inning [**Intermediate (50-70) Division/Junior/Senior League:** seventh inning], or its half of an extra inning after a tie, the game ends immediately when the winning run is scored.

NOTE: Once a game becomes regulation and it is called with the home team taking the lead in an incomplete inning, the game ends with the home team the winner.

EXCEPTION: If the last batter in a game hits a home run out of the playing field, the batter-runner and all runners on base are permitted to score, in accordance with the base-running rules, and the game ends when the batter-runner touches home plate.

> A.R. - The batter hits a home run out of the playing field to win the game in the last half of the sixth [**Intermediate (50-70) Division/Junior/Senior League:** seventh inning] or an extra inning, but is called out for passing a preceding runner. The game ends immediately when the winning run is scored.

(d) A called game ends at the moment the umpire terminates play.

EXCEPTION: If the game is called during an incomplete inning, the game ends at the end of the last previous completed inning in each of the following situations:

(1) The visiting team scores one or more runs to tie the score in the incomplete inning, and the home team does not score in the incomplete inning.

(2) The visiting team scores one or more runs to take the lead in the incomplete inning, and the home team does not tie the score or retake the lead in the incomplete inning.

(e) A regulation game that is tied after four [**Intermediate (50-70) Division/Junior/Senior League:** five] or more completed innings and halted by the umpire, shall be resumed from the exact point that play was halted. The game shall continue in accordance with Rule 4.10(a) and 4.10(b).

NOTE: When a TIE game is halted, the pitcher of record may continue pitching in the same game on any subsequent date provided said pitcher has observed the required days of rest for his/her particular age group. For scorekeeping purposes, it shall be considered the same game, and all batting, fielding, and pitching records will count.

LITTLE LEAGUE (MAJOR)/MINOR LEAGUE EXAMPLE:
Rule 4.11

	1	2	3	4	5	6
VISITORS	0	0	0	4	1	
HOME	0	0	0	5		

Game called in top of 5th inning on account of rain. Score reverts to last completed inning (4th) and the home team is the winner 5 to 4.

INTERMEDIATE (50-70) DIVISION/JUNIOR/SENIOR LEAGUE EXAMPLE:
Rule 4.11

	1	2	3	4	5	6	7
VISITORS	0	0	0	0	4	1	
HOME	0	0	0	0	5		

Game called in top of 6th inning on account of rain. Score reverts to last completed inning (5th) and the home team is the winner 5 to 4.

4.12 - TIE games halted due to weather, curfew, or light failure shall be resumed from the exact point at which they were halted in the original game. It can be completed preceding the next scheduled game between the same teams. A player may not pitch in more than one game in a day. (**EXCEPTION: Junior and Senior League:** If a pitcher reaches 30 pitches while facing a batter in the first game, the pitcher may continue to pitch, and maintain their eligibility to pitch in the second game on that day, until any one of the following conditions occurs: (1) that batter reaches base; (2) that batter is retired; or (3) the third out is made to complete the half-inning or the game. The pitcher would be allowed to pitch in a second game provided that pitcher is moved, removed, or the game is completed before delivering a pitch to another batter. If a player delivers 31 or more pitches in the first game, and is not covered under the threshold exception, the player may not pitch in the second game that day).

The lineup and batting order of both teams shall be the same as the lineup and batting order at the moment the game was halted, subject to the rules governing substitution. Any player may be replaced by a player who was not in the game prior to halting the original game. Substitutions, including entry and re-entry, are covered by Rule 3.03. **NOTE:** When a TIE game is halted, the pitcher of record may continue pitching in the same game on any subsequent date provided said pitcher has observed the required days of rest for his/her particular age group. For scorekeeping purposes, it shall be considered the same game, and all batting, fielding, and pitching records will count.

LITTLE LEAGUE (MAJOR)/MINOR LEAGUE EXAMPLE:

Rule 4.12

Tie games halted due to weather, curfew, or light failure shall be resumed from the exact point at which they were halted in the original game.

	1	2	3	4	5	6
VISITORS	0	0	0	0	4	5
HOME	0	0	0	4		

Game called in top of 6th inning, visiting team batting with two out, no base runners - this is a tie game. Resume the game in the top of the 6th, visiting team at bat, two out.

INTERMEDIATE (50-70) DIVISION/JUNIOR/SENIOR LEAGUE EXAMPLE:

Rule 4.12

Tie games halted due to weather, curfew, or light failure shall be resumed from the exact point at which they were halted in the original game.

	1	2	3	4	5	6	7
VISITORS	0	0	0	0	0	4	5
HOME	0	0	0	0	4		

Game called in top of 7th inning, visiting team batting with two out, no base runners - this is a tie game. Resume the game in the top of the 7th, visiting team at bat, two out.

4.13 - DOUBLE HEADERS

Little League (Major) Division: A team may play one (1) doubleheader in a calendar week. No team shall play three games in a day. (Exception under condition of Rule 4.12.)

Tee Ball and Minor League: No team shall be scheduled to play two games in one day. (See Rule 4.12).

Intermediate (50-70) Division/Junior/Senior League: Doubleheaders are permitted.

4.14 - The Umpire-in-Chief shall order the playing field lights turned on whenever in such umpire's opinion that darkness makes further play in daylight hazardous.

4.15 - A game may be forfeited by the Umpire-in-Chief of the game in progress to the opposing team when a team -

(a) being upon the field, refuses to start play within 10 minutes after the appointed hour for beginning the game, unless such delay, in the umpire's judgment, is unavoidable;

(b) refuses to continue play unless the game was terminated by the umpire;

(c) fails to resume play, after the game was halted by the umpire, within one minute after the umpire has called "Play";

(d) fails to obey within a reasonable time the umpire's order to remove a player from the game;

(e) after warning by the umpire, willfully and persistently violates any rules of the game;

(f) employs tactics designed to delay, shorten or make a travesty of the game.

4.16 - If a game cannot be played because of the inability of either team to:

(a) place nine players on the field before the game begins, and/or,

(b) place at least one adult in the dugout as manager or acting manager, this shall not be grounds for automatic forfeiture, but shall be referred to the Board of Directors for a decision.

NOTE: A game may not be started with less than nine (9) players on each team, nor without at least one adult manager or substitute manager.

4.17 - If during a game either team is unable to place nine (9) players on the field due to injury or ejection, the opposing manager shall select a player to re-enter the line-up. A player ejected from the game is not eligible for re-entry. If no players are available for re-entry, or if a team refuses to place nine (9) players on the field, this shall not be grounds for automatic forfeiture but shall be referred to the Board of Directors for a decision. **NOTE:** A game may not be continued with less than nine (9) players on each team.

4.18 - Forfeited games shall be so recorded in the scorebook and the book signed by the Umpire-in-Chief. A written report stating the reason for the forfeiture shall be sent to the league president within 24 hours, but failure of the umpire to file this report shall not affect the forfeiture.

4.19 - PROTESTING A GAME

(a) Protest shall be considered only when based on the violation or interpretation of a playing rule, use of an ineligible pitcher or the use of an ineligible player. No protest shall be considered on a decision involving an umpire's judgment. Equipment which does not meet specifications must be removed from the game. **Exception:** Illegal bat [see Rule 6.06(d)].

(b) The managers of contesting teams only shall have the right to protest a game (or in their absence, coaches). However, the manager or acting manager may not leave the dugout until receiving permission from an umpire.

(c) Protests shall be made as follows:

(1) The protesting manager shall immediately, and before any succeeding play begins, notify the umpire that the game is being played under protest.

(2) Following such notice the umpire shall consult with the other umpire(s). If the umpire is convinced that the decision is in conflict with the rules, the umpire shall reverse that decision. If, however, after consultation, the umpire is convinced that the decision is not in conflict with the rules, said

umpire shall announce that the game is being played under protest. Failure of the umpire to make such announcement shall not affect the validity of the protest.

(d) Protest made due to the use of an ineligible pitcher or an ineligible player may be considered only if made to the umpire before the umpire(s) leave the field at the end of the game. Whenever it is found that an ineligible pitcher or ineligible player is being used, said pitcher shall be removed from the mound, or said player shall be removed from the game, and the game shall be continued under protest or not as the protesting manager decides.

(e) Any protest for any reason whatsoever must be submitted by the manager first to the umpire on the field of play and then in writing to the local league president within 24 hours. The Umpire-in-Chief shall also submit a report immediately.

(f) A committee composed of the president, player agent, league's Umpire-in-Chief, and one or more other officers or directors who are not managers or umpires shall hear and resolve any such protest as above, including playing rules. If the protest is allowed, resume the game from the exact point when the infraction occurred.

NOTE 1: This rule does not pertain to charges of infractions of regulations such as field decorum or actions of the league personnel or spectators which must be considered and resolved by the Board of Directors.

NOTE 2: All Little League officials are urged to take precautions to prevent protests. When a protest situation is imminent, the potential offenders should be notified immediately. **Example**: Should a manager, official scorer, league official, or umpire discover that a pitcher is ineligible at the beginning of the game, or will become ineligible during the game or at the start of the next inning of play, the fact should be brought to the attention of the manager of the team involved. Such action should not be delayed until the infraction has occurred. However, failure of personnel to notify the manager of the infraction does not affect the validity of the protest.

A.R. - A substitute pitcher who is ineligible DOES NOT have to pitch to a batter. It is not a violation until the ineligible pitcher has delivered a "Pitch" as defined in Rule 2.00.

(g) **Minor League:** A local league may adopt a rule that protests must be resolved before the next pitch or play.

(h) There are no protests in Tee Ball.

Rule 5.00
Putting the Ball in Play - Live Ball

5.01 - At the time set for beginning the game, the Umpire-in-Chief shall order the home team to take its defensive positions and the first batter of the visiting team to take a position in the batter's box. As soon as all players are in position, the Umpire-in-Chief shall call "Play."

5.02 - After the umpire calls "Play," the ball is alive and in play and remains alive and in play until, for legal cause, or at the umpire's call of "Time" suspending play, the ball becomes dead. While the ball is dead, no player may be put out, no bases may be run, and no runs may be scored, except that runners may advance one or more bases as the result of acts which occurred while the ball was alive (such as, but not limited to an illegal pitch and/or a balk in **Intermediate (50-70) Division/Junior/Senior League**, an overthrow, interference, or a home run or other fair ball hit out of the playing field).

5.03 - The pitcher shall deliver the pitch to the batter who may elect to strike the ball, or who may not offer at it, as such batter chooses.

5.04 - The offensive team's objective is to have its batter become a runner, and its runners advance.

5.05 - The defensive team's objective is to prevent offensive players from becoming runners, and to prevent their advance around the bases.

5.06 - When a batter becomes a runner and touches all bases legally, one run shall be scored for the offensive team.

5.07 - When three offensive players are legally put out, that team takes the field and the opposing team becomes the offensive team (side retired). **Minor League:** The side is retired when three offensive players are legally put out, called out by an umpire, or when all players on the roster have batted one time in the half-inning, or when the offensive team scores five (5) runs. (**OPTION:** The local league Board of Directors may suspend the five-run rule in the last half-inning for either team.) **Tee Ball:** The side is retired when three offensive players are legally put out, called out by an umpire, or when all players on the roster have batted one time in the half-inning.

5.08 - If a thrown ball accidentally touches a base coach, or a pitched or thrown ball touches an umpire, the ball is alive and in play. However, if the base coach interferes with a thrown ball, the runner is out.

5.09 - The ball becomes dead and runners advance one base, or return to their bases, without liability to be put out, when -

(a)   a pitched ball touches a batter, or the batter's clothing, while in a legal batting position; runners, if forced, advance (see 6.08);

(b)   the plate umpire interferes with the catcher's act of throwing (when the throw is in an attempt to retire a runner); runners return. If the catcher's throw gets the runner out, the out stands. No umpire interference;

(c)   an illegal pitch [a balk in **Intermediate (50-70) Division/Junior/Senior League**] is committed (see Penalty 8.05);

(d)   a ball is illegally batted either fair or foul; runners return;

(e)   a foul ball not caught, runners return. The umpire shall not put the ball in play until all runners have retouched their bases;

(f)   a fair ball touches a runner or an umpire on fair territory before it touches an infielder including the pitcher, or touches an umpire before it has passed an infielder other than the pitcher. Runner hit by a fair batted ball is out;

NOTE: If a fair ball goes through, or by an infielder and touches a runner immediately back of said infielder, or touches a runner after being deflected by an infielder, the ball is in play and the umpire shall not declare the runner out. In making such decision, the umpire must be convinced that the ball passed through, or by, the infielder and that no other infielder had the chance to make a play on the ball; runners advance, if forced;

(g)   A pitched ball lodges in the catcher's or umpire's mask or paraphernalia; runners advance;

> A.R. - If a pitched ball lodges in the umpire's or catcher's mask or paraphernalia, and remains a dead ball, on the third strike [**Majors/Intermediate (50/70) Division/Junior/Senior League**] or fourth ball, then the batter is entitled to first base and all runners advance one base. If the count on the batter is less than three balls, runners advance one base.

(h)   **Intermediate (50-70) Division/Junior/Senior League:** Any legal pitch touches a runner trying to score; runners advance.

5.10 - The ball becomes dead when an umpire calls "Time." The Umpire-in-Chief shall call "Time" -

(a)   when in said umpire's judgment, weather, darkness, or similar conditions make immediate further play impossible;

(b)   when light failure makes it difficult or impossible for the umpires to follow the play; **NOTE:** A league may adopt its own regulations governing games interrupted by light failure.

(c)   when an accident incapacitates a player or an umpire;

    (1)   If an accident to a runner is such as to prevent said runner from proceeding to an entitled base, as on a home run hit out of the playing field or an award of one or more bases, a substitute runner shall be permitted to complete the play.

(d)   when a manager requests "Time" for a substitution, or for a conference with one of the players; (**NOTE:** Only one offensive time-out, for the purpose of a visit or conference, will be permitted each inning.)

(e)   when the umpire wishes to examine the ball, to consult with either manager, or for any similar cause;

(f)   when a fielder, after catching a fly ball, falls into a stand, or falls across ropes into a crowd when spectators are on the field, or any other dead-ball area. As pertains to runners, the provisions of 7.04(b) shall prevail. If a fielder after making a catch steps into a dead ball area, the ball is dead;

(g)   when an umpire orders a player or any other person removed from the playing field;

(h)   except in the cases stated in paragraphs (b) and (c)(1) of this rule, no umpire shall call "Time" while a play is in progress.

5.11 - After the ball is dead, play shall be resumed when the pitcher takes a position on the pitcher's plate with a new ball or the same ball in said pitcher's possession and the plate umpire calls "Play." The plate umpire shall call "Play" as soon as the pitcher takes a position on the plate with possession of the ball.

Rule 6.00
The Batter

6.01 -

(a) Each player of the offensive team shall bat in the order that their name appears in the team's batting order.

(b) The first batter in each inning after the first inning shall be the player whose name follows that of the last player who legally completed a time at bat in the preceding inning.

NOTE: In the event that while a batter is in the batter's box, the third out of an inning is made on a base runner, the batter then at bat shall be the first batter of the next inning and the count of balls and strikes shall start over.

6.02 -

(a) The batter shall take a position in the batter's box promptly when it is said batter's time at bat.

(b) The batter shall not leave that position in the batter's box after the pitcher comes to Set Position, or starts a windup.

PENALTY: If the pitcher pitches, the umpire shall call "Ball" or "Strike" as the case may be.

(c) **Local League Option:** After entering the batter's box, the batter must remain in the box with at least one foot throughout the at bat.

Exceptions:

1. On a swing, slap, or check swing.

2. When forced out of the box by a pitch.

3. When the batter attempts a "drag bunt."

4. When the catcher does not catch the pitched ball.

5. When a play has been attempted.

6. When time has been called.

7. When the pitcher leaves the dirt area of the pitching mound or takes a position more than five feet from the pitcher's plate after receiving the ball or the catcher leaves the catcher's box.

8. On a three ball count pitch that is a strike that the batter thinks is a ball.

PENALTY: If the batter leaves the batter's box or delays play and none of the exceptions apply, the umpire shall warn the batter. After one warning on a batter, the umpire shall call a strike. Any number of strikes can be called on each batter. **Minor/Major Division:** No pitch has to be thrown, the ball is dead, and no runners may advance. **Intermediate (50-70) Division/Junior/Senior:** No pitch has to be thrown and ball is live.

NOTE: The batter may return their position in the batter's box and assume the new count at any time during the at-bat, unless such enforced penalty is the third strike.

6.03 - The batter's legal position shall be with both feet within the batter's box.

A.R. - The lines defining the box are within the batter's box.

6.04 - A batter has legally completed a time at bat when he/she is retired or becomes a runner.

6.05 - A batter is out when -

(a)   a fair or foul fly ball (other than a foul tip) is legally caught by a fielder;

> A.R. - A fielder may reach into, but not step into, a dugout to make a catch, and if he/she holds the ball, the catch shall be allowed. A fielder, in order to make a catch on a foul ball nearing a dugout or other dead ball area (such as the stands), must have one or both feet on or over the playing surface (including the dugout) and neither foot on the ground inside the dugout or in any other dead ball area. Ball is in play, unless the fielder, after making a legal catch, falls into a dugout or other dead ball area, in which case the ball is dead.

(b)   **Majors/Intermediate (50-70) Division/Junior/Senior League –**
   (1)   a third strike is legally caught by the catcher;
   (2)   a third strike is not caught by the catcher when first base is occupied before two are out; **Minor League and Tee Ball**: A third strike is caught or not caught by the catcher. **Option:** A local league may elect to apply the Minor League and Tee Ball rule for the Little League (Major) Division for the regular season.

> A.R. - **(Majors/Intermediate (50-70) Division/Junior/Senior League)** When a batter becomes a runner on a third strike that is not caught, and starts for the bench or his/her position, that batter may advance to first base at any time before entering the dugout or any other dead ball area. To put the batter out, the defense must tag the batter or first base before the batter touches first base.

(c)   bunting foul on a third strike;

(d)   an Infield Fly is declared;

(e)   that batter attempts to hit a third strike and is touched by the ball;

(f)   a fair ball touches said batter before touching a fielder;

(g)   after hitting or bunting a fair ball, the bat hits the ball a second time in fair territory. The ball is dead and no runners may advance. If the batter-runner drops the bat and the ball rolls against the bat in fair territory and, in the umpire's judgment there was no intention to interfere with the course of the ball, the ball is alive and in play;

> A.R. - If a bat is thrown into fair or foul territory and interferes with a defensive player attempting to make a play, interference shall be called, whether intentional or not.

(h)   after hitting or bunting a foul ball, the batter-runner intentionally deflects the course of the ball in any manner while running to first base. The ball is dead and no runners may advance;

(i)   after hitting a fair ball, the batter-runner or first base is tagged before said batter-runner touches first base; or **Majors/Intermediate (50-70) Division/Junior/**

Senior League: after a third strike as defined in Rule 6.09(b), the batter-runner or first base is tagged before said batter-runner touches first base;

(j) in running the last half of the distance from home base to first base, while the ball is being fielded to first base, the batter-runner runs outside (to the right of) the three-foot line, or inside (to the left of) the foul line, and in the umpire's judgment in so doing interferes with the fielder taking the throw at first base; except that the batter-runner may run outside (to the right of) the three-foot line or inside (to the left of) the foul line to avoid a fielder attempting to field a batted ball;

> A.R. - The lines marking the three-foot lane are a part of that lane and a batter-runner is required to have both feet within the three-foot lane or on the lines marking the lane.

(k) an infielder intentionally drops a fair fly ball or line drive, with first; first and second; first and third; or first, second, and third bases occupied before two are out. The ball is dead and runner or runners shall return to their original base or bases;

> A.R. - In this situation, the batter is not out if the infielder permits the ball to drop untouched to the ground, except when the Infield Fly rule applies.

(l) a preceding runner shall, in the umpire's judgment, intentionally interfere with a fielder who is attempting to catch a thrown ball or to throw a ball in an attempt to complete a play.

(m) **Intermediate (50-70) Division/Junior/Senior League:** with two out, a runner on third base, and two strikes on the batter, the runner attempts to steal home base on a legal pitch and the ball touches the runner in the batter's strike zone. The umpire shall call "Strike Three," the batter is out and the run shall not count; before two are out, the umpire shall call "Strike Three," the ball is dead, and the run counts.

6.06 - A batter is out for illegal action when -

(a) hitting the ball with one or both feet on the ground entirely outside the batter's box.

> A.R. - If a batter hits a ball fair or foul while out of the batter's box, he/she shall be called out.

(b) stepping from one batter's box to the other while the pitcher is in position ready to pitch;

(c) interfering with the catcher's fielding or throwing by:
   (1) stepping out of the batter's box, or;

   (2) making any other movement that hinders the catcher's actions at home plate or the catcher's attempt to play on a runner, or;

   (3) failing to make a reasonable effort to vacate a congested area when there is a throw to home plate and there is time for the batter to move away.

EXCEPTION: Batter is not out if any runner attempting to advance is retired, or if runner trying to score is called out for batter's interference.

(d)   the batter enters the batter's box with one or both feet entirely on the ground with an illegal bat (see bat specifications rule 1.10) or is discovered having used an illegal bat prior to the next player entering the batter's box. The ball is dead. Runners must return if they advanced on the play.

NOTE: If the infraction is discovered before the next player enters the batter's box following the turn at bat of the player who used an illegal bat:

(1)   The manager of the defense may advise the plate umpire of a decision to decline the penalty and accept the play. Such election shall be made immediately at the end of the play.

(2)   For the first violation, the offensive team will lose one eligible adult base coach for the duration of the game.

> A.R. - Any of the three adults in the dugout may be used as the one adult base coach at any time during the duration of the game.

(3)   For the second violation, the manager of the team will be ejected from the game. Any subsequent violation will result in the newly designated manager being ejected.

> A.R. - When an illegal bat is discovered, it MUST be removed from the game at that point.

6.07 - BATTING OUT OF TURN

(a)   A batter shall be called out, on appeal, when failing to bat in his/her proper turn, and another batter completes a time at bat in place of the proper batter. (1) The proper batter may take a position in the batter's box at any time before the improper batter becomes a runner or is retired, and any balls and strikes shall be counted in the proper batter's time at bat.

(b)   When an improper batter becomes a runner or is retired, and the defensive team appeals to the umpire before the first pitch to the next batter of either team, or before any play or attempted play, the umpire shall (1) declare the proper batter out; and (2) nullify any advance or score made because of a ball batted by the improper batter or because of the improper batter's advance to first base on a hit, an error, a base on balls, a hit batter, or otherwise.

NOTE: If a runner advances, while the improper batter is at bat, on a stolen base, illegal pitch [**Intermediate (50-70) Division/Junior/Senior League:** balk], wild pitch, or passed ball, such advance is legal.

(c)   When an improper batter becomes a runner or is retired, and a pitch is made to the next batter of either team before an appeal is made, the improper batter thereby becomes the proper batter, and the results of such time at bat become legal.

(d)   (1) When the proper batter is called out for failing to bat in turn, the next batter shall be the batter whose name follows that of the proper batter thus called out; (2) When an improper batter becomes a proper batter because no appeal is made before the next pitch, the next batter shall be the batter whose name follows that of such legalized improper batter. The instant an improper batter's actions are legalized, the batting order picks up with the name following that of the legalized improper batter.

BATTING OUT OF TURN - APPROVED RULINGS

To illustrate various situations arising from batting out of turn, assume a first-inning batting order as follows:

Abel - Baker - Charles - Daniel - Edward - Frank - George - Henry - Irwin.

PLAY (1) Baker bats. With the count 2 balls and 1 strike, (a) the offensive team discovers the error or (b) the defensive team appeals.

RULING: In either case, Abel replaces Baker, with the count 2 balls and 1 strike.

PLAY (2) Baker bats and doubles. The defensive team appeals (a) immediately or (b) after a pitch to Charles.

RULING: (a) Abel is called out and Baker is the proper batter; (b) Baker stays on second and Charles is the proper batter.

PLAY (3) Abel walks. Baker walks. Charles forces Baker. Edward bats in Daniel's turn. While Edward is at bat, Abel scores and Charles goes to second on a wild pitch. Edward grounds out, sending Charles to third. The defensive team appeals (a) immediately or (b) after a pitch to Daniel.

RULING: (a) Abel's run counts and Charles is entitled to second base since these advances were not made because of the improper batter batting a ball or advancing to first base. Charles must return to second base because the advance to third resulted from the improper batter batting a ball. Daniel is called out and Edward is the proper batter; (b) Abel's run counts and Charles stays on third. The proper batter is Frank.

PLAY (4) With the bases full and two out, Henry bats in Frank's turn, and triples, scoring three runs. The defensive team appeals (a) immediately or (b) after a pitch to George.

RULING: (a) Frank is called out and no runs score. George is the proper batter to lead off the second inning; (b) Henry stays on third and three runs score. Irwin is the proper batter.

PLAY (5) After Play (4) (b) above, George continues to bat. (a) Henry is picked off third base for the third out, or (b) George flies out, and no appeal is made. Who is the proper leadoff batter in the second inning?

RULING: (a) Irwin became the proper batter as soon as the first pitch to George legalized Henry's triple; (b) Henry. When no appeal was made, the first pitch to the leadoff batter of the opposing team legalized George's time at bat.

PLAY (6) Daniel walks and Abel comes to bat. Daniel was an improper batter and if an appeal is made before the first pitch to Abel, Abel is out, Daniel is removed from base, and Baker is proper batter. There is no appeal and a pitch is made to Abel. Daniel's walk is now legalized, and Edward thereby becomes the proper batter. Edward can replace Abel at any time before Abel is put out, or becomes a runner. Edward does not do so. Abel flies out, and Baker comes to bat. Abel was an improper batter, and if an appeal is made before the first pitch to Baker, Edward is out, and the proper batter is Frank. There is no appeal, and a pitch is made to Baker. Abel's out is now legalized, and the proper batter is Baker. Baker walks. Charles is the proper batter. Charles flies out. Now Daniel is the proper batter, but Daniel is on second base. Who is the proper batter?

RULING: The proper batter is Edward. When the proper batter is on base, that batter is passed over, and the following batter becomes the proper batter.

(**NOTE:** The umpire and scorekeeper shall not direct the attention of any person to the presence in the batter's box of an improper batter. This rule is designed to require constant vigilance by the players and managers of both teams. There are two fundamentals to keep in mind: (1) When a player bats out of turn, the proper batter is the player called out. (2) If an improper batter bats and reaches base or is out and no appeal is made before a pitch to the next batter, or before any play or attempted play, that improper batter is considered to have batted in proper turn and establishes the order that is to follow.)

Tee Ball: The scorekeeper shall inform the manager that a player has batted out of order. There shall be no penalty and that player shall not have another turn at bat, but shall resume the normal position next time up.

6.08 - The batter becomes a runner and is entitled to first base without liability to be put out (provided said runner advances to and touches first base) when -

(a) (1) four "balls" have been called by the umpire; ball is live and base runners may advance; or,

(2) **Minor/Major Division:** Prior to a pitch being thrown, the defense elects to "Intentionally Walk" the batter by announcing such decision to the plate umpire.

NOTE 1: Such notification must be made by the defensive manager. The manager must request and be granted "time" by the umpire and then inform the umpire of the defense's intent to walk the batter.

NOTE 2: The ball is dead and no other runners may advance unless forced by the batter's award. Four (4) pitches will be added to the pitch count.

(b) the batter is touched by a pitched ball which the batter is not attempting to hit unless (1) The ball is in the strike zone when it touches the batter, or (2) The batter makes no attempt to avoid being touched by the ball;

NOTE: If the ball is in the strike zone when it touches the batter, it shall be called a strike, whether or not the batter tries to avoid the ball. If the ball is outside the strike zone when it touches the batter, it shall be called a ball if that batter makes no attempt to avoid being touched.

A.R. - When the batter is touched by a pitched ball which does not entitle that batter to first base, the ball is dead and no runner may advance.

(c) the catcher or any fielder interferes with the batter. If a play follows the interference, the manager of the offense may advise the plate umpire of a decision to decline the interference penalty and accept the play. Such election shall be made immediately at the end of the play. However, if the batter reaches first base on a hit, an error, a base on balls, a hit batter, or otherwise, and all other runners advance at least one base, the play proceeds without reference to the interference;

A.R. 1 - **Intermediate (50-70) Division/Junior/Senior League:** If a runner is trying to score by a steal or squeeze from third base, note the additional penalty set forth in Rule 7.07.

A.R. 2 - If the catcher interferes with the batter before the pitcher delivers the ball, it shall not be considered interference on the batter under Rule 6.08(c). In such cases, the umpire shall call "Time" and the pitcher and batter resume the count.

(d) a fair ball touches an umpire or a runner on fair territory before touching a fielder.

> A.R. - Ball is dead. Runner(s) who are forced advance and any runners not forced will return to their bases at the time of the pitch.

NOTE: If a fair ball touches an umpire after having passed a fielder other than the pitcher, or having touched a fielder, including the pitcher, the ball is in play.

6.09 - The batter becomes a runner when-

(a) a fair ball is hit;

(b) **Majors/Intermediate (50-70) Division/Junior/Senior League**: the third strike is not caught, providing (1) first base is unoccupied or (2) first base is occupied with two out; (**NOTE:** A batter forfeits his/her opportunity to advance to first base when he/she enters the dugout or other dead ball area);

(c) a fair ball, after having passed a fielder other than the pitcher, or after having been touched by a fielder, including the pitcher, shall touch an umpire or runner in fair territory;

(d) a fair fly ball passes over a fence or into the stands at a distance from home base of 165 feet [**Intermediate (50-70) Division:** 200 feet; and **Junior/Senior League:** 250 feet] or more. Such hit entitles the batter to a home run when all bases have been legally touched. A fair fly ball that passes out of the playing field at a point less than 165 feet [**Intermediate (50-70) Division:** 200 feet; and **Junior/Senior League:** 250 feet] from home base shall entitle the batter to advance to second base only;

(e) a fair ball, after touching the ground, bounds into the stands; passes through, over, or under a fence; through or under a scoreboard; or through or under shrubbery or vines on the fence, in which case the batter and runners shall be entitled to advance two bases;

(f) any fair ball which, either before or after touching the ground, passes through or under a fence, through or under a scoreboard, through any opening in the fence or scoreboard, through or under shrubbery or vines on the fence, or which sticks in a fence or scoreboard, in which case the batter and the runners shall be entitled to two bases;

(g) any bounding fair ball is deflected by the fielder into the stands, or over or under a fence on fair or foul territory, in which case the batter and all runners shall be entitled to advance two bases;

(h) any fair fly ball is deflected by the fielder into the stands, or over the fence into foul territory, in which case the batter shall be entitled to advance to second base; but if deflected into the stands or over the fence in fair territory, the batter shall be entitled to a home run. However, should such a fair fly be deflected at a point less than 165 feet [**Intermediate (50-70) Division:** 200 feet; and **Junior/Senior League:** 250 feet] from home plate, the batter shall be entitled to two bases only.

Rule 7.00
The Runner

7.01 - A runner acquires the right to an unoccupied base when that runner touches it before being retired. The runner is then entitled to it until retired or forced to vacate it for another runner legally entitled to that base. If a runner legally acquires title to a base, and the pitcher assumes his/her position on the pitcher's plate, the runner may not return to a previously occupied base.

7.02 - In advancing, a runner shall touch first, second, third, and home base in order. If forced to return, the runner shall retouch all bases in reverse order, unless the ball is dead under any provision of Rule 5.09. In such cases, the runner may go directly to the original base.

7.03 - Two runners may not occupy a base, but if, while the ball is alive, two runners are touching the base, the following runner shall be out when tagged. The preceding runner is entitled to the base.

(a) If two runners are on a base and both are tagged, then the lead runner is out if forced.

7.04 - Each runner, other than the batter, may, without liability to be put out, advance one base when -

(a) the batter's advance without liability to be put out forces the runner to vacate a base, or when the batter hits a fair ball that touches another runner or the umpire before such ball has been touched by, or has passed a fielder, if the runner is forced to advance, or in **Intermediate (50-70) Division/Junior/Senior League**, there is a balk;

(b) a fielder, after catching a fly ball, falls into a stand, falls across ropes into a crowd when spectators are on the field, or falls into any other dead-ball areas;

(c) **Intermediate (50-70) Division/Junior/Senior League:** while the runner is attempting to steal a base, the batter is interfered with by the catcher or any other fielder.

NOTE: When a runner is entitled to a base without liability to be put out, while the ball is in play, or under any rule in which the ball is in play after the runner reaches an entitled base, and the runner fails to touch the base to which that runner is entitled before attempting to advance to the next base, the runner shall forfeit the exemption from liability to be put out and may be put out by tagging the base or by tagging the runner before that runner returns to the missed base.

> A.R. - A runner forced to advance without liability to be put out, may advance past the base to which he/she is entitled at his/her own risk.

7.05 - Each runner including the batter-runner may, without liability to be put out, advance -

(a) to home base scoring a run, if a fair ball goes out of the playing field in flight and the runner touches all bases legally; or if a fair ball which, in the umpire's judgment, would have gone out of the playing field in flight [165 feet from home plate; **Intermediate (50-70) Division:** 200 feet; and **Junior/Senior League:** 250

feet], is deflected by the act of a fielder in throwing a glove, cap, or any article of apparel;

(b) three bases, if a fielder deliberately touches a fair ball with a cap, mask, or any part of that fielder's uniform detached from its proper place on the person of said fielder. The ball is in play and the batter may advance to home plate at the batter's peril;

(c) three bases, if a fielder deliberately throws a glove and touches a fair ball. The ball is in play and the batter may advance to home base at that batter's peril;

(d) two bases, if a fielder deliberately touches a thrown ball with a cap, mask, or any part of the uniform detached from its proper place on the person of said fielder. The ball is in play;

(e) two bases, if a fielder deliberately throws a glove at and touches a thrown ball. The ball is in play;

(f) two bases, if a fair ball bounces or is deflected into the stands outside the first or third base foul line; if it goes through or under a field fence; through or under a scoreboard; through or under shrubbery or vines on the fence; or if it sticks in such fence, scoreboard, shrubbery, or vines;

(g) two bases when, with no spectators on the playing field, a thrown ball goes into the stands; into a bench (whether or not the ball rebounds into the field); over, under, or through a field fence; on a slanting part of the screen above the backstop; or remains in the meshes of a wire screen protecting spectators. The ball is dead. When such wild throw is the first play by an infielder, the umpire, in awarding such bases, shall be governed by the position of the runners at the time the ball was pitched; in all other cases the umpire shall be governed by the position of the runners at the time the wild throw was made;

> A.R. - If all runners, including the batter-runner, have advanced at least one base when an infielder makes a wild throw on the first play after the pitch, the award shall be governed by the position of the runners when the wild throw was made.

(h) one base, if a ball, pitched to the batter, or thrown by the pitcher from the position on the pitcher's plate to a base to catch a runner, goes into a stand or a bench, or over or through a field fence or backstop. The ball is dead;

(i) one base, if the batter becomes a runner on a ball four when the pitch passes the catcher and lodges in the umpire's mask or paraphernalia;

Majors/Intermediate (50-70) Division/Junior/Senior League: one base, if the batter becomes a runner on a ball four or strike three when the pitch passes the catcher and lodges in the umpire's mask or paraphernalia.

NOTE 1: If the batter becomes a runner on a wild pitch which entitles the runners to advance one base, the batter-runner shall be entitled to first base only but can advance beyond first base at their own risk if the ball stays in play.

NOTE 2: In Tee Ball, the runner or runners will be permitted to advance at their own risk on an overthrow that remains in play, but not more than one base.

(j)   one base, if a fielder deliberately touches a pitched ball with his/her cap, mask, or any part of his/her uniform detached from its proper place on his/her person. The ball is in play, and the award is made based on the position of the runner at the time the ball was touched.

7.06 - When the obstruction occurs, the umpire shall call or signal "Obstruction."

(a)   If a play is being made on the obstructed runner, or if the batter-runner is obstructed before touching first base, the ball is dead and all runners shall advance without liability to be put out, to the bases they would have reached, in the umpire's judgment, if there had been no obstruction. The obstructed runner shall be awarded at least one base beyond the base last legally touched by such runner, before the obstruction. Any preceding runners forced to advance by the award of bases as the penalty for obstruction shall advance without liability to be put out;

(b)   If no play is being made on the obstructed runner, the play shall proceed until no further action is possible. The umpire shall then call "Time" and impose such penalties, if any, as in that umpire's judgment will nullify the act of obstruction. **NOTE 1:** When the ball is not dead on obstruction and an obstructed runner advances beyond the base which, in the umpire's judgment, the runner would have been awarded because of being obstructed, the runner does so at his/her own risk and may be tagged out. This is a judgment call. **NOTE 2:** If the defensive player blocks the base (plate) or base line clearly without possession of the ball, obstruction shall be called. The runner is safe and a delayed dead ball shall be called.

7.07 – Intermediate (50-70) Division/Junior/Senior League: If, with a runner on third base and trying to score by means of a squeeze play or a steal, the catcher or any other fielder steps on, or in front of home base without possession of the ball, or touches the batter or the bat, the pitcher shall be charged with a balk, the batter shall be awarded first base on the interference and the ball is dead.

7.08 - Any runner is out when -

(a)   (1)   running more than three feet away from his/her baseline to avoid being tagged, unless such action is to avoid interference with a fielder fielding a batted ball. A runner's baseline is established when the tag attempt occurs and is a straight line from the runner to the base to which he/she is attempting to reach; or

(2)   after touching first base, the runner leaves the baseline, obviously abandoning all effort to touch the next base; or

(3)   the runner does not slide or attempt to get around a fielder who has the ball and is waiting to make the tag; or

> A.R. - There is no "must slide rule."

(4)   **Little League (Major) and below only**: the runner slides head first while advancing.

(b)   intentionally interferes with a thrown ball; or hinders a fielder attempting to make a play on a batted ball (**NOTE:** A runner who is adjudged to have hindered a fielder who is attempting to make a play on a batted ball is out whether it was intentional or not);

(c) that runner is tagged, when the ball is alive, while off a base;

EXCEPTION: A batter-runner cannot be tagged out after overrunning or over sliding first base if said batter-runner returns immediately to the base.

> A.R. 1 - This includes a batter-runner who overruns first after being awarded a base on balls.
>
> A.R. 2 - If the impact of a runner breaks a base loose from its position, no play can be made on that runner at that base if the runner had reached the base safely.
>
> A.R. 3 - If a base is dislodged from its position during a play, any following runner on the same play shall be considered as touching or occupying the base if, in the umpire's judgment, that runner touches or occupies the dislodged bag, or the point marked by the original location of the dislodged bag.

(d) failing to retouch the base after a fair or foul ball is legally caught before that runner, or the base, is tagged by a fielder. The runner shall not be called out for failure to retouch the base after the first following pitch, or any play or attempted play. This is an appeal play.

NOTE: Base runners can legally retouch their base once a fair ball is touched in flight and advance at their own risk if a fair or foul ball is caught.

(e) failing to reach the next base before a fielder tags said runner or the base after that runner has been forced to advance by reason of the batter becoming a runner. However, if a following runner is retired on a force play, the force is removed and the runner must be tagged to be put out. The force is removed as soon as the runner touches the base to which that runner is forced to advance, and if oversliding or overrunning the base, the runner must be tagged to be put out. However, if the forced runner, after touching the next base, retreats for any reason towards the base last occupied, the force play is reinstated and the runner can again be put out if the defense tags the base to which the runner is forced;

(f) touched by a fair ball in fair territory before the ball has touched or passed an infielder. The ball is dead and no runner may score, no runners may advance, except runners forced to advance;

EXCEPTION: If a runner is touching a base when touched by an Infield Fly, that runner is not out, although the batter is out.

NOTE 1: If a runner is touched by an Infield Fly when not touching a base, both runner and batter are out.

NOTE 2: If two runners are touched by the same fair ball, only the first one is out because the ball is instantly dead.

(g) attempting to score on a play in which the batter interferes with the play at home base before two are out. With two out, the interference puts the batter out and no score counts;

(h) passes a preceding runner before such runner is out;

(i) after acquiring legal possession of a base, the runner runs the bases in reverse order for the purpose of confusing the defense or making a travesty of the game. The umpire shall immediately call "Time" and declare the runner out;

(j) failing to return at once to first base after overrunning or oversliding that base. If attempting to run to second the runner is out when tagged. If, after overrunning or oversliding first base the runner starts toward the dugout, or toward a position, and fails to return to first base at once, that runner is out, on appeal, when said runner or the base is tagged;

(k) in running or sliding for home base, the runner fails to touch home base and makes no attempt to return to the base, when a fielder holds the ball in hand, while touching home base, and appeals to the umpire for the decision. (**NOTE:** This rule applies only where the runner is on the way to the bench and a fielder would be required to chase the runner to tag him/her. It does not apply to the ordinary play where the runner misses the plate and then immediately makes an effort to touch the plate before being tagged. In that case, the runner must be tagged.)

7.09 - It is interference by a batter or runner when -

(a) the batter hinders the catcher in an attempt to field the ball;

(b) the batter intentionally deflects the course of a foul ball in any manner;

(c) before two are out and a runner on third base, the batter hinders a fielder in making a play at home base; the runner is out;

(d) any member or members of the offensive team stand or gather around any base to which a runner is advancing, to confuse, hinder, or add to the difficulty of the fielders. Such runner shall be declared out for the interference of a teammate or teammates;

(e) any batter or runner who has just been retired hinders or impedes any following play being made on a runner. Such runner shall be declared out for the interference of a teammate;

(f) if, in the judgment of the umpire, a base runner willfully and deliberately interferes with a batted ball or a fielder in the act of fielding a batted ball with the obvious intent to break up a double play, the ball is dead. The umpire shall call the runner out for interference and also call out the batter-runner because of the action of the runner. In no event may bases be run or runs scored because of such action by a runner;

(g) if, in the judgment of the umpire, a batter-runner willfully and deliberately interferes with a batted ball or a fielder in the act of fielding batted ball, with the obvious intent to break up a double play, the ball is dead; the umpire shall call the batter-runner out for interference and shall also call out the runner who advanced closest to the home plate regardless where the double play might have been possible. In no event shall bases be run because of such interference;

(h) in the judgment of the umpire, the base coach at third base or first base, by touching or holding the runner, physically assists that runner in returning to or leaving third base or first base;

> A.R. - When a play is being made on the assisted runner, the runner is out and all runners return to the bases occupied at the time of the interference (dead ball). If no play is being made on the assisted runner, the runner is out and play continues (delayed dead ball).

(i) with a runner on third base, the base coach leaves the box and acts in any manner to draw a throw by a fielder;

(j) the runner fails to avoid a fielder who is attempting to field a batted ball, or intentionally interferes with a thrown ball, provided that if two or more fielders attempt to field a batted ball, and the runner comes in contact with one or more of them, the umpire shall determine which fielder is entitled to the benefit of this rule, and shall not declare the runner out for coming in contact with a fielder other than the one the umpire determines to be entitled to field such a ball;

(k) a fair ball touches the batter or runner in fair territory before touching a fielder. If a fair ball goes through or by an infielder and touches a runner immediately back of said infielder or touches the runner after having been deflected by a fielder, the umpire shall not declare the runner out for being touched by a batted ball. In making such decision, the umpire must be convinced that the ball passed through or by the infielder and that no other infielder had the chance to make a play on the ball. If in the judgment of the umpire, the runner deliberately and intentionally kicks such a batted ball on which the infielder had missed a play, then the runner shall be called out for interference.

PENALTY FOR INTERFERENCE: The runner is out and the ball is dead.

7.10 - Any runner shall be called out, on appeal, when-

(a) after a fly ball is caught, the runner fails to retouch the base before said runner or the base is tagged (**NOTE:** "Retouch" in this rule, means to tag up and start from a contact with the base after the ball is caught. A runner is not permitted to take a flying start from a position in back of, and not touching, the base);

(b) with the ball in play, while advancing or returning to a base, the runner fails to touch each base in order before said runner, or a missed base, is tagged;

> A.R. - (1) No runner may return to touch a missed base after a following runner has scored. (2) When the ball is dead, no runner may return to touch a missed base or one abandoned after said runner has advanced to and touched a base beyond the missed base.

Play A - Batter hits the ball out of the park, or hits a ground rule double, and misses first base (ball is dead). The runner may return to first base to correct the mistake before touching second. But if the runner touches second, he/she may not return to first and if the defensive team appeals, the runner is declared out at first. (**Appeal play**.)

Play B - Batter hits a ground ball to shortstop, who throws wild into the stands (ball is dead). Batter-runner misses first base but is awarded second base on the overthrow. Even though the umpire has awarded the runner second base on the overthrow, the runner must touch first base before proceeding to second base. (**Appeal play.**)

(c)   the runner overruns or overslides first base and fails to return to the base immediately, and said runner or the base is tagged;

(d)   the runner fails to touch home base and makes no attempt to return to that base, and home base is tagged. **NOTE:** A runner forfeits his/her opportunity to return to home base when he/she enters the dugout or other dead ball area.

Any appeal under this rule must be made before the next pitch, or any play or attempted play. No appeal can be made if the ball is dead. If the violation occurs during a play which ends a half-inning, the appeal must be made before all the defensive players have left fair territory on their way to the bench or dugout. **EXCEPTION:** If an otherwise proper appeal is being made by a player who has to go into foul territory to retrieve the ball in order to make an appeal or if the appeal is being made by the catcher (who may never have been in fair territory at all), the appeal will be adjudged to have been properly executed.

An appeal is not to be interpreted as a play or an attempted play.

Successive appeals may not be made on a runner at the same base. If the defensive team on its first appeal errs, a request for a second appeal on the same runner at the same base shall not be allowed by the umpire. (Intended meaning of the word "err" is that the defensive team in making an appeal threw the ball into a dead ball area. For example, if the pitcher threw to first base to appeal and threw the ball into the stands, no second appeal would be allowed.)

NOTE 1: Appeal plays may require an umpire to recognize an apparent "fourth out." If the third out is made during a play in which an appeal play is sustained on another runner, the appeal play decision takes precedence in determining the out. If there is more than one appeal during a play that ends a half-inning, the defense may elect to take the out that gives it the advantage. For the purposes of this rule, the defensive team has "left the field" when all players have left fair territory on their way to the bench or dugout.

NOTE 2: If a pitcher makes an illegal pitch [a balk in **Intermediate (50-70) Division/Junior/Senior League**] when making an appeal, such act shall be a play. An appeal should be clearly intended as an appeal, either by a verbal request by the player or an act that unmistakably indicates an appeal to the umpire. A player, inadvertently stepping on the base with a ball in hand, would not constitute an appeal. The ball must be live and in play.

7.11 - The players, coaches, or any member of an offensive team shall vacate any space (including both dugouts) needed by a fielder who is attempting to field a batted or thrown ball.

PENALTY: Interference shall be called and the batter or runner on whom the play is being made shall be declared out.

7.12 - Unless two are out, the status of a following runner is not affected by a preceding runner's failure to touch or retouch a base. If, upon appeal, the preceding runner is the third out, no runners following the preceding runner shall score. If such third out is the result of a force play, neither preceding nor following runners shall score.

7.13 - **Little League (Major) and Minor League:** When a pitcher is in contact with the pitcher's plate and in possession of the ball and the catcher is in the catcher's box ready to receive delivery of the ball, base runners shall not leave their bases until the ball has been delivered and has reached the batter. **NOTE: Tee Ball:** Base runners must stay in contact with the base until the ball is hit. When players have advanced as far as possible without being put out or having been retired, the umpire shall call "time" and place the ball on the tee.

The violation by one base runner shall affect all other base runners -

(a) when a base runner leaves the base before the pitched ball has reached the batter and the batter does not hit the ball, the runner is permitted to continue. If a play is made on the runner and the runner is out, the out stands. If said runner reaches safely the base to which the runner is advancing, that runner must be returned to the base occupied before the pitch was made, and no out results;

(b) when a base runner leaves the base before the pitched ball has reached the batter and the batter hits the ball, the base runner or runners are permitted to continue. If a play is made and the runner or runners are put out, the out or outs will stand. If not put out, the runner or runners must return to the original base or bases or to the unoccupied base nearest the one that was left; In no event shall the batter advance beyond first base on a single or error, second base on a double or third base on a triple. The Umpire-in-Chief shall determine the base value of the hit ball.

(c) when any base runner leaves the base before the pitched ball has reached the batter and the batter bunts, hits a ball within the infield or advances on an uncaught third strike, no run shall be allowed to score. If three runners were on the bases and the batter reaches first base safely, each runner shall advance to the base beyond the one they occupied at the start of the play except the runner who occupied third base, that runner shall be removed from the base without a run being scored.

NOTE: See exceptions following this rule.

EXCEPTION: If at the conclusion of the play there is an open base, paragraphs (a) and (b) will apply.

EXAMPLES:

1. Runner on first leaves too soon, batter reaches first safely, runner goes to second.
2. Runner on second leaves too soon, batter reaches first safely, runner returns to second.
3. Runner on third leaves too soon, batter reaches first safely, runner returns to third.
4. Runner on first leaves too soon, batter hits clean double, runner goes to third only.
5. Runner on second leaves too soon, batter hits clean double, runner goes to third only.
6. Runner on third leaves too soon, batter hits clean double, runner returns to third.
7. All runners on base will be allowed to score when the batter hits a clean triple or home run, regardless of whether any runner left too soon.
8. Runners on first and second, either leaves too soon, batter reaches first safely, runners go to second and third.
9. Runners on first and second, either leaves too soon, batter hits clean double, runner on first goes to third, runner on second scores.
10. Runners on first and third, either leaves too soon, batter reaches first safely, runner on first goes to second, runner on third remains there.
11. Runners on first and third, either leaves too soon, batter hits a clean double, runner on first goes to third, runner on third scores.

12. Runners on second and third, either leaves too soon, batter reaches first safely, neither runner can advance.

13. Runners on second and third, either leaves too soon, batter hits a clean double, runner on third scores, runner on second goes to third.

14. Runners on first, second, and third, any runner leaves too soon, batter hits clean double, runners on second, third score, runner on first goes to third.

15. Bases full, any runner leaves too soon, batter reaches first safely on any ball bunted or hit within the infield, all runners advance one base except runner advancing from third. Runner advancing from third is removed, no run is scored and no out charged. If on the play, a putout at any base results in an open base, runner who occupied third base returns to third base.

16. Bases full, any runner leaves too soon, batter received a base on balls or is hit by a pitch, each runner will advance one base and a run will score.

NOTE 1: When an umpire detects a base runner leaving the base too soon, that umpire shall drop a signal flag or handkerchief immediately to indicate the violation.

NOTE 2: For purpose of these examples, it is assumed that the batter-runner remains at the base last acquired safely.

NOTE 3: Tee Ball: Base runners must stay in contact with the base until the ball is hit. When players have advanced as far as possible without being put out or having been retired the umpire shall call "time" and place the ball on the tee.

7.14 - Once each inning a team may utilize a player who is not in the batting order as a special pinch-runner for any offensive player. A player may only be removed for a special pinch-runner one time during a game. The player for whom the pinch-runner runs is not subject to removal from the lineup. If the pinch-runner remains in the game as a substitute defensive or offensive player, the player may not be used again as a pinch-runner while in the batting order. However, if removed for another substitute that player or any player not in the line-up, is again eligible to be used as a pinch-runner. A local league may adopt Tournament Rule 3(d) for 7.14. **NOTE: Does not apply if the local league adopts the continuous batting order. See Rule 4.04.**

7.15 - Procedures for Use of a Double First Base: The double base may be used for first base only. The base must be rectangular, with two sides not less than 14 inches and not more than 15 inches, and the other two sides not less than 29 inches and not more than 30 inches. The longer sides shall face toward home plate and the right field corner. The outer edges shall not be more than two and one-fourth (2¼) inches thick, filled with soft material, and covered with canvas or rubber. Half the base shall be white (entirely over fair territory) and half shall be orange or green (entirely over foul territory). When using the double first base, the following rules must be observed:

(a) A batted ball that hits the white section of the double base shall be declared fair. A batted ball that hits the colored (orange or green) section without first touching or bounding over the white section shall be declared foul.

(b) Whenever a play is being made on the batter-runner, the defense must us the white section of the double first base.

NOTE 1: A play is being made on the batter-runner when he/she is attempting to reach first base while the defense is attempting to retire him/her at that base.

NOTE 2: If there is a play on the batter-runner, and the batter-runner touches only the white portion and the defense appeals prior to the batter-runner returning to first base, it is treated the same as missing the base. **PENALTY:** Batter-runner is out.

(c)   Whenever a play is being made on the batter-runner, the batter-runner must use the colored (orange or green) section on his/her first attempt to tag first base. **NOTE:** On extra-base hits or other balls hit to the outfield when there is no chance for a play to be made at the double first base, the batter-runner may touch either the white or colored (orange or green) section of the base. Should, however, the batter-runner reach and go beyond first base, he/she may only return to the white section of the base. **PENALTY:** If there is a play on the batter-runner, and the batter-runner touches only the white portion and the defense appeals prior to the batter-runner returning to first base, it is treated the same as missing the base. If properly appealed, the batter-runner is out.

(d)   When tagging up on a fly ball, the white section of the base must be used by the runner. One foot is permitted to extend behind or on the base into foul territory, as long as the front foot is touching the white section of the base. **PENALTY:** If properly appealed, runner is out.

(e)   When leaving base on a pitched ball in **Little League (Major) and below**, the runner must maintain contact with the white section of the base until the ball has reached the batter. Runners may extend a foot behind the white portion of the base, but must maintain contact with the white section until the ball has reached the batter. **PENALTY:** See Rule 7.13.

(f)   On an attempted pick-off play, the runner must return to the white section of the base only. This includes a throw from the pitcher, catcher, or any other player, in an attempt to retire the runner at the double first base.

(g)   In **Majors, Intermediate (50-70) Division, Junior, and Senior League** divisions, when the batter becomes a runner on a third strike not caught by the catcher, the batter-runner and the defensive player may use either the colored (orange or green) or the white section.

(h)   Use of the double first base does not change any other rule concerning interference or obstruction at first base. (An errant throw into the three-foot running lane could still result in an obstruction call. Also, the batter-runner must still avoid interference with the fielder attempting to field a batted ball.)

Rule 8.00
The Pitcher

8.01 - Legal pitching delivery. There are two legal pitching positions, the Windup Position and the Set Position, and either position may be used at any time. Pitchers shall take signs from the catcher while standing on the pitcher's plate.

Pitchers may disengage the pitcher's plate after taking their signs but may not step quickly onto the pitcher's plate and pitch. This may be judged a quick pitch by the umpire. When the pitcher disengages the pitcher's plate, he/she must drop the hands to the sides.

(a) The Windup Position. The pitcher shall stand facing the batter, the pivot foot in contact with the pitcher's plate, and the other foot free. From this position any natural movement associated with the delivery of the ball to the batter commits the pitcher to pitch without interruption or alteration. The pitcher shall not raise either foot from the ground, except that in the actual delivery of the ball to the batter, said pitcher may take one step backward, and one step forward with the free foot. From this position the pitcher may:

   (1) deliver the ball to the batter, or

   (2) step and throw to a base in an attempt to pick-off a runner, or

   (3) disengage the pitcher's plate. In disengaging the pitcher's plate, the pitcher must step off with the pivot foot and not the free foot first. The pitcher may not go into a set or stretch position. If the pitcher does, it is an illegal pitch [a balk in **Intermediate (50-70) Division/Junior/Senior League**].

   NOTE: When a pitcher holds the ball with both hands in front of the body, with the pivot foot in contact with the pitcher's plate, and the other foot free, that pitcher will be considered in a Windup Position.

(b) The Set Position. Set Position shall be indicated by the pitcher when that pitcher stands facing the batter with the pivot foot in contact with, and the other foot in front of, the pitcher's plate, holding the ball in both hands in front of the body and coming to a complete stop. From such Set Position the pitcher may deliver the ball to the batter, throw to a base, or step backward off the pitcher's plate with the pivot foot. Before assuming the Set Position, the pitcher may elect to make any natural preliminary motion such as that known as "the stretch." But if the pitcher so elects, that pitcher shall come to the Set Position before delivering the ball to that batter.

   NOTE: In Little League (Major) and below the pitcher need not come to a complete stop. **Intermediate (50-70) Division/Junior/Senior League:** the pitcher must come to a complete and discernible stop.

(c) At any time during the pitcher's preliminary movements and until the natural pitching motion commits that pitcher to the pitch, said pitcher may throw to any base provided the pitcher steps directly toward such base before making the throw. The pitcher shall step "ahead of the throw." A snap throw followed by the step toward the base is an illegal pitch [a balk in **Intermediate (50-70) Division/ Junior/Senior League**]. (See Penalty for illegal pitch/balk under Rule 8.05.)

(d)   If the pitcher makes an illegal pitch with the bases unoccupied, it shall be called a ball unless the batter reaches first base on a hit, an error, a base on balls, a hit batter, or otherwise. A ball which slips out of the pitcher's hand and crosses the foul line shall be called a ball; otherwise it will be called "no pitch" without runners on base, and an illegal pitch [a balk in **Intermediate (50-70) Division/ Junior/Senior League**] with runners on base. (See Penalty for illegal pitch under Rule 8.05.)

(e)   If the pitcher removes the pivot foot from contact with the pitcher's plate by stepping backward with that foot, that pitcher thereby becomes an infielder and in the case of a wild throw from that position, it shall be considered the same as a wild throw by any other infielder.

(f)   A pitcher must indicate visually to the Umpire-in-Chief, the batter, and any runners the hand with which he/she intends to pitch, which may be done by wearing his/her glove on the other hand while touching the pitcher's plate. The pitcher is not permitted to pitch with the other hand until the batter is retired, the batter becomes a runner, the inning ends, the batter is substituted for by a pinch-hitter, or the pitcher incurs an injury. In the event a pitcher switches pitching hands during an at-bat because he/she has suffered an injury, the pitcher may not, for the remainder of the game, pitch with the hand from which he/she has switched. The pitcher shall not be given the opportunity to throw any preparatory pitches after switching pitching hands. Any change of pitching hands must be indicated clearly to the Umpire-in-Chief.

(g)   **Tee Ball:** The pitcher shall keep both feet on the pitcher's plate until the ball is hit.

8.02 - The pitcher shall not -

(a)   (1)   bring the pitching hand in contact with the mouth or lips while in contact with the pitcher's plate. **EXCEPTION:** The pitcher may bring the hand in contact with the mouth or lips while in the 10-foot circle (**Intermediate (50-70) Division/Junior/Senior:** 18-foot circle) surrounding the pitcher's plate provided he/she distinctly wipes off the pitching hand before contacting the ball.

       PENALTY: For violation of this part of the rule the umpires shall immediately call a ball and warn the pitcher that repeated violation of any part of this rule can cause the pitcher to be removed from the game. However, if the pitch is made and a batter reaches first base on a hit, an error, a hit batter, or otherwise, and no other runner is put out before advancing at least one base, the play shall proceed without reference to the violation.

       (2)   apply a foreign substance of any kind to the ball;

       (3)   expectorate on the ball, either hand or the glove;

       (4)   rub the ball on the glove, person, or clothing;

       (5)   deface the ball in any manner; or

       (6)   deliver what is called the "shine" ball, "spit" ball, "mud" ball, or "emery" ball. The pitcher is allowed to rub off the ball between the bare hands;

PENALTY: For violation of any part of Rules 8.02(a)(2) through (6) the umpire shall: Call the pitch a ball and warn the pitcher. If a play occurs on the violation, the manager of the offense may advise the plate umpire of acceptance of the play. (Such election must be made immediately at the end of play.)

NOTE: A pitcher may use a rosin bag for the purpose of applying rosin to the bare hand or hands. Neither the pitcher nor any other player shall dust the ball with the rosin bag; neither shall the pitcher nor any other player be permitted to apply rosin from the bag to their glove or dust any part of the uniform with the rosin bag.

(b) Intentionally delay the game by throwing the ball to players other than the catcher, when the batter is in position, except in an attempt to retire a runner, or commit an illegal pitch for the purpose of not pitching to the batter (i.e. intentional walk, etc.)

PENALTY: If, after warning by the umpire, such delaying action is repeated, the pitcher can be removed from the game.

(c) Intentionally pitch at the batter. If in the umpire's judgment, such violation occurs, the umpire shall warn the pitcher and the manager of the defense that another such pitch will mean immediate expulsion of the pitcher. If such pitch is repeated during the game, the umpire shall eject the pitcher from the game.

8.03 - When a pitcher takes a position at the beginning of each inning, that pitcher shall be permitted to pitch not to exceed eight preparatory pitches to the catcher, or other teammate acting in the capacity of catcher, during which play shall be suspended. Such preparatory pitches shall not consume more than one minute of time. If a sudden emergency causes a pitcher to be summoned into the game without any opportunity to warm up, the Umpire-in-Chief shall allow the pitcher as many pitches as the umpire deems necessary.

8.04 - When the bases are unoccupied, the pitcher shall deliver the ball to the batter within 20 seconds after the pitcher receives the ball. Each time the pitcher delays the game by violating this rule, the umpire shall call "Ball."

NOTE: The intent of this rule is to avoid unnecessary delays. The umpire shall insist that the catcher return the ball promptly to the pitcher, and that the pitcher take a position on the pitcher's plate promptly.

8.05 – With a runner or runners on base, it is an illegal pitch – **Major/Minor League** [a balk in **Intermediate (50-70) Division/Junior/Senior League**] when -

(a) the pitcher, while touching the plate, makes any motion naturally associated with the pitch and fails to make such delivery;

(b) the pitcher, while touching the plate, feints a throw to first base and fails to complete the throw;

(c) the pitcher, while touching the plate, fails to step directly toward a base before throwing to that base;

(d) the pitcher, while touching the plate, throws, or feints a throw to an unoccupied base, except for the purpose of making a play;

(e) the pitcher makes a quick pitch; Umpires will judge a quick pitch as one delivered before the batter is reasonably set in the batter's box.

NOTE: Rule 8.05(e) is an illegal pitch (Rule 2.00). **Little League (Major)/ Minor League:** The penalty for Rule 8.05(e), regardless of whether there are runners present or not, is a ball. This is an instance in which an illegal pitch, by Little League (Major)/Minor League definition, can occur without runners on base. **Intermediate (50-70) Division/Junior/Senior League**: With runners on base, Rule 8.05(e) is penalized with a balk; with no runners on base, Rule 8.05(e) is penalized with a ball. (See exceptions in "PENALTY.")

(f)   the pitcher delivers the ball to the batter while not facing the batter;

(g)   the pitcher makes any motion naturally associated with the pitch while not touching the pitcher's plate;

NOTE: Rule 8.05(g) is an illegal pitch (Rule 2.00). **Little League (Major)/ Minor League:** The penalty for Rule 8.05(g), regardless of whether there are runners present or not, is a ball. This is an instance in which an illegal pitch, by Little League (Major)/Minor League definition, can occur without runners on base. **Intermediate (50-70) Division/Junior/Senior League**: With runners on base, Rule 8.05(g) is penalized with a balk; with no runners on base, Rule 8.05(g) is penalized with a ball. (See exceptions in "PENALTY.")

(h)   the pitcher unnecessarily delays the game;

(i)   the pitcher, without having the ball, stands on or astride the pitcher's plate or while off the plate feints a pitch;

(j)   the pitcher, while touching the plate, accidentally or intentionally drops the ball;

(k)   the pitcher, while giving an intentional base on balls, pitches when the catcher is not in the catcher's box;

(l)   **Intermediate (50-70) Division/Junior/Senior League only**: The pitcher, after coming to a legal position, removes one hand from the ball other than in an actual pitch, or in throwing to a base;

(m)   **Intermediate (50-70) Division/Junior/Senior League only:** The pitcher delivers the pitch from the set position without coming to a stop.

NOTE 1: Little League (Major) and Minor League - 8.05(l) and 8.05(m) shall not be enforced at any time.

NOTE 2: A batter hit by a pitch shall be awarded first base without reference to the illegal pitch.

PENALTY FOR AN ILLEGAL PITCH: Little League (Major)/Minor League: The ball is dead and no runners will advance. The pitch shall be called a ball even if the pitch is not actually thrown. **EXCEPTION**: If the pitch is delivered and a play follows the illegal pitch, the play shall be allowed to continue as a delayed dead ball. Upon completion of the play, the manager of the offense may advise the plate umpire of a decision to decline the illegal pitch penalty and accept the play. Such election shall be made immediately at the end of the play. However, if the batter hits the ball and reaches first base safely, and if all base-runners advance at least one base on the action resulting from the batted ball, the play proceeds without reference to the illegal pitch.

When an illegal pitch is called, regardless of whether the pitch is completed or not by the pitcher, a pitch will always be charged to the pitcher's pitch count. (Rule 2.00 Definitions: Pitch) **NOTE**: Under no circumstances shall a balk be called in Little League (Major) or Minor League.

PENALTY FOR A BALK: The balk applies only to **Intermediate (50-70) Division/ Junior/Senior League**. The ball is dead, and each runner shall advance one base without liability to be put out unless the batter reaches first on a hit, an error, a base on balls, a hit batter, or otherwise, and all other runners advance at least one base in which case the play proceeds without reference to the balk. When a balk is called and the pitch is delivered it will be considered neither a ball nor strike unless the pitch is ball four (4) awarding the batter first base and forcing all runners on base to advance.

When a balk is called, if the pitch is delivered, a pitch shall be charged against the pitch count regardless of whether the batter put the pitch into play. However, on a balk that is called on a pickoff attempt or in an instance that the pitcher does not deliver the pitch, no pitch shall be charged to the pitch count.

NOTE: Umpires should bear in mind that the purpose of the balk rule is to prevent the pitcher from deliberately deceiving the base runner. If there is doubt in the umpire's mind, the "intent" of the pitcher should govern. However, certain specifics should be borne in mind:

(1) Straddling the pitcher's plate without the ball is to be interpreted as intent to deceive and ruled a balk.

(2) With a runner on first base and the runner attempting to steal second, the pitcher may make a complete turn, without hesitating toward first, and throw to second. This is not to be interpreted as throwing to an unoccupied base.

> A.R. 1 - If the pitcher violates (a) through (m) in this rule and throws wild to a base, the runner or runners may advance at their own risk. (Delayed dead ball.)
>
> A.R. 2 - A runner who misses the first base to which that runner is advancing and who is called out on appeal shall be considered as having advanced one base for the purpose of this rule.

8.06 - This rule, which applies to each pitcher who enters a game, governs the visits of the manager or coach to the pitcher **at the mound.**

(a) A manager or coach may come out once (**Minor Division**: twice) in one inning to visit with the pitcher, but the second time (**Minor Division:** third time) out, the player must be removed as a pitcher. **Example:** If a manager visits Pitcher A once in the first inning, then makes a pitching change in the same inning, Pitcher B would be allowed one visit in that inning before being removed on the second visit.

(b) A manager or coach may come out twice (**Minor Division:** three times) in one game to visit with the pitcher, but the third time (**Minor Division:** fourth time) out, the player must be removed as a pitcher. **Example**: If a manager visits Pitcher A twice in the first three innings, then makes a pitching change in the fourth inning, Pitcher B would be allowed two visits in that game before being removed on the third visit, subject to the limits in (a) above.

NOTE: A pitcher moving to a different position and returning as the pitcher of record shall retain the number of visits from their previous appearance as pitcher. To calculate the number of visits for a pitcher, all visits, regardless of the pitcher being removed and returned to the pitcher's position, shall be applied.

(c) A manager or coach may confer with any other player(s), including the catcher, during the visit with the pitcher. A manager or coach who is granted a time out to talk to any defensive player will be charged with a visit to the pitcher.

A.R. 1 - When a manager requests timeout to make a pitching change, it shall not be considered a visit to the pitcher provided the manager makes the pitching substitution prior to speaking to any defensive player. **Intermediate (50-70) Division/Junior/Senior**: This applies when a pitcher moves to another position and returns as a pitcher later in the same game.

A.R. 2 - A conference with the pitcher or any other fielder to evaluate the player's condition after an injury shall not be considered a visit for the purposes of this rule. The manager or coach should advise the umpire of such a conference, and the umpire should monitor the conference.

Rule 9.00
The Umpire

9.01 -

(a) The league president shall appoint one or more adult umpires to officiate at each league game. The umpire shall be responsible for the conduct of the game in accordance with these official rules and for maintaining discipline and order on the playing field during the game.

   NOTE 1: Plate umpire must wear mask, shin guards, and chest protector. Male umpire must wear protective cup. **NOTE 2:** It is highly recommended all umpires attach a "dangling" type throat protector to their mask.

(b) Each umpire is the representative of the league and of Little League International, and is authorized and required to enforce all of these rules. Each umpire has authority to order a player, coach, manager, or league officer to do or refrain from doing anything which affects the administering of these rules and to enforce the prescribed penalties.

(c) Each umpire has authority to rule on any point not specifically covered in these rules.

(d) Each umpire has authority to disqualify any player, coach, manager, or substitute for objecting to decisions or for unsportsmanlike conduct or language, and to eject such disqualified person from the playing field. If an umpire disqualifies a player while a play is in progress, the disqualification shall not take effect until no further action is possible in that play.

   NOTE: The local league has the option to adopt this rule application. The stealing and relaying of signs to alert the batter of pitch selection and/or location is unsportsmanlike behavior. If, in the judgment of the umpire, this behavior is occurring, those responsible including any player(s), coach(es), and/or manager shall be ejected from the game.

(e) A manager, coach, or player shall not leave their position in the field or bench area during a fight or physical confrontation; a manager or coach who attempts to prevent a fight or restore order, in the umpire's judgment, is not in violation of this rule.

   PENALTY: The umpire shall eject the offender(s) from the game immediately. Failure to comply with the ejection may result in the umpire suspending the game and referring it to the Board of Directors for further action.

(f) All umpires have authority at their discretion to eject from the playing field (1) any person whose duties permit that person's presence on the field, such as ground crew members, photographers, newsmen, broadcasting crew members, etc., and (2) any spectator or other person not authorized to be on the playing field.

(g) Umpires may order both teams into their dugouts and suspend play until such time as league officials deal with unruly spectators. Failure of league officials to adequately handle an unruly spectator can result in the game remaining suspended until a later date.

9.02 -

(a) Any umpire's decision which involves judgment, such as, but not limited to, whether a batted ball is fair or foul, whether a pitch is a strike or a ball, or whether a runner is safe or out, is final. No player, manager, coach, or substitute shall object to any such judgment decisions.

(b) If there is reasonable doubt that any umpire's decision may be in conflict with the rules, the manager may appeal the decision and ask that a correct ruling be made. Such appeal shall be made only to the umpire who made the protested decision.

(c) If a decision is appealed, the umpire making the decision may ask another umpire for information before making a final decision. No umpire shall criticize, seek to reverse, or interfere with another umpire's decision unless asked to do so by the umpire making it.

(d) No umpire may be replaced during a game unless injured or ill.

9.03 -

(a) If there is only one umpire, that umpire must be an adult and shall have complete jurisdiction in administering the rules. This umpire may take any position on the playing field which will enable said umpire to discharge all duties (usually behind the catcher, but sometimes behind the pitcher if there are runners.)

(b) If there are two or more umpires, one shall be designated Umpire-in-Chief and the others field umpires or a plate umpire.

(c) The Umpire-in-Chief may be a plate umpire or a field umpire. The Umpire-in-Chief's duties, in addition to any field or plate duties, shall be to:

    (1) take full charge of, and be responsible for, the proper conduct of the game;

    (2) make all decisions except those commonly reserved for the other field umpires or plate umpire; and

    (3) announce any special ground rules.

(d) If no adult umpire is available for a game, and non-adult umpires are used exclusively for that game, the local Little League must assign an adult as Game Coordinator, or the game cannot be played. The Game Coordinator must not be a manager or coach of either team in the game, and cannot be assigned as Game Coordinator for more than one game at a time. The Game Coordinator's duties shall be:

    (1) To be included in the pregame meeting as noted in Rule 4.01;

    (2) To remain at the game at all times, including between half-innings, in a position to see all actions on the field and in close proximity to the field (not in any enclosure). If, for some reason, the Game Coordinator is not present or is unable to perform his/her duties for any reason, the game must be suspended until the Game Coordinator returns, or until a new adult Game Coordinator is present and assumes the duties of Game Coordinator for the remainder of the game;

    (3) To oversee the conduct of all players, managers, coaches, and umpires in the game;

(4) To have the authority to disqualify any player, coach, manager, or substitute for objecting to the decisions of an umpire, for unsportsmanlike conduct or language, or for any of the reasons enumerated in these Playing Rules, and to eject such disqualified person from the playing field. If the Game Coordinator disqualifies a player while a play is in progress, the disqualification shall not take effect until no further action is possible in that play;

(5) To have the sole ability to judge as to whether and when play shall be suspended during a game because of inclement weather conditions or the unfit condition of the playing field; as to whether and when play shall be resumed after such suspension; and as to whether and when a game shall be terminated after such suspension. Said Game Coordinator shall not call the game until at least thirty minutes after play as suspended. The Game Coordinator may continue suspension as long as there is any chance to resume play. (This supersedes Rule 3.10.)

> A.R. - The Game Coordinator should not interrupt or stop a game until all play and action ends. At that time, the Game Coordinator can alert the plate umpire to stop the game, and at that time enforce any part of 9.03(d).

9.04 -

(a) The plate umpire shall stand behind the catcher. This umpire usually is designated as the Umpire-in-Chief. The plate umpire's duties shall be to:

(1) call and count balls and strikes;

(2) call and declare fair balls and fouls except those commonly called by field umpires;

(3) make all decision on the batter except those specifically reserved to the Umpire-in-Chief, or field umpire;

(4) inform the official scorer of the official batting order, and any changes in the lineups and batting order, on request.

(b) A field umpire may take any position on the playing field best suited to make impending decisions on the bases. A field umpire's duties shall be to:

(1) make all decisions on the bases except those specifically reserved to the Umpire-in-Chief, or the plate umpire;

(2) take concurrent jurisdiction with the Umpire-in-Chief in calling "Time," illegal pitches, **Intermediate (50-70) Division/Junior/Senior League:** balks, or defacement or discoloration of the ball by any player;

(3) aid the Umpire-in-Chief in every manner in enforcing the rules, excepting the power to forfeit the game, shall have equal authority with the Umpire-in-Chief in administering and enforcing the rules and maintaining discipline.

(c) If different decisions should be made on one play by different umpires, the Umpire-in-Chief shall call all the umpires into consultation, with no manager or player present. After consultation, the Umpire-in-Chief shall determine which decision shall prevail, based on which umpire was in the best position and which decision was most likely correct. Play shall proceed as if only the final decision had been made.

9.05-

(a) The umpire shall report to the league president within 24 hours after the end of a game all violations of rules and other incidents worthy of comment, including the disqualification of any manager, coach, or player, and the reasons therefore.

(b) When any manager, coach, or player is disqualified for a flagrant offense such as the use of obscene or indecent language, or an assault upon an umpire, manager, coach, or player, the umpire shall forward full particulars to the league president within 24 hours after the end of the game.

(c) After receiving the umpire's report that a manager, coach, or player has been disqualified, the league president shall require such manager, coach, or player to appear before at least three members of the Board of Directors to explain their conduct. In the case of a player, the manager shall appear with the player in the capacity of an advisor. The members of the Board present at the meeting shall impose such penalty as they feel is justified. **NOTE:** The Board may impose such penalties that it feels are warranted, but may not lessen the requirements of Rule 4.07.

9.06 - Umpires shall not wear shoes with metal spikes or cleats.

IMPORTANT

Carry your Rulebook. It is better to consult the rules and hold up the game long enough to solve a problem than to have a game protested and possibly replayed.

Tournament Rules and Guidelines
Little League Baseball®, 8- to 10-Year Old Division, 9- to 11-Year-Old Division, Intermediate (50-70) Division, Junior League, and Senior League Baseball
Points of Emphasis in Bold Italic

Tournament play started in Little League in 1947. Conduct of tournament play by District Administrators began in 1956 following the first Little League International Congress. Today, responsibility for scheduling and supervising all District tournament games comes under jurisdiction of the District Administrator. Little League International has the right to appoint Tournament Directors at other levels of tournament play.

The Tournaments of Little League have grown year by year until today they have become the outstanding, in fact, the only exposure that the majority of the public sees. In many cases, they are the criterion by which Little League is judged. Proper conduct at tournament time imposes a large responsibility upon all concerned. Good judgment and exemplary disciplines are demanded if Little League tournaments of the future are to remain worthwhile in the public esteem.

The Little League Baseball Tournament, 8- to 10-Year-Old Division Baseball Tournament, 9- to 11-Year-Old Division Baseball Tournament, Intermediate (50-70) Division, Junior League, and Senior League Tournaments are authorized by the Little League International Board of Directors. Leagues which exercise the option to participate in Tournament Play must pledge they will do so with full knowledge of the rules and in agreement that the rules will be upheld.

RULES: Except where noted in these Tournament Rules and Guidelines, the Little League Baseball Official Regulations and Playing Rules will be used in the conduct of the 8- to 10-Year-Old Division Tournament, the 9- to 11-Year-Old Division Tournament, the Little League Baseball Tournament, the Intermediate (50-70) Division, Junior League, and Senior League Tournaments.

8- to 10-Year-Old Division & 9- to 11-Year-Old Division: The objective of the 8- to 10-Year-Old Division and 9- to 11-Year-Old Division Tournament is to provide eight-, nine-, and ten-year-old players, and nine-, ten-, and eleven-year-old players, the opportunity to participate in a baseball tournament at the District, Sectional, and State levels at the conclusion of the regular season. Leagues are strongly encouraged to place the maximum number of players (14) on the Tournament Affidavit, thereby giving more players the opportunity to participate.

Responsibility and Chain of Command

It should be clearly understood by Tournament Directors and league presidents that operation of the annual tournaments in Little League come under a different authority and jurisdiction from that normally observed during the playing season. It is, in fact, a whole new ball game. Once the tournament season starts, authority is vested solely in the Tournament Committee at Williamsport.

There will be no waivers, resorting to local rules, or other variation unless granted explicitly from Williamsport. To administer the tournament properly and scale down thousands of teams to two finalists in the limited time afforded by the tournament season is an undertaking requiring considerable discipline. Once the tournament starts, it must proceed without interruption. If protests or disputes occur which cannot be settled by the umpires or Tournament Director through immediate and concise application of the rules, an appeal must be made through proper channels promptly to prevent a major blockage or loss of momentum.

Revocation of tournament privileges or forfeiture of a tournament game may be decided only by the Tournament Committee at Williamsport. Should a problem arise that cannot be resolved while a game is in progress, the game must be suspended by the Umpire-in-Chief and the problem referred immediately to the Tournament Director. If not resolved, it must be referred to the Regional Director. If still unresolved, it will be referred to the Tournament Committee in Williamsport. If the Tournament Committee deems any player to be ineligible, by league age, residency or school attendance, participation in other programs, or participation in less than sixty (60) percent of the regular season games, it may result in forfeiture of tournament game(s), and/or suspension or removal of personnel from tournament play, and/or suspension or removal of personnel or teams from further Little League activities, and/or suspension or revocation of the local league's charter. These actions can only be taken by the Tournament Committee in Williamsport.

The Tournament Committee and the individual Regional Directors may appoint agents to act on their behalf, and any person so appointed shall have the authority to act as, and exercise the duties of, the Tournament Committee or the individual Regional Directors.

The Tournament Committee also reserves the right in its sole discretion to impose any penalties if, in its judgment, any player, manager, coach, umpire, or other volunteer conducts him/herself in any manner, on or off the field, that does not positively reflect the high standard Little League holds for sportsmanship, citizenship, and decorum. This includes displays of unsportsmanlike conduct, "making a travesty of the game," or violating any rules, regulations, or policies contained herein during the game, at the game site, at any other location or time related to the International Tournament. The Committee also reserves the right to impose any penalty the Committee deems appropriate, if the committee determines action is necessary to correct a situation brought to its attention, regardless of the source of that information. The decision of the Tournament Committee is final and binding.

Knowledge of the rules must be guaranteed before a Tournament Director is declared qualified. All Tournament Directors will undergo a thorough and instructive briefing session prior to taking on their duties, must signify that they understand the rules, and regardless of personal feelings, they are in full agreement and can interpret them properly. At the time of the District tournament meeting, it will be required that each league president or the representative in attendance signify that the league and tournament team managing personnel are knowledgeable of Tournament Rules and are in full agreement with these conditions.

Selection of Tournament Teams (Recommended Method)

Little League would gain immeasurably in esteem of the public if all tournament teams were selected by the players themselves. Players relish the challenge of competition, but their anxiety to excel is in balance with an intuitive respect and admiration for teammate and opponent alike who demonstrate superior ability and skill.

1. It is not required that players be selected for the position they occupy during the regular season. For example, a pitcher who is also a good outfielder or infielder may

be placed on the roster and used in whatever position the manager deems to be of advantage.

2. Tournament team candidates should be selected upon their playing ability and eligibility. The roster should include sufficient pitching strength to meet tournament schedules.

3. The following plan was presented to the International Congress, Washington, D.C., 1965, as a guideline, taken from the experience of the International Advisory Council. The principle is to have all components of a league determine and participate in fair and democratic selection of the tournament team. This would eliminate many of the complaints, abuses, pressures, and charges of favoritism which are directed toward the league president. The following groups should each select its tournament team.

> Group 1 - Players
> Group 2 - League Officers
> Group 3 - Team Managers
> Group 4 - Team Coaches
> Group 5 - Volunteer Umpires

Every player on the eligible teams is entitled to vote. Each group submits its list of players at a meeting of the Board of Directors of the league. The names are to be read and counted from each of the groups, and the players in the order of total votes received will become eligible for the tournament team.

Where more than one player has an equal number of votes to qualify for the last position or positions, final selection should be made by a majority vote of the Board of Directors at the time of the meeting.

NOTE: Method of selection is to be determined by the local league Board of Directors.

Tournament Organization

Teams

Each chartered league shall be eligible to enter a team. Alternates are not authorized.

(NOTE: In the 8- to 10-Year-Old Division and 9- to 11-Year-Old Division, a league may enter more than one tournament team with the District Administrator's approval.)

Where two or more charters have combined to form a single program, a tournament team must be selected for each charter composed of players from within its own chartered area. Exceptions can only be made by the Charter Committee.

Tournament teams and Eligibility Affidavit shall consist of, and must be limited to, a maximum of fourteen (14) players, one (1) manager, and a maximum of two (2) coaches.

Senior League: Teams and Eligibility Affidavit shall consist of, and must be limited to, a maximum of sixteen (16) players, one (1) manager, and a maximum of two (2) coaches.

Managers and Coaches

The District Administrator or District Staff shall not serve as manager or coach. The league president may be eligible for selection by the local league Board of Directors to coach or manage with written approval from their respective District Administrator.

Little League: The manager and coach(es) shall be regular season team managers and/or coaches from the Little League Baseball (Major) Division.

8- to 10- Division & 9- to 11-Year Old Division: The manager and coach(es) shall be regular season team managers and/or coaches from the Little League Baseball (Major) Division or Minor League Division.

Intermediate (50-70) Division: The manager and coach(es) shall be regular season team managers and/or coaches from the Intermediate (50-70) Division.

Junior League: The manager and coach(es) shall be regular season team managers and/or coaches from the Junior Division or Senior Division.

Senior League: The manager and coach(es) shall be regular season team managers and/or coaches from the Junior Division or Senior Division.

Managers/Coaches in the Dugout – If a tournament team has twelve (12) or more eligible players in uniform at the game site at the start of a game, then the maximum of three (3) adults who are named on the affidavit (or authorized replacements as noted on the affidavit) will be permitted to act as manager/coaches for that game. However, if a tournament team has eleven (11) or fewer eligible players in uniform at the game site at the start of a game, then a maximum of two (2) adults must be named at the start of the game as manager and coach. The two named adults must be listed on the affidavit, or must be authorized temporary replacements as noted on the affidavit. If there is a third adult listed on the affidavit, that adult is not permitted to be in the dugout or on the field during that game. **NOTE:** Base coaches may be adults and/or players provided at least one adult manager or coach remains in the dugout. See 4.05(b).

Umpires

The Tournament Director shall have full responsibility for providing volunteer Little League umpires for tournament play. Umpires from leagues involved in the game should not be assigned. The District Administrator shall not umpire.

There should be at least two umpires in each game. More are recommended when available.

The designated Umpire-in-Chief for each game must be an adult.

Tournament Eligibility Affidavit

It shall be the league president's responsibility to review and certify the birth records (league age) by viewing the original birth record and residence or school attendance (as defined by Little League Baseball, Incorporated) of all players. When the league finally decides on the makeup of the team, names must be entered on the league's Eligibility Affidavit. Once the District Administrator certifies the Eligibility Affidavit, the tournament team will be required to have in its possession:

1. the Eligibility Affidavit;
2. a map, signed, and dated by the league president and District Administrator, showing the actual boundaries of the league, with locations noted for the residences of the parent or legal guardian (court-appointed) or location of the school for every participant named on the affidavit;

3. a tournament verification form for each player; **NOTE: Players who established "residence" or "school attendance" for regular season and/or tournament in a prior season using the Tournament Player Verification form, and can produce the form with proper proofs and signatures, will NOT need to complete a new Tournament Player Verification form.**

4. three or more documents to determine residency of the parent(s) or legal guardian (court-appointed) or a document to support school attendance/enrollment for each player named on the tournament affidavit;

5. **waivers [i.e. II(d), IV(h), Charter Committee, etc.]**

    IMPORTANT: Alternates are not authorized. They shall not accompany the team and shall not be listed on the Eligibility Affidavit.

Eligibility Affidavit must be certified by the District Administrator or his or her designated appointee and presented by the team manager to the Tournament Director before every game. Each Tournament team must have twelve (12) eligible players for the District Administrator to certify. **EXCEPTION**: A District Administrator may certify the Eligibility Affidavit for those teams that provide a justifiable reason for not having twelve (12) players. **NOTE:** The Eligibility Affidavit becomes official once the team plays its first tournament game.

Player Participation In Other Programs

Once Tournament team practice commences, subject to the provisions of "Tournament Team Practice," player participation in other programs during the International Tournament is permitted, subject to the specific provisions of Regulation I(g) and Regulation IV(a) NOTE 2.

Release of Names

The release of names of players selected for the tournament team shall not be made before June 1, and not until the availability and eligibility of all prospective team members have been established. (The Little League group accident insurance program underwritten by an AIG member company for tournament teams will not go into effect until June 1.)

Violation of this rule may be cause for revocation of tournament privilege by the Tournament Committee.

League Eligibility

In order for a Little League program to be eligible to enter a team or teams into the International Tournament (including 8- to 10-Year-Old Division and 9- to 11-Year-Old Division) the following must be accomplished as indicated:

1) The league must be chartered in an age appropriate division(s) for which it wishes to enter a tournament team(s), no later than June 1, 2019. **Examples**: Chartered in Little League (Majors) to enter a Major Division team (10- to 12-year-olds); chartered in Senior League to enter a Junior or Senior League Division team, etc.

2) The league must have scheduled and played, at a minimum, a 12-game [**Senior League: Ten (10) game**] (per team) regular season, exclusive of playoffs and tournament games, for each division, or age appropriate division, entering tournament prior to the first game in their respective tournament. See Reg. VII. **NOTE 1:** Forfeited games shall not count towards the 12-game [**Senior League:** Ten (10)-game] regular season. **NOTE 2:**

For Junior Tournament eligibility, Senior League players league age 13 and 14 must have played in a minimum of eight (8) Regular Season games.

3) All waiver requests (for the league, team, player, manager, and/or coach) of any kind must be submitted and approved not later than June 1, 2019.

4) Team number revisions and fees incurred by the league must be paid in full by June 1, 2019.

5) All combined team and interleague play requests that may involve tournament play must be submitted and approved not later than June 1, 2019.

Failure to meet any of the listed requirements could result in a team or teams being declared ineligible by the Tournament Committee at Little League International.

Player Eligibility

Players are eligible for Tournament Play, provided they meet the criteria established by the Little League "Residency and School Attendance Player Eligibility Requirement," "Player Participation In Other Programs," and the following:

8- to 10-Year-Old Division - Any player League Age 8, 9, or 10, with amateur status, who has participated as an eligible player in 60 percent (60%) of the regular season games by the start of Tournament Play in their respective District, with the exception of the school baseball season, on a:

1. Little League Baseball (Major) Division team, or;
2. Minor League Baseball team.

9- to 11-Year-Old Division - Any player League Age 9, 10, or 11, with amateur status, who has participated as an eligible player in 60 percent (60%) of the regular season games by the start of Tournament Play in their respective District, with the exception of the school baseball season, on a:

1. Little League Baseball (Major) Division team, or;
2. Minor League Baseball team.

Little League (Major) Division - Any player League Age 10, 11, or 12, with amateur status, who has participated as an eligible player in 60 percent (60%) of the regular season games (Special Games may NOT be counted toward this requirement) by the start of Tournament Play in their respective District, with the exception of the school baseball season, on a:

1. Little League Baseball (Major) Division team, or;
2. Intermediate (50-70) Division Baseball team.

Intermediate (50-70) Division – Any player League Age 11, 12, or 13, with amateur status, who has participated as an eligible player in 60 percent (60%) of the regular season games (Special Games may be counted toward this requirement - **See Regulation IX**) in the Intermediate (50-70) Division by the start of Tournament Play in their respective District, with the exception of the school baseball season.

Junior League - Any player League Age 12, 13, or 14, with amateur status, who has participated as an eligible player in 60 percent (60%) of the regular season games (Special Games may be counted toward this requirement - **See Regulation IX**) by the start of Tournament Play in their respective District, with the exception of the middle school, junior high school, or high school baseball season, on a:

1. Junior League Baseball Team, or;

2. Senior League Baseball Team. [For Junior Tournament eligibility, Senior League players must have played in a minimum of eight (8) regular season games or 60 percent (60%) of the regular season games, whichever is greater.]

Senior League - Any player League Age 13, 14, 15, or 16, with amateur status, who has participated as an eligible player in 60 percent (60%) of the regular season games (Special Games may be counted toward this requirement - **See Regulation IX**) by the start of Tournament Play in their respective District, with the exception of the middle school, junior high school or high school baseball season, on a:

1. Senior League Baseball Team, or;

2. Junior League Baseball Team.

EXCEPTION: The local league Board of Directors may permit a player to be eligible for selection, who does not meet the 60 percent (60%) requirement, if they provide a physician's note documenting an injury or illness prior to or during the current season prohibiting his/her participation and such note releases the player for the balance of the Regular Season and/or Tournament Play.

NOTE 1: Forfeited games shall not count towards a team's 12-game [**Senior League:** Ten (10)-game] regular season nor towards any player's 60% participation.

NOTE 2: Consistent with a manager's ability to conduct the affairs of his or her team, a manager may disqualify a player from the team for the current season, subject to Board of Directors approval, if the player repeatedly misses practice or games.

NOTE 3: The Senior League and Junior League Tournaments are divided by age, without regard to the regular season division in which a player participates, as noted above.

CONDITION 1: Participation must be within the chartered league/district named on the Eligibility Affidavit unless written approval is granted by the respective Regional Director and Charter Committee.

CONDITION 2: A player who is not able to participate in a number of local league regular season games because of participation in a school baseball program will receive an adjustment on the minimum participation in games required under this rule.

EXAMPLE: If, for any given division, Team A played 20 regular season games before June 15, and a player missed 10 games because of participation in a school baseball program, that player is required to have participated in only six (6) regular season games to be eligible for the Tournament Team.

CONDITION 3: A player may be named to the roster of, and practice with, only ONE Little League International Tournament Team. Once the affidavit is signed by the local league president, player agent, and District Administrator (or their representatives), the players listed on the affidavit shall not be eligible to participate on any other Little League International Tournament Team for the current year.

Baseball players league age 9, 10, 11, 12, 13, and 14 may be eligible for selection to multiple tournament teams. These players may only be selected to one tournament team. Under no circumstances may these players be chosen for, practice with, or participate with more than one tournament team.

Violation of this rule may be cause for revocation of tournament privilege by the Tournament Committee.

Tournament Requirement for Non-Citizens

A participant who is not a citizen of the country in which he/she wishes to play, but meets residency or school attendance requirements as defined by Little League, may participate in that country if:

1. his/her visa allows that participant to remain in that country for a period of at least one year, or;
2. the prevailing laws allow that participant to remain in that country for at least one year, or;
3. the participant has an established bona fide residence in that country for at least two years prior to the start of the regular season.

Exceptions can only be made by action of the Charter Committee in Williamsport.

Insurance

Accident: A league shall not be accepted for tournament play unless covered by accident insurance, which includes tournament play. It is strongly recommended that a medical release for each player on the Affidavit be carried by the team manager.

Liability: Liability Insurance must be carried by the league on whose field tournaments are played as well as all leagues who participate in the tournament. Minimum coverage of $1,000,000 single limit, bodily injury, and property damage. The policy must include coverage for claims arising out of athletic participants.

If insurance is purchased locally, a copy of the policy must be on file at Little League International.

Replacement of Player, Manager, or Coach

Any player, manager, or coach listed on the Eligibility Affidavit who is unable to participate because of injury, illness, vacation, or other justifiable reason may be replaced by another eligible person. If a player, manager, or coach is replaced, that person may not be returned to the Tournament Affidavit. Permanent replacements must be from the league's regular season teams and shall be recorded and approved by the District Administrator or Tournament Director in the space provided on the back of the Eligibility Affidavit. **Exception: If a manager or coach is unable to attend a game for a justifiable reason, a Tournament Director could approve a temporary replacement as outlined in the Little League Tournament Team Eligibility Affidavit. Temporary replacement of a manager or coach must be entered on the Eligibility Affidavit. A manager or coach who is ejected from a game may not be replaced for the team's next physically played game. (See Rule 4.07)**

Playing Equipment

The dimensions and other specifications of all playing equipment used must conform to those set forth in the Little League, Intermediate (50-70) Division, Junior League, and Senior League Baseball Playing Rules except for those noted below:

Every member of the team must wear a conventional uniform which includes shirt, pants, socks, and cap. This may be a regular season uniform.

Each team must provide at least six (6) [7 for **Intermediate (50-70) Division/Junior/Senior League**] NOCSAE approved safety helmets with warning labels. The batter, [all base runners, on-deck batter for **Intermediate (50-70) Division/Junior/Senior League**], and player base coaches must wear approved helmets. All male players must wear athletic supporters. Catchers (male) must wear the metal, fibre, or plastic type cup.

Catchers must wear a mask with (NOCSAE) approved catchers helmet (**skull cap type are not acceptable**) and "dangling" type throat guard during practice, infield/outfield, pitcher warm-up, and games.

All catchers must wear approved chest protector and shin guards. Catchers must wear approved long or short model chest protectors. Shoes with metal cleats or spikes shall not be worn by players, managers, coaches, or umpires. **Intermediate (50-70) Division/Junior/Senior League:** Players may wear shoes with metal spikes.

Schedules

Each District Administrator must finalize tournament schedules two (2) weeks prior to the start of the tournament or June 15 (whichever is earliest). Schedules for each level (District, Section, Division, State, Regional) must utilize Little League International approved single elimination brackets, double elimination brackets, modified double elimination brackets, or pool play/elimination format with pool play tie breaker format as noted in this section. All other tournament formats must be approved by the Tournament Committee. **NOTE:** Schedules shall not be altered once a tournament starts without Tournament Committee approval.

> A.R. - A District Administrator may utilize the modified double elimination format for Tournament Play. Modified double elimination must use an approved Little League double elimination bracket, eliminating the "if" game. No other modification are acceptable.

8- to 10-Year-Old, 9- to 11-Year-Old, and Little League Divisions: A team may play two games in one day with the approval of the Regional Director.

Intermediate (50-70) Division/Junior/Senior League: Teams may participate in a maximum of two (2) games in a day.

NOTE 1: Inclement weather may be justification to revert to single elimination in order to complete a tournament on schedule, with the approval of the Regional Director. **NOTE 2:** The 8- to 10- and 9- to 11-Year-Old Divisions advances to State level only. **NOTE 3:** Consult approved schedules for specific dates. Tournament dates may vary.

Tournament Team Practice

Try-outs, practices, or Special Games by tournament teams shall not be held before June 1. Tournament team practice may only take place against other Little League teams within the same or contiguous districts in the same division, providing such practice is done out of uniform. Tournament team practice with a non-Little League program and/or participation in any non-Little League program, event, or game is subject to the specific provisions of Regulation I(g) and Regulation IX. (The Little League group accident insurance program underwritten by an AIG member company for tournament teams will not go into effect until June 1.)

Violation of this rule may be cause for revocation of tournament privileges by the Tournament Committee.

Selection of Fields

Local leagues selected to host a Section, State, Division, Region, or World Series tournament must have an approved ASAP safety plan.

All games shall be played upon Little League fields approved by the Tournament Director. Exception to this rule can only be made with the consent of the Regional Director.

Fields must be enclosed with an outfield fence. Outfield fences for the **Little League Division** must be a maximum of 225 feet from home plate and a minimum of 195 feet; for **8- to 10- and 9- to 11-Divisions**, a maximum of 225 feet and a minimum of 180 feet; for **Intermediate (50-70) Division**, a maximum of 300 feet and a minimum of 225 feet; for **Junior League**, a maximum of 350 feet and a minimum of 250 feet; for **Senior League**, a maximum of 420 feet and a minimum of 280 feet. Tournament Directors should not permit portable outfield fences to exceed 200 feet [250 feet for **Intermediate (50-70) Division**; and 300 feet for **Junior/Senior League Baseball**]. Conventional dirt mounds are approved for tournament play. A Little League approved artificial mound is permitted at the District level. A request to use an artificial mound for the Section tournament level and above may be submitted to the Tournament Committee in Williamsport (through the District Administrator/Tournament Director and Regional Office). An artificial mound must not be used at the Section level and above unless approved in writing by the Tournament Committee for a specific tournament site/level, and only for the current year. The Tournament Director or assistant shall judge fitness of the playing field before the game starts.

8- to 10-Year-Old, 9- to 11-Year-Old, Little League Divisions: The on-deck batter's position is not permitted.

NOTE: For additional information about field selection see "Physical Conditions."

Games Under Lights

Games under lights may be scheduled at all levels of tournament play. The District Administrator having jurisdiction must determine that lighting installations meet minimum standards approved by Little League International.

Curfew

No inning shall start after midnight prevailing time [12:30 a.m. prevailing time for **Intermediate (50-70) Division/Junior League**; 1:00 a.m. prevailing time for **Senior League**].

NOTE 1: An inning starts the moment the third out is made completing the previous inning.

NOTE 2: Neither Tournament Directors and officials nor tournament teams are permitted to circumvent the curfews established above by continuing, suspending and restarting, or starting a game after curfew has been reached and play is required to be terminated. If the curfew noted above occurs during a game suspended in accordance with Tournament Playing Rule 11, that game must not be continued after the curfew. It must either be resumed on a subsequent day, or declared ended, as determined by rule.

Starting Time of Games

A game shall not be started unless the Tournament Director or assistant judges there is adequate time to complete the game before darkness or curfew.

Admission Charge

There shall be no charge for admission to Little League, 8- to 10-Year-Old, or 9- to 11-Year-Old Division Tournament games. An admission charge is permitted for **Intermediate (50-70) Division/Junior/Senior League**.

Conditions of Tournament Play

Protests

This rule replaces Rule 4.19.

No protest shall be considered on a decision involving an umpire's judgment. Equipment which does not meet specifications must be removed from the game.

Protest shall be considered only when based on:

A. The violation or interpretation of a playing rule;

When a manager claims that a decision is in violation of the playing rules, the following steps must be taken:

1. A formal (verbal) protest must be made to the Umpire-in-Chief at once by the manager or coach.

2. The Umpire-in-Chief must immediately call a conference of all umpires working the game.

3. If the problem cannot be resolved to the satisfaction of the managers, the Umpire-in-Chief shall be required to consult with the Tournament Director or District Administrator.

4. If the managers do not accept the decision of the Tournament Director, either manager may elect, without penalty, to discontinue play until the matter is referred to the Regional Headquarters. Either the Umpire-in-Chief, Tournament Director or District Administrator will call the Regional Headquarters at this time.

5. If the managers do not accept the decision of the Regional Director (or his/her designated agent), either may insist that the matter be referred to the Tournament Committee in Williamsport. The decision of the Tournament Committee shall be final and binding.

NOTE 1 - PROTESTS INVOLVING PLAYING RULES NOT RESOLVED BEFORE THE NEXT PITCH OR PLAY SHALL NOT BE CONSIDERED.

NOTE 2 - UMPIRES, TOURNAMENT DIRECTORS, AND DISTRICT ADMINISTRATORS DO NOT HAVE THE AUTHORITY TO DECLARE A FORFEITURE UNDER ANY CIRCUMSTANCES.

B. The use of an ineligible pitcher.

Ineligibility under this rule applies to violations of Tournament Playing Rule 4. If an ineligible pitcher delivers one or more pitches to a batter, that game is subject to protest and action by Tournament Committee in Williamsport.

1. If the facts establishing or verifying an ineligible pitcher become known DURING a game, and the ineligible pitcher participates in the game, subject to the following conditions:

   (a) A protest may be lodged by the manager or coach with the Umpire-in-Chief, who shall consult with the Tournament Director or District Administrator.

   (b) The Tournament Director or District Administrator must contact the Regional Director (or his/her appointed agent), who shall contact the Tournament Committee for a decision. The decision of the Tournament Committee shall be final and binding.

2. If the facts establishing or verifying an ineligible pitcher become known AFTER a game, and the ineligible pitcher participated in the game, subject to the following conditions:

   (a) A protest may be lodged by the manager or coach with the Tournament Director or District Administrator. Such protest must be made before either team affected by the protest begins another game.

   (b) The Tournament Director or District Administrator must contact the Regional Director (or his/her appointed agent), who shall contact the Tournament Committee for a decision. The decision of the Tournament Committee shall be final and binding.

PENALTY: See Tournament Rule 4(i).

C. The use of an ineligible player.

Ineligibility under this rule applies to league age, residence or school attendance (as defined by Little League Baseball, Incorporated), participation in other programs, or participation as an eligible player for sixty (60%) percent of the regular season in the proper division.

1. If the facts establishing or verifying the ineligibility of a player are known to the complainant, Tournament Official, or Tournament Director after the ineligible player participated in a game during the International Tournament, that team shall be disqualified and removed from the International Tournament, subject to any of the following conditions:

   (a) A protest is lodged by the manager or coach with the Umpire-in-Chief, who shall consult with the Tournament Director or District Administrator. The Tournament Director or District Administrator must contact the Regional Director (or his/her appointed agent), who shall contact the Tournament Committee for a decision. The decision of the Tournament Committee shall be final and binding.

   (b) The Tournament Director, District Administrator, or Tournament Official become aware of the circumstances by any means, they must contact the Regional Director (or his/her appointed agent), who shall contact the Tournament Committee for a decision. The decision of the Tournament Committee shall be final and binding.

In addition to the penalties described above in A, B, and C, the Tournament Committee may disqualify a player, team, or entire league from tournament play. The Tournament Committee may take action as a result of a protest or on its own initiative. Disqualification of a team or player(s) and/or forfeiture of a game must be the decision of the Tournament Committee at Williamsport, and such decisions will be made prior to the continuation of the affected team(s) or player(s) in further tournament play.

NOTE: All officials, including all managers, coaches, scorekeepers, umpires, Tournament Directors, District Administrators, etc., should make every effort to prevent a situation that may result in the forfeiture of a game or suspension of tournament privileges. However, failure by any party to prevent such situations shall not affect the validity of a protest.

Must Play To Advance

A team shall not advance from one level of Tournament to a higher level of tournament play without first having competed against and defeated a scheduled opponent at the tournament level from which it is seeking to advance. Any team advancing without play must do so with the approval of the Regional Director.

Tournament Playing Rules

The Little League, Intermediate (50-70) Division, Junior League, and Senior League Baseball Playing Rules shall govern tournament play except as noted below:

1. **BASEBALLS:** Baseballs licensed by Little League with the "RS-T" (regular season and tournament) designation must be used.

   NOTE: Specific baseball models for tournament play can be found at LittleLeague. org/TournamentBalls.

2. **FIELDS:** All fields are considered neutral. The home team shall be determined by the toss of a coin, the winner having the choice.

3. **PLAYING RULES:** A copy of the Little League, Intermediate (50-70) Division, Junior League, and Senior League Baseball Regulations and Playing Rules and the Tournament Rules and Guidelines must be available at each tournament site and at the time the game is to be played. This is the responsibility of the Tournament Director. Written ground rules established by the Tournament Director or assistant must be reviewed with both managers and Umpire-in-Chief at least ten (10) minutes before the start of the game. It is suggested the same be available to news media if requested.

   a. After entering the batter's box, the batter must remain in the box with at least one foot throughout the at bat.
   EXCEPTIONS:
   i. On a swing, slap, or check swing.
   ii. When forced out of the box by a pitch.
   iii. When the batter attempts a "drag bunt."
   iv. When the catcher does not catch the pitched ball.
   v. When a play has been attempted.
   vi. When time has been called.
   vii. When the pitcher leaves the dirt area of the pitching mound or takes a position more than five feet from the pitcher's plate after receiving the ball or the catcher leaves the catcher's box.
   viii. On a three ball count pitch that is a strike that the batter thinks is a ball.

   PENALTY: If the batter leaves the batter's box or delays play and none of the exceptions apply, the umpire shall warn the batter. After one warning on a batter, the umpire shall call a strike. Any number of strikes can be called on each batter. **Minor/Major Division:** No pitch has to be thrown, the ball is dead, and no runners may advance. **Intermediate (50-70) Division/Junior/Senior:** No pitch has to be thrown and ball is live.

   NOTE: The batter may return their position in the batter's box and assume the new count at any time during the at-bat, unless such enforced penalty is the third strike.

   b. In all Tournament levels and divisions, the penalty for use of an illegal bat [see Rule 6.06 (d)], if discovered before the next player enters the batter's box following the turn at bat of the player who used an illegal bat, is:

       i.   The batter is out (**NOTE:** The manager of the defense may advise the plate umpire of a decision to decline this portion of the penalty and accept the play. Such election shall be made immediately at the end of the play), and;

       ii.   The manager of the team will be ejected from the game, the batter who violated the rule will be ejected from the game, and the offensive team will lose one eligible adult base coach for the duration of the game.

  c.   **9- to 11-Year-Old Division**: The batter may advance on an uncaught third strike (6.05/6.09). This rule will not apply for the **8- to 10-Year-Old Division**.

  d.   Twice a game but not more than one time per inning, a team may utilize a player who is not in the batting order as a special pinch-runner for any offensive player. A player may only be removed for a special pinch-runner one time during a game. The player for whom the pinch-runner runs is not subject to removal from the lineup. If the pinch-runner remains in the game as a substitute defensive or offensive player, the player may not be used again as a pinch-runner while in the batting order. However, if removed for another substitute that player or any player not in the line-up, is again eligible to be used as a pinch-runner.

  e.   Each umpire has authority to disqualify any player, coach, manager, or substitute for objecting to decisions or for unsportsmanlike conduct or language and to eject such disqualified person from the playing field. If an umpire disqualifies a player while a play is in progress, the disqualification shall not take effect until no further action is possible in that play. The stealing and relaying of signs to alert the batter of pitch selection and/or location is unsportsmanlike behavior. If, in the judgment of the umpire this behavior is occurring, those responsible including any player(s), coach(es), and/or manager shall be ejected from the game.

4. **PITCHING RULES – LITTLE LEAGUE, 8- TO 10-YEAR-OLD, 9- TO 11-YEAR-OLD, INTERMEDIATE (50-70) DIVISION, AND JUNIOR LEAGUE**

These rules replace the regular season pitching regulations. *Violation of these pitching rules is subject to protest and action by the Tournament Committee in Williamsport if protested or brought to the Tournament Committee's attention.*

  a.   Any player on a tournament team may pitch. **Exception:** Any player, who has played the position of catcher in four (4) or more innings in a game, is not eligible to pitch on that calendar day.

A player who played the position of catcher for three (3) innings or less, moves to the pitcher position, and delivers 21 pitches or more in the same day, may not return to the catcher position on that calendar day. **EXCEPTION:** If the pitcher reaches the 20-pitch limit while facing a batter, the pitcher may continue to pitch, and maintain their eligibility to return to the catcher position, until any one of the following conditions occur: (1) that batter reaches base; (2) that batter is retired; or (3) the third out is made to complete the half-inning or the game.

  b.   A tournament pitcher may not pitch in regular season or Special Games while the team is still participating in the tournament.

  c.   Pitchers once removed from the mound may not return as pitchers. **Intermediate (50-70) Division/Junior League:** A pitcher remaining in the game, but moving to a different position, can return as a pitcher anytime in the remainder of the game, but only once per game.

d. The manager must remove the pitcher when said pitcher reaches the pitch limit for his/her age group as noted below, but the pitcher may remain in the game at another position:

League Age:		
	13 - 14	95 pitches per day
	11 - 12	85 pitches per day
	9 - 10	75 pitches per day
	8	50 pitches per day

EXCEPTION: If a pitcher reaches the pitch limit imposed above for his/her league age while facing a batter, the pitcher may continue to pitch until any one of the following conditions occurs: (1) That batter reaches base; (2) That batter is retired; (3) The third out is made to complete the half-inning or the game. (**NOTE: If a pitcher reaches 40 pitches while facing a batter, the pitcher may continue to pitch, and maintain their eligibility to play the position of catcher for the remainder of that day, until any one of the following conditions occurs: (1) that batter reaches base; (2) that batter is retired; or (3) the third out is made to complete the half-inning or the game. The pitcher would be allowed to play the catcher position provided that pitcher is moved, removed, or the game is completed before delivering a pitch to another batter.** If a player delivers 41 or more pitches, and is not covered under the threshold exception, the player may not play the position of catcher for the remainder of that day.)

e. Pitchers league age 14 and under must adhere to the following rest requirements:
   * If a player pitches 66 or more pitches in a day, four (4) calendar days of rest must be observed.
   * If a player pitches 51-65 pitches in a day, three (3) calendar days of rest must be observed.
   * If a player pitches 36-50 pitches in a day, two (2) calendar days of rest must be observed.
   * If a player pitches 21-35 pitches in a day, one (1) calendar day of rest must be observed.
   * If a player pitches 1-20 pitches in a day, no (0) calendar day of rest is required.

NOTE: Under no circumstance shall a player pitch in three (3) consecutive days.

EXCEPTION: If a pitcher reaches a day(s) of rest threshold while facing a batter, the pitcher may continue to pitch until any one of the following conditions occurs: (1) That batter reaches base; (2) That batter is retired; (3) The third out is made to complete the half-inning or the game. The pitcher will only be required to observe the calendar day(s) of rest for the threshold he/she reached during that at-bat, provided that pitcher is removed or the game is completed before delivering a pitch to another batter.

f. **A player cannot pitch in two games in a day.**

(EXCEPTION: Junior League - If a pitcher reaches 30 pitches while facing a batter in the first game, the pitcher may continue to pitch, and maintain their eligibility to pitch in the second game on that day, until any one of the following conditions occurs: (1) that batter reaches base; (2) that batter is retired; or (3) the third out is made to complete the half-inning or the game. The pitcher would be allowed to pitch in a second game provided that pitcher is moved, removed, or the game is completed before delivering a pitch to

another batter. If a player delivers 31 or more pitches in the first game, and is not covered under the threshold exception, the player may not pitch in the second game that day);

g. In a game suspended by darkness, weather, or other causes and resumed the following calendar day, the pitcher of record at the time the game was halted may continue to the extent of his/her eligibility, provided he/she delivered 40 or less pitches, and subject to each of these conditions:

   1. If the pitcher delivered 20 or less pitches before the game was suspended, that pitcher's pitch count will begin at zero for the continuation portion of the game.

   2. If the pitcher delivered between 21 and 40 pitches before the game was suspended, that pitcher's pitch count will begin with the number of pitches delivered in that game.

h. In a game ("Game A") suspended by darkness, weather, or other causes and resumed more than one calendar day later, the provisions of (g) above shall apply, unless the pitcher of record pitched in another game or games after Game A was halted. In that event, eligibility to pitch in the continuation portion of Game A shall be determined by the number of pitches delivered in the game or games after Game A was halted.

i. Failure to remove a pitcher who has reached his/her maximum number of pitches required by league age or use of an ineligible pitcher is basis for protest. Violations protested or brought to the Tournament Committee's attention, shall result (by action of the Tournament Committee) in the suspension of the team's manager for the next two scheduled tournament games, even if those games are played at the next tournament level. Additional penalties (up to and including forfeiture of a game and/or disqualification of the team, managers, or coaches from further tournament participation) may be imposed if, in the opinion of the Tournament Committee:

   1. a manager or coach takes any action that results in making a travesty of the game, or;

   2. a team fails to meet the requirements of this rule more than once during the International Tournament, which begins with District play and ends at the World Series level (State level for 8- to 10- and 9- to 11-), or;

   3. a manager willfully and knowingly disregards the requirements of this rule.

   A manager or coach suspended for any reason is not permitted to be at the game site and must not take any part in the game, nor have any communications whatsoever with any persons at the game site. This includes pregame and postgame activities. Violation may result, by action of the Tournament Committee, in further suspension; forfeiture of a game; and/or disqualification of the team, managers, or coaches from further tournament participation.

4. PITCHING RULES – SENIOR LEAGUE

These rules replace the regular season pitching regulations. Violation of these pitching rules is subject to protest and action by the Tournament Committee in Williamsport if protested or brought to the Tournament Committee's attention.

a. Any player on a tournament team may pitch. **EXCEPTION**: Any player, who has played the position of catcher in four (4) or more innings in a game, is not eligible to pitch on that calendar day.

A player who played the position of catcher for three (3) innings or less, moves to the pitcher position, and delivers 31 pitches or more in the same day, may not return to the catcher position on that calendar day. **EXCEPTION:** If the pitcher reaches the 30-pitch limit while facing a batter, the pitcher may continue to pitch, and maintain their eligibility to return to the catcher position, until any one of the following conditions occur: (1) that batter reaches base; (2) that batter is retired; or (3) the third out is made to complete the half-inning or the game.

b. A Tournament pitcher may not pitch in regular season or Special Games while the team is still participating in the Tournament.

c. A pitcher remaining in the game, but moving to a different position, can return as a pitcher anytime in the remainder of the game, but only once per game.

d. The manager must remove the pitcher when said pitcher reaches the pitch limit for his/her age group as noted below, but the pitcher may remain in the game at another position:

  League Age: 13 – 16 (Senior League) 95 pitches per day

EXCEPTION: If a pitcher reaches the pitch limit imposed above for his/her league age while facing a batter, the pitcher may continue to pitch until any one of the following conditions occurs: (1) That batter reaches base; (2) That batter is retired; (3) The third out is made to complete the half-inning or the game. **NOTE: If a pitcher reaches 40 pitches while facing a batter, the pitcher may continue to pitch, and maintain their eligibility to play the position of catcher for the remainder of that day, until any one of the following conditions occurs: (1) that batter reaches base; (2) that batter is retired; or (3) the third out is made to complete the half-inning or the game. The pitcher would be allowed to play the catcher position provided that pitcher is moved, removed, or the game is completed before delivering a pitch to another batter. If a player delivers 41 or more pitches, and is not covered under the threshold exception, the player may not play the position of catcher for the remainder of that day.**

e. Pitchers league age 13-16 must adhere to the following rest requirements:
  - If a player pitches 76 or more pitches in a day, four (4) calendar days of rest must be observed.
  - If a player pitches 61-75 pitches in a day, three (3) calendar days of rest must be observed.
  - If a player pitches 46-60 pitches in a day, two (2) calendar days of rest must be observed.
  - If a player pitches 31-45 pitches in a day, one (1) calendar day of rest must be observed.
  - If a player pitches 1-30 pitches in a day, no (0) calendar day of rest is required.

NOTE: Under no circumstance shall a player pitch in three (3) consecutive days.

EXCEPTION: If a pitcher reaches a day(s) of rest threshold while facing a batter, the pitcher may continue to pitch until any one of the following conditions occurs: (1) That batter reaches base; (2) That batter is retired; (3) The third out is made to complete the half-inning or the game. The pitcher will only be required to observe the calendar day(s) of rest for the threshold he/she reached during that at-bat, provided that pitcher is removed or the game is completed before delivering a pitch to another batter.

f.   **A player may be used as a pitcher in up to two games in a day.**

(EXCEPTION: If a pitcher reaches 30 pitches while facing a batter in the first game, the pitcher may continue to pitch, and maintain their eligibility to pitch in the second game on that day, until any one of the following conditions occurs: (1) that batter reaches base; (2) that batter is retired; or (3) the third out is made to complete the half-inning or the game. The pitcher would be allowed to pitch in a second game provided that pitcher is moved, removed, or the game is completed before delivering a pitch to another batter. If a player delivers 31 or more pitches in the first game, and is not covered under the threshold exception, the player may not pitch in the second game that day);

g.   In a game suspended by darkness, weather, or other causes and resumed the following calendar day, the pitcher of record at the time the game was halted may continue to the extent of his/her eligibility, provided he/she delivered 60 or less pitches, and subject to each of these conditions:

1.   If the pitcher delivered 30 or less pitches before the game was suspended, that pitcher's pitch count will begin at zero for the continuation portion of the game;

2.   If the pitcher delivered between 31 and 60 pitches before the game was suspended, that pitcher's pitch count will begin with the number of pitches delivered in that game;

h.   In a game ("Game A") suspended by darkness, weather, or other causes and resumed more than one calendar day later, the provisions of (g) above shall apply, unless the pitcher of record pitched in another game or games after Game A was halted. In that event, eligibility to pitch in the continuation portion of Game A shall be determined by the number of pitches delivered in the game or games after Game A was halted.

i.   Failure to remove a pitcher who has reached his/her maximum number of pitches required by league age or use of an ineligible pitcher is basis for protest. Violations protested or brought to the attention of the Tournament Committee, shall result (by action of the Tournament Committee) in the suspension of the team's manager for the next two scheduled tournament games, even if those games are played at the next tournament level. Additional penalties (up to and including forfeiture of a game and/or disqualification of the team, managers or coaches from further tournament participation) may be imposed if, in the opinion of the Tournament Committee:

1.   a manager or coach takes any action that results in making a travesty of the game,

2.   a team fails to meet the requirements of this rule more than once during the International Tournament, which begins with District play and ends at the World Series level or;

3. a manager willfully and knowingly disregards the requirements of this rule.

A manager or coach suspended for any reason is not permitted to be at the game site and must not take any part in the game, nor have any communications whatsoever with any persons at the game site. This includes pregame and postgame activities. Violation may result, by action of the Tournament Committee, in further suspension, forfeiture of a game and/or disqualification of the team, managers or coaches from further tournament participation.

5. **FORFEITS:** No game may be forfeited or a team disqualified without the authorization of the Tournament Committee. Violations which may result in forfeiture or disqualification must be reported immediately to the Regional Director before further play takes place which would involve a team or teams affected by such action.

6. **BENCH/DUGOUT:** No one except the players, manager, and coach(es) shall occupy the bench or dugout during a game. Base coaches may be players or adults. Two (2) adult base coaches are permitted at all levels subject to playing rule 4.05(b).

7. **VISITS:** A manager or coach may not leave a dugout for any reason during a game without receiving permission from an umpire. The manager or coach may be removed from the field for the remainder of the game for violation of this rule. When permission is granted, the manager or coach will be permitted to go to the mound to confer with the pitcher or any defensive player(s). A manager or coach who is granted a time out to talk to any defensive player will be charged with a visit to the pitcher.

9- to 11-Year-Old Division, Little League, Intermediate (50-70) Division, Junior League, and Senior League: A manager or coach may come out once in one inning to visit with the pitcher, but the second time out, the player must be removed as a pitcher. The manager or coach may come out twice in a game to visit with the pitcher, but third time out, the player must be removed as a pitcher. The rule applies to each pitcher who enters a game.

8- to 10-Year-Old Division: A manager or coach may come out twice in one inning to visit with the pitcher, but the third time out, the player must be removed as a pitcher. The manager or coach may come out three times in a game to visit with the pitcher, but the fourth time out, the player must be removed as a pitcher. The rule applies to each pitcher who enters a game.

NOTE: Only one offensive time-out will be permitted each inning.

8. **INJURY/ILLNESS:** If a player is injured or becomes ill during a game, the decision of a doctor (if present) or medical personnel will be final as to whether or not the player may continue in the game.

9. **MANDATORY PLAY: 8- to 10-Year-Old Division, 9- to 11-Year-Old Division, Little League, Intermediate (50-70) Division and Junior League: If a tournament team has thirteen (13) or more eligible players in uniform at a game, then every player on a team roster shall participate in each game for a minimum of one (1) at bat. If a tournament team has twelve (12) or fewer eligible players in uniform at a game, then every player on a team roster shall participate in each game for a minimum of six (6) consecutive defensive outs and bat at least one (1) time.**

a. Prior to the start of play in the top of the fourth inning [**Intermediate (50-70) Division/Junior League:** fifth inning], the umpire-in-chief or other individual designated by the game Tournament Director in consultation with the official scorekeeper, shall advise both team managers of their obligation to insert all players who have not completed their mandatory play requirement into the line-up as outlined below. A manager's failure/refusal to insert players into the line-up as outlined below shall result in immediate ejection of the manager and removal for the remainder of the International Tournament.

1. If a team has 12 or fewer players in uniform at the start of a game, and is:

   a. **Visiting Team:** Any player(s) who has yet to enter the game to meet the defensive requirement of mandatory play must be inserted prior to the first pitch or play in the bottom half of the fourth inning [**Intermediate (50-70) Division/Junior League:** fifth inning] into one of the next six (6) positions in the line-up, that will ensure all requirements of mandatory play will be satisfied, absent a shortened game, including one at-bat.

   b. **Home Team:** Any player(s) who has yet to enter the game to meet the defensive requirement of mandatory play must be inserted prior to the first pitch or play in the top half of the fifth inning [**Intermediate (50-70) Division/Junior League:** sixth inning] into one of the next three (3) positions in the line-up, that will ensure all requirements of mandatory play will be satisfied, absent a shortened game, including one at-bat.

2. If a team has 13 or more players in uniform at the start of a game, players must be inserted into the line-up to bat offensively during the:

   a. **Visiting Team:** fourth or fifth inning, or as one of the first three batters in the sixth inning [**Intermediate (50-70) Division/Junior League:** fifth or sixth inning, or as one of the first three batters in the seventh inning], that will allow their one at-bat to be satisfied.

   b. **Home Team:** fourth inning or as one of the first three batters in the fifth inning [**Intermediate (50-70) Division/Junior League:** fifth inning or as one of the first three batters in sixth inning], that will allow their one at-bat to be satisfied.

b. Managers are solely responsible for ensuring that all players fulfill the requirements of mandatory play, even if notification is not made.

c. There is no exception to this rule unless the game is shortened for any reason. **NOTE:** A game is not considered shortened if the home team does not complete the offensive half of the sixth or seventh inning (or any extra inning) due to winning the game.

d. **Failure to meet the mandatory play requirements in this rule is a basis for protest. If one or more players on a roster do not meet this requirement, and if protested or brought to the Tournament Committee's attention, in the removal of the team's manager, without replacement, for the remainder of the International Tournament. Additional penalties (including but not limited to forfeiture of a game, additional mandatory play requirements for players who failed to meet mandatory play, and/or disqualification of the team or coaches from further tournament participation) may be imposed if, in the opinion of the Tournament Committee:**

1. a manager or coach takes any action that results in making a travesty of the game, causing players to intentionally perform poorly for the purpose of extending or shortening a game, or;

2. a team fails to meet the requirements of this rule more than once during the International Tournament, which begins with District play and ends at the World Series level (State level for 8- to 10- and 9- to 11-Year-Old Divisions), or;

3. a manager willfully and knowingly disregards the requirements of this rule.

A manager or coach suspended for any reason is not permitted to be at the game site and must not take any part in the game, nor have any communications whatsoever with any persons at the game site. This includes pregame and postgame activities. Violation may result, by action of the Tournament Committee, in further suspension; forfeiture of a game; and/or disqualification of the team, managers, or coaches from further tournament participation.

e. For the purposes of this rule, "six (6) consecutive defensive outs" is defined as: A player enters the field in one of the nine defensive positions when his/her team is on defense and occupies such position while six consecutive outs are made; "bat at least one (1) time" is defined as: A player enters the batter's box with no count and completes that time at bat by being retired or by reaching base safely.

10. **SUBSTITUTIONS/RE-ENTRY:** This tournament rule replaces regular season Rule 3.03 (re-entry) for all levels of tournament play.

a. If illness, injury, or the ejection of a player prevents a team from fielding nine (9) players, a player previously used in the lineup may be inserted, but only if there are no other eligible substitutes available. The opposing team manager shall select the player to re-enter the lineup. A player ejected from the game is not eligible for re-entry.

b. Any player who has been removed for a substitute may re-enter the game in the **SAME** position in the batting order.

c. **A substitute entering the game for the first time may not be removed prior to completion of her/his mandatory play requirements.**

NOTE 1: See definitions in Rule 9(d) above on complying with this rule defensively and offensively. Tournament Playing Rule 10(c) does not apply to Senior League.

NOTE 2: A player who has met the mandatory play requirements, and is a pitcher at the time she/he is removed, may be removed for a substitute batter and re-enter the game as a pitcher once, provided the pitcher was not physically replaced on the mound. If a team has thirteen (13) or more players in uniform at the start of a game and is the visiting team, they may substitute a batter for the starting pitcher listed in the line-up prior to the pitcher facing a batter without violating Rule 3.03(c) provided that the pitcher of record pitches to the first batter in the bottom of the first inning in accordance with Rule 3.05. All other rules governing the pitcher are still in effect.

EXCEPTION: Does not apply to Senior League.

EXAMPLE: Player A is a starter and not a pitcher, Player B substitutes into the game for player A. Both players have met mandatory play by completing one time at bat and/or 6 consecutive outs and both occupy the same spot in the batting order. In the fifth inning player A becomes a pitcher and is scheduled to bat in the sixth inning, but player B bats for player A. Both players have met mandatory play requirements and player A was not physically replaced on the mound as a pitcher, therefore, player A can return to pitch the sixth inning.

d. Defensive substitutions must be made while the team is on defense. Offensive substitutions must be made at the time the offensive player has her/his turn at bat or is on base.

e. A starter and her/his substitute must not be in the lineup at the same time, except as provided in Playing Rule 10(a).

f. Improper substitution is a basis for protest. Protests involving improper substitution not resolved before the next pitch or play shall not be considered.

g. Tournament Rule 3(d) will replace Rule 7.14, as the Special Pinch Runner rule.

h. **Intermediate (50-70) Division/Junior/Senior League only**: A pitcher remaining in the game, but moving to a different position, can return as a pitcher anytime in the remainder of the game, but only once per game. **Senior League only:** Rule 3.03, Designated Hitter, WILL apply during the tournament.

I. **Senior League:** Any player in the starting line-up, including the designated hitter, who has been removed for a substitute may re-enter the game ONCE, provided such player occupies the same batting position as he or she did in the starting line-up. A substitute (non-starter) may not re-enter the game in any position once that player is removed from the line-up.

11. **SUSPENDED GAMES:** Any game in which a winner cannot be determined in accordance with the playing rules shall be resumed from the exact point at which it was suspended regardless of the number of innings played. Incomplete (not regulation) or tie games are considered suspended games. **NOTE:** A contest decided by forfeit does not constitute a "game" for the purposes of this rule, unless one complete inning was physically played before the game was forfeited. (Forfeits are only by decree of the Tournament Committee in Williamsport.)

12. **RUN RULE:** If at the end of three (3) innings [**Intermediate (50-70) Division/Junior/Senior League:** four innings], two and one-half innings [**Intermediate (50-70) Division/Junior/Senior League:** three and one-half innings] if the home team is ahead, one team has a lead of fifteen (15) runs or more, the manager of the team with the least runs shall concede the victory to the opponent. If at the end of a regulation game one team has a lead of ten (10) runs or more, the manager of the team with the least runs shall concede the victory to the opponent. **NOTE 1:** If the visiting team has a lead of fifteen (15) or ten (10) or more runs respectively, the home team must bat in its half of the inning. **NOTE 2:** A game determined by the 15-run rule, shall be considered a regulation game.

13. **REGULATION GAME:** Each tournament game must be played to the point of being an official game:

    a. Regulation games are of four or more innings [five or more innings for **Intermediate (50-70) Division/Junior/Senior League**] in which one team has scored more runs than the other [three and one-half (3½) if the home team is ahead or four and one-half (4½) if the home team is ahead in **Intermediate (50-70) Division/Junior/Senior League**].

    b. Regulation games (when a winner can be determined) terminated because of weather, darkness, or curfew must be resumed if the visiting team ties the game or takes the lead in its half of the inning and the home team does not complete its at bat or take the lead in an incomplete inning. This does not apply to games suspended or delayed by weather that may still be resumed before darkness or curfew (as defined in Tournament Rules and Guidelines – Curfew) on the same day.

    c. If two games are scheduled for the same site, no "time limit" may be imposed on the first game.

14. **TIE GAME:** When the completion of six innings [**Intermediate (50-70) Division/ Junior/Senior League:** seven innings] and the score is tied, the following tie-breaker will be played to determine a winning team:

    a. The seventh inning [**Intermediate (50-70) Division/Junior/Senior League:** eighth inning] will be played as normal.

    b. Starting in the top of the eighth inning [**Intermediate (50-70) Division/Junior/ Senior League:** ninth inning], and each half inning thereafter, the offensive team shall begin its turn at bat with the player who is scheduled to bat last in that respective half inning being placed on second base. **EXAMPLE:** If the number five batter is the lead-off batter, the number four batter in the batting order will be placed on second base. An eligible substitute or special pinch runner may be inserted for the runner.

15. **REPLAYING GAMES:** No tournament game may be replayed without specific approval from the Tournament Committee at Williamsport.

16. **UNAUTHORIZED AGREEMENTS:** No agreements shall be made between managers, and/or Tournament Directors, and/or umpires contrary to Tournament Rules.

17. **ALTERCATIONS:** A manager, coach, or player shall not leave their position in the field or bench area during a fight or physical confrontation; a manager or coach who attempts to prevent a fight or restore order, in the umpire's judgment, is not in violation of this rule.

    Penalty: The umpire shall eject the offender(s) from the game immediately. Failure to comply with the ejection may result in the umpire suspending the game. The Tournament Director shall refer all incidents to the Tournament Committee who may impose additional penalties and/or actions towards individuals and/or teams up to and including forfeiture of a game, further suspension and/or disqualification.

18. **EJECTIONS:** Any manager, coach, or player ejected from a game will be suspended for the next physically played game (See Rule 4.07). This includes pregame and postgame activities. Ejections shall be noted in the tournament team's affidavit in the Record of Ejections on page 4. Entry should include member's name and date ejected and be signed by the Tournament Director or District Administrator.

OFFICIALS

Scorers

The Tournament Director having jurisdiction shall appoint and provide an official scorer for each game.

The official scorer shall, immediately following each game, enter on the reverse side of each team's Eligibility Affidavit:

1. Date of game.
2. Name of each player who pitched.
3. Number of pitches.
4. Name of opponent
5. Score of game.
6. Signature of Tournament Director or assistant. This record shall be accepted as official.

Financial Responsibility

Unless officially notified to the contrary by Williamsport, each league shall assume full responsibility for expenses incurred in tournament competition. Participating teams which choose not to accept housing and/or meals provided by the host shall reside and eat elsewhere at their own expense, and shall be responsible for their own local transportation.

Compensation to defray travel expenses for teams traveling 150 miles or more per one round trip, to Section tournaments and beyond will be paid by Little League Baseball, Incorporated, to local leagues in the form of a credit toward the next year's fees (U.S. leagues only). All Tournament fees and adjustments to Tournament Teams enrolled must be submitted through the Little League Data Center (LittleLeague.org/DataCenter) by the local league to Little League International by September 15, 2019. **NOTE:** A maximum of one round trip will be compensated per tournament site at each level of play. Mileage forms must be completed and submitted through the Little League Data Center (LittleLeague.org/DataCenter) by the local league to Little League International by September 15, 2019, in order for reimbursement to be paid. **EXCEPTION:** The local league president may request, in writing, reimbursement by check. This request must accompany the mileage reimbursement form.

Mileage compensation is $1 per mile. Little League International, Williamsport, Pennsylvania, will make all arrangements and reservations for transporting the Regional champions to and from the World Series.

Guidelines for Conduct of Tournament

The following standards for the conduct of tournament play are for the guidance and information of Tournament Directors and participating leagues. Experience of hundreds of field directors responsible for the conduct of the tournament at all levels over many years is reflected in these guidelines which should be studied carefully and applied totally to assure successful staging of the various levels of play.

District Administrators

District Administrators or their appointed assistants will direct the tournaments. This responsibility may not be delegated to a local league. The Tournament Director conducts or supervises play up to and including the final game of that level; collects or directs the collection of all funds belonging to the tournament; pays or directs payments from moneys so collected or received; and makes required reports to leagues involved and to the Regional Office.

The league or leagues hosting tournaments may not assume responsibility for, nor physically operate, the tournament. The league or leagues may not retain tournament income, may not make payments from nor obligate tournament funds for any purpose.

At the district tournament meeting the Tournament Rules should be reviewed in briefing league representatives, umpires, and others involved in the tournament. Before assigning tournament games, the District Administrators should inspect all prospective sites. It cannot be emphasized too strongly that providing the best possible playing conditions on regular fields is the obligation of the District Administrator.

Tournament Director

1. District, Sectional, Divisional, State, or Regional Tournament Director may provide appropriate awards to participating teams and players.

2. Each Tournament Director shall report as follows:

   a. Advise each participating league of schedule, time, and site of games.

   b. Forward completed schedule to the Regional Director showing winners at each level of play.

   c. Pay allowable expenses and distribute balance of tournament income to the District Fund and/or leagues on a per-game basis. Where one or more teams travel greater distances than others, a mileage allowance may be paid before distributing the per-game shares.

   d. Forward completed financial report to the Regional Director within ten (10) days following final game of each level of tournament.

   NOTE: 8- to 10-Year-Old Division and 9- to 11-Year-Old Division advances to State level only.

Physical Conditions

It is essential that the best possible playing conditions be provided at every level of the tournament. The following conditions are recommended for tournament games:

1. Facilities:

   a. Grass outfield (Regional, Divisional, State, and Sectional Tournaments). Grass infield (Regional, Divisional, and State Tournaments).

   b. Outfield fences must be a maximum of 225 feet from home plate and a minimum of 195 feet (**Little League**); For **8- to 10- and 9- to 11-Year Old,** a maximum of 225 feet and a minimum of 180 feet; For **Intermediate (50-70) Division,** a maximum of 300 feet and a minimum of 225 feet; For **Junior League**, a maximum of 350 feet and a minimum of 250 feet; For **Senior League**, a maximum of 420 feet and a minimum of 280 feet.

c. Outfield fences of safe-type construction, a minimum of 4 feet in height, maximum of 6 feet.

d. Batter's eye 24 feet wide minimum at center field.

e. Backstop not less than 20 feet from home plate. **Intermediate (50-70) Division/ Junior/Senior League** backstop should not be less than 35 feet from home plate.

f. Back drop of 6 to 8 feet of canvas in back of home plate if no press box is in that position.

g. Two foul poles at least 6 feet above the top of the fence.

h. A protective screen in front of dugouts.

i. Lights, if used, must meet minimum Little League standards.

j. Only conventional dirt pitching mounds are approved for tournament play. **Exception**: A Little League approved artificial mound is permitted at the District level. A list of licensed and approved artificial mounds can be found at LittleLeague.org/FieldSupplies.

2. Groundskeeper's services:

a. Grass cut to proper height. No holes or other unsafe conditions.

b. Infield dragged and in playable condition.

c. Markings according to regulations. Bases must be regulation size and properly secured.

3. Additional Facilities:

a. Public address system and announcer.

b. Scoreboard and operator(s).

c. Adequate seating (Sectional - 500; Divisional/State - 1,000; Regional - 1,500 minimum).

d. Adequate parking.

e. Policing. Local police departments should be advised of the event and requested to cooperate with league personnel.

f. First aid, medical, and ambulance services available.

g. Rest rooms.

h. Baseballs (if not otherwise provided by Tournament Director).

i. Adult volunteer insurance should be provided by each league involved.

NOTE 1: 8- to 10-Year-Old and 9- to 11-Year-Old Divisions advance to State level only. **NOTE 2:** Host leagues may retain concession income.

Assistants and Committees

To assure a successful tournament, it is desirable that the director (particularly at Sectional, Divisional, State, and Regional levels) appoint assistants and committee chairpersons to undertake the various functions which are essential. The following are suggested:

1. **Finance:** To solicit donations, supervise collections at games, sale of advertising and programs, etc. Host leagues may not conduct fund raising projects unless approved by the Tournament Director.

2. **Housing:** Players, managers, coaches, and umpires may be provided hotel or motel accommodations and food allowance.

3. **Publicity:** Obtain and make available to all news media names of teams, players, time of games and sites, results of games, and other information essential to news media in the interest of promoting the tournament. Addresses and/or telephone numbers of players must not be released to anyone for any purpose.

4. **Transportation:** Arrangements for meeting teams upon arrival and delivery to points of departure. Arrange for transportation of managers and coaches.

5. **Program:** When authorized by the Tournament Director as a fund raising project, the Program Chairperson should work with the Finance Chairperson to assemble material, sell ads, etc. Programs should not be published unless self-supporting.

6. **Parking and Police:** If deemed necessary, arrange for traffic control, parking, and related functions.

7. **Medical:** Have names and phone numbers of doctors, nurses, ambulance, and hospital available and arrangements made for their services, if required. If possible, a doctor or nurse should be in attendance.

8. **Ceremonies:** Arrange for flag raising, welcome, introductions, etc. These should be brief and meaningful.

9. **Umpires:** Recommended minimum of two, a maximum of six. Services on a voluntary basis. Normal expenses may be provided.

10. **Official scorekeepers.**

Expenses

Tournament Directors are authorized to pay from tournament income the following costs:

1. Championship pennant.
2. Approved Little League pins for players, managers, coaches (all teams), and umpires.
3. Postage, telephone, and out-of-pocket expenses.
4. Housing and food allowance for players, managers, coaches, and umpires.

NOTE: Tournament Director should secure, at no cost to the tournament, baseballs (if not provided by host league), umpires, scorekeepers, and housing for players.

Radio

Broadcasting of tournament games is permitted with authorization from the Tournament Director. Commercial sponsorship must be consistent with Little League policy. Fees or donations paid for the broadcasting rights must accrue to the tournament fund at that level.

Television

Only Little League International may authorize the televising (live or taped) of tournament games. The District Administrator or Tournament Director may recommend approval, but may not make commitments or sign any agreement or contracts for the televising of games.

Not later than two weeks prior to the start of the tournament at the level to be televised, the director having jurisdiction shall submit in writing complete details of the proposal to

Little League International. Videotaping of games is permissible provided tapes are not sold or used for any commercial purposes.

Brief, televised reports on tournament games and activities on news programs are permitted.

Live-Streaming

With live-streaming becoming much easier to accomplish, local leagues may be interested in webcasting or live-streaming games through their own local league website, official social media account, or other digital platform. Leagues are permitted to stream/webcast games through these league-owned platforms granted they follow all Little League policies regarding commercialization and trademarks and have the appropriate releases from all participants and notices for attendees. For any stream/webcast that is through any outlet that is not fully owned and/or operated by a local league, Little League International is the only body that can authorize or disallow the live-streaming or web-casting of tournament games. A contract (provided by Little League International) must originate with the local District Administrator, tournament director, or local Little League president. (See Regulation XV.)

Programs

The District Administrator or Tournament Director may authorize the publication of a program or scorecard as a means of providing additional financing for the tournament at that level. However, they may not execute contracts or other commitments in the name of, or as agents for, Little League International.

All funds (net) realized from advertising and/or sale of programs must be applied to the tournament fund at that level.

Regional Directors

The following Regional Directors or their appointed agents should be contacted by the Tournament Director when protests cannot be resolved at the tournament level.

U.S. OFFICES

U.S. CENTRAL
Director - Nina Johnson-Pitt;
Assistant Director - Ashlea Nash

U.S. EAST
Director - Corey Wright;
Assistant Director - Amry Shelby; Assistant Director - Ty Knopp

U.S. SOUTHEAST
Director - Jennifer Colvin;
Assistant Director - Matt Weber

U.S. SOUTHWEST
Director - Angela Garcia;
Assistant Director - Kiley Johnson

U.S. WEST
Director - April Meehleder;
Assistant Director - Brian Pickering; Assistant Director - Aaron Torres

INTERNATIONAL OFFICES

ASIA-PACIFIC
Director - B.H. Chow

CANADA
Director - Joe Shea;
Assistant Director - Wendy Thomson

EUROPE AND AFRICA
Director - Beata Kaszuba-Baker;
Assistant Director - Bart Sochacki

LATIN AMERICA AND CARIBBEAN
Director - Carlos Pagan;
Assistant - Jose Berrios

International Tournament Pool Play Format
Section I – Guidelines

The Pool Play Format should only be used in divisions in which there is a reasonable expectation for all teams to play all games for which they are scheduled. In divisions in which teams traditionally drop out at the last moment, or partway through the tournament, the standard double-elimination or single-elimination formats should be used instead.

The following conditions must apply to all Pool Play Format tournaments, unless specified as optional:

A. In the event a team or teams drop out of a pool play format tournament before the first game of the tournament is played (by any team in the tournament), the pools must be redrawn. If a team or teams drop out or is/are removed by action of the Tournament Committee after the first game is played, the matter must be referred to the Tournament Committee for a decision.

B. A Pool Play Format tournament may have one or more pools.

C. The pool assignments (or "draw") must either be a blind draw, or must be based on geographic considerations. Pool assignments must never be "seeded" based on the expected ability of the teams.

D. In all cases, the results of Pool Play have no bearing on the next segment of play, with the exception of rules and regulations regarding rest periods for pitchers, (i.e., losses do not "carry over").

E. It is preferable for each team in a given pool to be scheduled to play all other teams in that pool once.

F. Each team within any one pool must be scheduled to play an equal number of games as the other teams in that pool.

G. In the case of a one-pool tournament, one team may advance to become the tournament champion, based solely on the results of pool play, at the discretion of the tournament director. More commonly in a one-pool tournament, however, two teams advance to play each other for the tournament championship.

H. If more than one pool is used, and the total number of teams in the largest and smallest of the pools combined is less than ten (10), the number of teams in the largest pool must be no more than one team greater than the number of teams in the smallest pool. Example:

Acceptable		Not Acceptable	
Pool A	**Pool B**	**Pool A**	**Pool B**
4 teams	5 teams	3 teams	6 teams

I. If more than one pool is used, and the total number of teams in the largest and smallest of the pools is ten (10) or more, the number of teams in the largest pool must be no more than two teams greater than the number of teams in smallest pool. Example:

Acceptable		Not Acceptable	
Pool A	**Pool B**	**Pool A**	**Pool B**
4 teams	6 teams	3 teams	7 teams

J. In the case of tournaments involving more than one pool, one or more teams may advance out of each pool to the next segment. In most cases, when two teams advance, the schedule may be arranged so that teams will "cross over" for the purpose of seeding in the next round. For example, in a two-pool tournament:

1. The first-place team in Pool A plays the second-place team in Pool B.

2. The first-place team in Pool B plays the second-place team in Pool A.

3. The winners of those two games play each other for the championship.

4. A consolation game may be scheduled between the losing teams. The crossover method, however, is not required. At the discretion of the tournament director, the teams advancing from pool play could be re-drawn for placement in the next round via blind draw.

K. In the case of tournaments involving more than one team advancing out of pool play into a playoff, the playoff format may be single- or double elimination, at the discretion of the tournament director. However, if the published format calls for double-elimination, and the tournament director subsequently wishes for it to revert to single-elimination because of delays caused by weather, etc., this can only be approved by the Tournament Committee in Williamsport.

L. The tournament director may, at his/her discretion, use a format in which all teams that finish the pool play round with a specific won-lost record will advance. In the following examples, the format calls for advancing all teams (from a 10-team pool in which each team plays only seven games) that finish pool play with zero or one loss. Example 1: Among the 10 teams in the pool, two finished with 7-0 records, while two others finished with 6-1 records. Result – These four teams advance and the other six teams are eliminated. Example 2: Among the 10 teams in the pool, one finished with a 7-0 record, while two others finished with 6-1 records. Result – These three teams advance and the other seven teams are eliminated.

M. The tiebreaker methods published herein by Little League International are the only methods that will be used when a tiebreaker is required. If any question or controversy arises, it must be referred to the Regional Headquarters before advancing a team.

N. A manager is not permitted to purposely forfeit any game for the purpose of engineering the outcome of pool play, and may be removed from the tournament by action of the Tournament Committee in Williamsport. Additionally, the Tournament Committee may remove such a team from further tournament play.

O. Only the Tournament Committee can forfeit a game in the International Tournament, and reserves the right to disregard the results of a forfeited game in computing a team's won-lost record and Runs-Allowed Ratio. (Section IV)

P. When a manager or coach instructs his/her players to play poorly for any reason, such as, but not limited to the following, such action may result in the manager's removal by the Umpire-in-Chief, and/or removal of the manager, coach(es) and/or team from further tournament play. **NOTE:** This policy is not intended to prevent a manager from using lesser-skilled players more frequently if he or she wishes, even if such action may result in losing a game:

1. losing a game to effect a particular outcome in a Pool Play Format tournament;

2. so as to lose a game by the 10-run rule;

3. to delay the game until the curfew; to allow an opponent to tie the score so that more innings may be played, etc.

Section II – Segments of a Pool Play Tournament

A. Under this format, there are two distinct segments to a pool play format tournament.
    1. In Segment 1 – The Pool Play Round, the teams are divided into a number of pools (usually two to four pools). Each team in each of the pools should play the other teams in that pool once. By decision of the tournament director, one or more teams with the best records(s) in the pool will advance to the next segment. **NOTE**: In a one-pool format, one or more teams may advance to become the tournament champion. If only one team advances, there is no second segment.
    2. In Segment 2 – The Elimination Round, the teams advancing out of Segment 1 are matched up in either a standard single-elimination format, or a standard double-elimination format.

B. Once a segment is completed, games played previously have no bearing on the next segment, with the exception of:
    1. rules and regulations regarding the required rest periods for pitchers;
    2. rules and regulations regarding players, managers and/or coaches that were ejected and the prescribed penalties resulting from the ejection.

Section III – Tiebreaker Procedures

A. In all cases, the team(s) advancing past Segment 1 must be the team(s) with the best won-lost record(s) during pool play. The tournament director will decide the number of teams that will advance beyond pool play, and such determination must be made available to the leagues/teams involved before the tournament begins.

B. When records are tied, however, the following procedures must be applied in order, so that the tie can be broken. These procedures also apply to determining the seeding for Segment 2 (the playoff round), if seeding for Segment 2 is based on results of pool play.
    1. The first tiebreaker is the result of the head-to-head match-up(s) during pool play (Segment 1) of the teams that are involved in the tie.
        a. If one of the teams involved in the tie has accomplished EVERY ONE of the following, then that team will advance:
            i.   Defeated all of the other teams involved in the tie at least once; AND,
            ii. Defeated all of the other teams involved in the tie in every one of the pool play games it played against those teams; AND,
            iii. Played each of the teams involved in the tie an equal number of times. **Example**: Three teams are tied with identical records for first place at the end of pool play, and one team is to advance to Segment 2. Teams A, B and C played against each other once in pool play. Team A won all of its games against Team B and Team C during pool play. Result – Team A advances, while Team B and Team C are eliminated.
    2. If the results of the head-to-head match-up(s) during pool play of the teams that are involved in the tie cannot break the tie (because no team defeated each of the other teams in the tie each time they played, or because no team has defeated all of the other teams involved in the tie in every one of the pool play games played between those teams, or because the teams involved in the tie did not play one another an equal number of times during pool play), then the tie is broken using the Runs-Allowed Ratio (see Section IV).

C. In all cases, if the tie-breaking principles herein are correctly applied and fail to break the tie, or if these guidelines are not applied correctly (in the judgment of the Tournament Committee in Williamsport), then the matter will be referred to the Tournament Committee, which will be the final arbiter in deciding the issue. If a tie cannot be broken through the proper application of these guidelines (in the opinion of the Tournament Committee), then a playoff, blind draw or coin flip will determine which team(s) will advance. This is a decision of the Tournament Committee.

Section IV – Runs-Allowed Ratio

A. For each team involved in a tie in which head-to-head results cannot be used (because no team defeated each of the other teams in the tie each time they played, or because no team has defeated all of the other teams involved in the tie in every one of the pool play games played between those teams, or because the teams involved in the tie did not play one another an equal number of times during pool play), the tournament director will calculate: The total number of runs given up in all pool play games played by that team, divided by 6 innings for **Little League and below** [7 innings for **Intermediate (50-70) Division/Junior/Senior League**]. This provides the Runs-Allowed Ratio.

1. Example: The Hometown Little League (Major) team has given up eight (8) runs in all four (4) of its pool play games. 8 divided by 24 equals .3333.

2. The Runs-Allowed Ratio for Hometown Little League (.3333 in the example above) is compared to the same calculation for each of the teams involved in the tie.

B. The Runs-Allowed Ratio is used to advance ALL teams after it is determined that head-to-head cannot be used.

C. If, after computing the Runs-Allowed Ratio using results of all pool play games played by the teams involved in the tie:

1. one team has the lowest Runs-Allowed Ratio, that team advances. After one team has advanced using the Runs-Allowed Ratio, each subsequent team needed to advance is determined by the Runs-Allowed Ratio until all teams are determined and seeded.

2. two or more teams remain tied with the same runs-Allowed Ratio, and the methods detailed in Section III – Tiebreaker Procedures cannot be used (because no team defeated each of the other teams in the tie each time they played, or because no team has defeated all of the other teams involved in the tie in everyone of the pool play games played between those teams, or because the teams involved in the tie did not play one another an equal number of times during pool play), then the Runs-Allowed Ratio must be recomputed using statistics only from the pool play games played between the teams involved in the tie. The results are used to advance ONE team, and any other ties must revert to the Runs-Allowed Ratio using all remaining teams.

D. If a game is forfeited, in most cases the score of the game will be recorded as 6-0 (for **Little League Divisions and below**) or 7-0 [for **Intermediate (50-70) Division/Junior/Senior League**]. However, only the Tournament Committee in Williamsport can decree a forfeit, and the Tournament Committee reserves the right to disregard the results of the game, to assign the score as noted above, or to allow the score to stand (if any part of the game was played).

E. In the event a team (defined for this purpose as a minimum of nine players) fails to attend a scheduled game, and it is determined by the Tournament Committee in Williamsport that the failure to attend was designed to cause a forfeit or delay the tournament for any reason, the Tournament Committee reserves the right to remove the team from further play in the International Tournament and/or remove those adults it deems responsible from the team and/or local league.

Rules, Regulations, and Policies

It is important for all Little League® volunteers and parents to be familiar with the most up-to-date version of Little League's Official Regulations, Playing Rules, and Operating Policies.

2019 RULES AND REGULATION UPDATES

BACKGROUND CHECKS

RESIDENCY REQUIREMENTS

2019 AGE CHARTS

BAT INFORMATION

PITCHING RULES

WAIVERS OF RULES

POLICY STATEMENTS

PATCH REQUIREMENTS

LIGHTING STANDARDS

For information on new rules, significant changes, and helpful resources visit:

LittleLeague.org/Rules

LITTLE LEAGUE® UNIVERSITY

Tips, Tutorials, and Training for Volunteers, Coaches, Umpires, Parents, and More!

LittleLeague.org

Appendix A
Lightning Safety Guidelines

Each year across the United States, thunderstorms produce an estimated 25 million cloud-to-ground flashes of lightning - each one of those flashes is a potential killer. According to the National Weather Service, an average of 73 people are killed by lightning each year and hundreds more are injured, some suffering devastating neurological injuries that persist for the rest of their lives. A growing percentage of those struck are involved in outside recreational activities.

Officials responsible for sports events often lack adequate knowledge of thunderstorms and lightning to make educated decisions on when to seek safety. Without knowledge, officials base their decisions on personal experience and, sometimes, on the desire to complete the activity. Due to the nature of lightning, personal experience can be misleading.

While many people routinely put their lives in jeopardy when thunderstorms are nearby, few are actually struck by lightning. This results in a false sense of safety. Unfortunately, this false sense of safety has resulted in numerous lightning deaths and injuries during the past several decades because people made decisions that unknowingly put their lives or the lives of others at risk.

For organized outdoor activities, the National Weather Service recommends those in charge have a lightning safety plan, and that they follow the plan without exception. The plan should give clear and specific safety guidelines in order to eliminate errors in judgment. Prior to an activity or event, organizers should listen to the latest forecast to determine the likelihood of thunderstorms. NOAA Weather Radio is a good source of up-to-date weather information. Once people start to arrive, the guidelines in your league's lightning safety plan should be followed.

A thunderstorm is approaching or nearby. Are conditions safe, or is it time to head for safety? Not wanting to appear overly cautious, many people wait far too long before reacting to this potentially deadly weather threat. The safety recommendations outlined here based on lightning research and the lessons learned from the unfortunate experiences of thousands of lightning strike victims.

Thunderstorms produce two types of lightning flashes, 'negative' and 'positive.' While both types are deadly, the characteristics of the two are quite different. Negative flashes occur more frequently, usually under or near the base of the thunderstorm where rain is falling. In contrast, positive flashes generally occur away from the center of the storm, often in areas where rain is not falling. There is no place outside that is safe in or near a thunderstorm. Consequently, people need to stop what they are doing and get to a safe place immediately. Small outdoor buildings including dugouts, rain shelters, sheds, etc., are NOT SAFE. Substantial buildings with wiring and plumbing provide the greatest amount of protection. Office buildings, schools, and homes are examples of buildings that would offer protection. Once inside, stay away from windows and doors and anything that conducts electricity such as corded phones, wiring, plumbing, and anything connected to these. In the absence of a substantial building, a hard topped metal vehicle with the windows closed provides good protection. Occupants should avoid contact with metal in the vehicle and, to the extent possible, move away from windows.

Who should monitor the weather and who is responsible for making the decision to stop activities?

Lightning safety plans should specify that someone be designated to monitor the weather for lightning. The 'lightning monitor' should not include the coaches, umpires, or referees, as they are not able to devote the attention needed to adequately monitor conditions. The 'lightning monitor' must know the plan's guidelines and be empowered to assure that those guidelines are followed.

When should activities be stopped?

The sooner activities are stopped and people get to a safe place, the greater the level of safety. In general, a significant lightning threat extends outward from the base of a thunderstorm cloud about 6 to 10 miles. Therefore, people should move to a safe place when a thunderstorm is 6 to 10 miles away. Also, the plan's guidelines should account for the time it will take for everyone to get to a safe place. Here are some criteria that could be used to halt activities.

1. If lightning is observed. The ability to see lightning varies depending on the time of day, weather conditions, and obstructions such as trees, mountains, etc. In clear air, and especially at night, lightning can be seen from storms more than 10 miles away provided that obstructions don't limit the view of the thunderstorm.

2. If thunder is heard. Thunder can usually be heard from a distance of about 10 miles provided that there is no background noise. Traffic, wind, and precipitation may limit the ability to hear thunder less than 10 miles away. If you hear thunder, though, it's a safe bet that the storm is within ten miles.

3. If the time between lightning and corresponding thunder is 30 seconds or less. This would indicate that the thunderstorm is 6 miles away or less. As with the previous two criteria, obstructions, weather, noise, and other factors may limit the ability to use this criterion. In addition, a designated person must diligently monitor any lightning. In addition to any of the above criteria, activities should be halted if the sky looks threatening. Thunderstorms can develop directly overhead and some storms may develop lightning just as they move into an area.

When should activities be resumed?

Because electrical charges can linger in clouds after a thunderstorm has passed, experts agree that people should wait at least 30 minutes after the storm before resuming activities.

What should be done if someone is struck by lightning?

Most lightning strike victims can survive a lightning strike; however, medical attention may be needed immediately - have someone call for medical help. Victims do not carry an electrical charge and should be attended to at once. In many cases, the victim's heart and/or breathing may have stopped and CPR may be needed to revive them. The victim should continue to be monitored until medical help arrives; heart and/or respiratory problems could persist, or the victim could go into shock. If possible, move the victim to a safer place away from the threat of another lightning strike.

Appendix B
Safety Code for Little League

- Responsibility for safety procedures should be that of an adult member of the local league.

- Arrangements should be made in advance of all games and practices for emergency medical services.

- Managers, coaches, and umpires should have some training in first-aid. First-Aid Kit should be available at the field.

- No games or practice should be held when weather or field conditions are not good, particularly when lighting is inadequate. (See Lightning Safety Guidelines.)

- Play area should be inspected frequently for holes, damage, glass, and other foreign objects.

- Dugouts and bat racks should be positioned behind screens.

- Only players, managers, coaches, and umpires are permitted on the playing field during play and practice sessions.

- Responsibility for keeping bats and loose equipment off the field of play should be that of a regular player assigned for this purpose.

- Procedure should be established for retrieving foul balls batted out of the playing area.

- During practice sessions and games, all players should be alert and watching the batter on each pitch.

- During warm up drills, players should be spaced so that no one is endangered by errant balls.

- Equipment should be inspected regularly. Make sure it fits properly.

- Pitching machines, if used, must be in good working order (including extension cords, outlets, etc.) and must be operated only by adult managers and coaches.

- Batters must wear protective NOCSAE helmets during practice, as well as during games.

- Catchers must wear catcher's helmet (with face mask and throat guard), chest protector, and shin guards. Male catchers must wear a protective supporter and cup at all times.

- Except when runner is returning to a base, head first slides are not permitted. This applies only to Little League (Majors) and below.

- At no time should "horse play" be permitted on the playing field.

- Parents of players who wear glasses should be encouraged to provide "Safety Glasses."

- Players must not wear watches, rings, pins, jewelry, hard cosmetic, or hard decorative items.

- Catchers must wear catcher's helmet, face mask, and throat guard in warming up pitchers. This applies between innings and in bullpen practice. Skull caps are not permitted.

- Batting/catcher's helmets should not be painted unless approved by the manufacturer.

- Regulations prohibit on-deck batters. This means no player should handle a bat, even while in an enclosure, until it is his/her time at bat. This applies only to Little League (Majors) and below.

- Players who are ejected, ill, or injured should remain under supervision until released to the parent or guardian.

Appendix C
Communicable Disease Procedures

Proper precautions are needed to minimize the potential risk of the spread of communicable disease and skin infections during athletic competition. These conditions include skin infections that occur due to skin contact with competitors and equipment. The transmission of infections such as Methicillin-Resistant Staphylococcus aureus (MRSA) and Herpes Gladiatorum, blood-borne pathogens such as HIV and Hepatitis B, and other infectious diseases such as Influenza can often be greatly reduced through proper hygiene.

Infectious Skin Diseases

Strategies for reducing the potential exposure to these infectious agents include:

- Athletes must notify a parent/guardian and coach of any skin lesion prior to any competition or practice. An appropriate health-care professional shall evaluate all skin lesions before returning to practices or competition.

- If an outbreak occurs on a team, especially in a contact sport, all team members should be evaluated to help prevent the potential spread of the infection. All shared equipment shall be properly cleaned/disinfected prior to use.

- Coaches, officials, and appropriate health-care professionals must follow Little League, state, or local guidelines on "time until return to competition." Participation with a covered lesion may be considered if in accordance with Little League, state, or local guidelines and the lesion is no longer contagious.

Blood-borne Infectious Diseases

Strategies for reducing the potential exposure to these agents include following Universal Precautions such as:

- An athlete who is bleeding, has an open wound, has any amount of blood on his/her uniform, or has blood on his/her person, shall be directed to leave the activity (game or practice) until the bleeding is stopped, the wound is covered, the uniform and/or body is appropriately cleaned, and/or the uniform is changed before returning to activity.

- Athletic trainers or other caregivers must wear gloves and use Universal Precautions to prevent blood or body fluid-splash from contaminating themselves or others.

- In the event of a blood or body fluid-splash, immediately wash contaminated skin or mucous membranes with soap and water.

- Clean all contaminated surfaces and equipment with disinfectant before returning to competition. Be sure to use gloves when cleaning.

- Any blood exposure or bites to the skin that break the surface must be reported and immediately evaluated by an appropriate health-care professional.

Other Communicable Diseases

Means of reducing the potential exposure to these agents include:

- Appropriate vaccination of athletes, coaches, officials and staff as recommended by the Centers for Disease Control (CDC).

- During times of outbreaks, follow the guidelines set forth by the CDC as well as state and local Health Departments.

Additional information is available from your state high school association and from the National Federation TARGET program.

This Policy was modified with permission from the National Federation of State High School Associations' Communicable Disease and Skin Infection Procedures Policy.

Appendix D
Bat Modifications and Alterations

While Little League International has not received any reports of Little League volunteers or players making alterations to bats designed to increase their performance, it has been an issue in some upper levels of play.

In an effort to ensure this does not become a problem in Little League, this policy statement has been prepared.

No bat, in any level of Little League Baseball or Softball play, is permitted to be altered. This is of particular concern especially when it is clearly done to enhance performance and violate bat standards. Making such alterations to bats is clearly an inappropriate attempt to gain an unfair advantage, and cheating has no place in our program. Umpires, managers, and coaches are instructed to inspect bats before games and practices - as they always should - to determine if bats might have been altered.

This includes using the appropriate Little League Bat Ring. If a bat does not clearly pass through the correct size ring, or if it has a flat spot on it, the bat must not be used. (This may simply indicate the bat has become misshapen with use, and does not necessarily indicate it was purposely altered. Still, the bat must be removed.)

Other signs to look for include contorted or mangled end-caps or knobs on non-wood bats. This could indicate that machinery was used to "shave" the inside of the bat to make it lighter. Bats with evidence of this type of tampering also must not be used.

Little League International wishes to make it clear that tampering with bats (or any other piece of equipment) is dangerous, and the equipment must not be used in any Little League game or practice.

Appendix E
Heat Illness Prevention Protection Policy

Take steps to protect your league's members from heat illness. Heat stroke, heat exhaustion, and heat cramps are all highly possible outcomes for your players and volunteers if they are not protected from the sun's power. When games are played in high heat or heat and high humidity, precautions should be in place.

According to the American Association of Pediatrics (AAP), children's bodies can't tolerate heat as well as adults, so don't expect them to perform in the same conditions you can.

Watch for heat illness signs: weakness, dizziness, slow pulse, and clammy skin. If sweating can't cool the body, especially because the player is dehydrated, heat stroke could develop. Signs of this are confusion, collapse, rapid pulse, and dry skin (no longer sweating).

The AAP notes heat stroke may cause convulsions or even unconsciousness. This is a medical emergency and professional help should be sought immediately. In some cases, heat stroke can kill, but it can also cause permanent brain damage in victims who survive.

Drink Early, Drink Often: Remember, the best protection for heat illness is water and rest. The maxim is: drink early, drink often, even when players aren't thirsty. Players should arrive for games/practices adequately hydrated and drink at least five (5) ounces of water every 15-20 minutes while they are active in the heat.

Ask players to bring water or a sports drink with modest amounts of electrolytes, but nothing with caffeine that acts as a diuretic and drains water from the body.

Try to provide water for players wherever possible at your facility.

Evidence shows that sunscreen of at least SPF 15 should be applied to exposed skin every time children will be in the sun for extended periods, to help keep the player cool and to protect against future skin cancer risk.

Take first steps:
- Provide sunshades for all dugouts and spectator areas as possible.
- Provide cool water and wet towels (with or without ice) for players and umpires to apply to necks.
- Recommend participants utilize topical sunscreen on a regular basis and encourage its use on all exposed skin.
- Take breaks in the shade between innings, or every 20 minutes.
- Set up a sprinkler in a grassy or paved area where players can cool off.

Take it to the next level:
- Install a water mister near or in dugouts to boost cooling.
- Provide umpires with a Camelback-style water container for hydrating during innings.
- Develop a "cool room" in your concession stand, or just a tent with walls, with fans or air-conditioning for those overcome by heat.

Anyone who begins to develop cramps, dizziness, or other signs of heat stress should be removed from the game, given cool water, and placed in as cool a place as possible: in a car with air-conditioning or in a cool, shaded area.

Make sure volunteers know to call 9-1-1 if the player becomes disoriented or confused, as this is a sign of the more serious heat stroke.

Appendix F
Privacy Policy

The Little League® International ("Little League") Privacy Policy has been written to answer questions you might have about our information and privacy practices. As a youth organization, we are very concerned about privacy. Therefore, we have taken measures to tailor our content and offerings to help protect the privacy of players, parents/guardians, coaches and managers, volunteers and fans.

This Privacy Policy applies to information collected on Little League authored websites, including LittleLeague.org, LittleLeagueStore.net, LittleLeague.org/Videos, LittleLeagueU. org, LittleLeagueUmpire.org, and other affiliated websites as well as our official pages on Facebook, Twitter, Snapchat, YouTube, Instagram and other social media (collectively, the "Sites"), as well as information received from other sources such as charter enrollment, player registration, events, volunteer reporting, and advertising.

This policy was last updated on November 9, 2018.

Advice to Children and Parents

For parents and guardians, we urge you to repeatedly discuss with your children the risks of giving personal information to anyone (online or in person) whom they do not personally know. We also encourage parents to spend time online with their children monitoring and reviewing their children's online activity. For additional tips on how to help children stay safe on the Internet, we recommend the following site: Consumer.ftc.gov/features/feature-0002-parents.

As a policy, no person under the age of 13 is permitted without parental authorization to register to receive Little League's electronic communications or participate in Little League's website or social media activities.

What Personal Information Do We Collect?

Registration and Volunteer Data. For players, we require chartered Little Leagues to collect limited personal information, including names, genders and dates of birth. For parents or guardians of players, we require chartered Little Leagues to collect more comprehensive personal information, including names, mailing addresses, telephone numbers, and email addresses. We require this information for registration purposes, to allow us to communicate with you, and to provide the information about the Little League program and additional services or promotions that may be relevant to you.

Similarly, for coaches, managers, parents/guardians of registered players, umpires, league officers, district officers, and other Little League employees and event staff including volunteers, we may collect or require chartered Little Leagues to collect personal information including names, mailing addresses, telephone numbers, and email addresses. We require this information for registration purposes and to allow us to communicate with you. Umpires, Little League employees and event staff including volunteers may also be required to provide their dates of birth, social security numbers, and other government issued identification card numbers for the limited purpose of conducting background checks.

Event Data. If you attend Little League events or the *World of Little League®: Peter J. McGovern Museum* ("Museum"), we may ask you to provide your personal information on a voluntary basis. For example, at the Museum, we make a kiosk available for attendees to complete a voluntary survey about their experience at the Museum, and if you voluntarily elect to complete a survey, we ask for your personal information, including name, mailing address, and email address, to help us improve our Museum experience and services.

If you attend certain events or participate in certain activities at events, we may require you to provide certain personal information. For example:

- If you attend our summer camp program, we require your personal information in order to enroll, including name, mailing address, telephone number, email address, date of birth, medical information for safety and emergency purposes, and financial information to pay the fee.

- If you attend the Family Fun Zone at the Little League Baseball® World Series or at any other event operated by Little League, we use radio-frequency identification ("RFID") technology to provide attendees with convenient access to various activities, and we require certain personal information, including name, mailing address, and email address for participants 18 years and older, in order to register the account and keep track of which activities were participated in.

If you attend an event at the Little League International complex, you may be under video surveillance on premises of the event for security purposes and to ensure the safety of all attendees.

Website Data. If you visit any of the Sites, we may ask you to provide your personal information in order to provide the quality services requested, such as subscribing to our email newsletters, participating in promotions, finding local leagues through League Finder, or registering for events. We may collect information as you interact with our Sites, such as making purchases, expressing your opinion, or simply browsing, for a variety of reasons including fulfilling online orders and improving your experience and our services. We may also collect information from other legitimate sources, such as our promotional partners, from public sources, advertising metrics, or personal information that is part of your social media accounts that you have made available to us.

Payment Information. If you place any orders for goods or services on the Sites or at our camps and events, we or our payment processing partners may ask you to provide your personal information in order to process your transactions and ship your orders. This information may include your name, mailing address, telephone number, email address, and financial account information including payment card information. Details regarding the terms and conditions, privacy and security policies of our payment processing partners are made available at the point of collection.

What is the Source of Personal Information We Collect?
We may collect personal information from the following sources:

- **Sites.** This includes Little League authored websites and other affiliated websites, as well as our official pages on third party platforms, including Facebook, Twitter, Snapchat, YouTube, Instagram, and other social media.

- **Fans, Members, and Volunteers.** This includes chartered leagues, and camps, events as well as their attendees, players, parent or guardians of players, coaches, managers, league official, district officers, umpires, administrators or volunteers. It also includes information provided directly to Little League from chartered Little Leagues and Districts through the Little League Data Center at LittleLeague.org/DataCenter ("Data Center") or through the DICK'S Sporting Goods Team Sports HQ platform at TeamSportsHQ.dsg.com ("DICK'S Platform").

- **Advertising.** This includes user interactions with our advertisements, as well as our coupons, special discounts, contests, games, and promotions.

- **Correspondence.** This includes any communication by electronic or non-electronic means between Little League or its members/affiliates and you.

- **Events.** We may collect information from attendees on site at the Museum, the Little League Baseball® World Series, regional tournaments, clinics, meetings and other events, including but not limited to completing a voluntary survey about their experience, check in or register for a clinic or meeting, or register an account for RFID technology used at our events.

- **Direct Inquiries.** We collect information from those individuals who email us or request information via our online submission forms in order to service your request accordingly.

How Do We Use Your Personal Information?

Any personal information collected by Little League will be used for the purpose of furthering the mission of Little League and as described in this Privacy Policy. We collect your personal information to meet contractual and other legal obligations, protect the interests of individuals and the public, and to serve our legitimate interests, such as: providing our products, services and events and assuring their quality; improving and developing new products, services and events; and protecting our assets, systems, staff, participants and attendees. We may also rely on your consent given for particular uses of your personal information, if required by applicable law. Specifically, we may use your personal information in the following ways:

Services. We may use your personal information in order to provide services to our volunteers, parents, fans, customers, and other constituents which include managing a network of organized youth sports programs across the world and ensuring that sporting events are successful. Without limitation, this typically requires the use of certain personal information, including registration data, event data, and other personal information, in order to provide program information, special offers or services through Little League and/or its trusted sponsors, partners, or licensees, to fulfill your requests for information or products/services, to maintain a list of verified and eligible participants, to maintain a list of volunteers and provide them with the operating tools to manage leagues, or to respond to your inquiries about our programs. We may also use this information to communicate with you, such as to update you on new rules, regulations, or risk management and operational issues.

Order Fulfillment. We use your personal information to process and ship orders for goods and services, to provide you with information related to your order, to improve your e-commerce experience, and for fraud detection purposes. This typically requires the use of certain personal information, payment information, and website data.

Marketing, Research, and Promotions. The information you provide in connection with our Sites and email communications, online submissions and surveys, social media sites, and communities is used to create an interactive experience. We may combine your registration data with other information that you have provided through social media or other platforms, and we may use this combined information to facilitate conversation and to occasionally offer you information, programs, and services, both directly from us and on behalf of affiliated third parties. We may also ask for your opinion through surveys and research, seek to register you for contests and notify you if you have won, or to provide you with the latest news or program updates distributed by Little League.

Archival. We may use, disclose, or share basic information (particularly identifying the names of players, their teams, team achievements, and years players played) for archival, record keeping, honorary, newsworthy or promotional purposes (including selecting, arranging and describing such records, and making them available to the public).

Legal. We may be required to use, disclose, or share your personal information with third parties when required by applicable law, in response to legal proceedings, in response to a request from a competent law enforcement agency, to protect our rights, privacy, safety or property, or the public, or to enforce the terms of any agreement or the terms of the Sites.

Mergers and Acquisitions. In the event that Little League or its assets are acquired by, or merged with, another organization or company including through bankruptcy, we may use, disclose, or share your personal information with any of our legal successors.

Fraud Detection. We may use, disclose, or share your personal information and non-personal information in order to investigate, prevent, or take action regarding illegal activities, suspected fraud, situations involving potential threats to the physical safety of any person, violations of this Privacy Policy, or as otherwise required by law.

Disclosure to Third Parties

We may share personal information with certain types of third parties:

- **Subsidiaries and Affiliates.** Little League International, regional offices, tournament volunteers, and other associated personnel or volunteers that assist with implementation of the Little League program.

- **Members and Volunteers.** Each chartered league is a self-organizing community made up of the players, parent or guardians of players, coaches, managers, league official, district officers, umpires, and volunteers that are a part of that league. Each chartered league is also a controller, along with Little League, of the personal information provided to that chartered league, and personal information provided by each of the above categories of individuals may be shared with others within that league. This includes information provided directly through the Data Center or DICK'S Sporting Goods Team Sports HQ Platform (TSHQ), as the DICK'S Platform is also a controller, along with Little League, of any information submitted through the Dick's Platform. A copy of the DICK'S Platform Privacy Policies can be found here: DicksSportingGoods. com/s/privacy-policy and BlueSombrero.com/privacy-statement.

- **Service Providers.** This includes service and platform providers that enable us to run many aspects of our organization, such as online event registration and ticketing platforms, pre-event and in-event marketing and consumer engagement technology providers, online form/survey and data collection platforms, internet marketing companies, e-commerce payment processors, and email marketing tool providers.

- **Experts.** This includes consultants and legal counsel that assist us in managing and operating our organization, such as safety consultants for league facilities and operations and outside law firms.

- **Sponsors, Licensees, Agents, or Partners.** This includes organizations that sponsor or associate with Little League to offer information, coupons, special discounts, contests, games, promotions, and special events. However, we only share your personal information with these third parties based on your consent given at the point of collection.

- **Legal, Mergers and Acquisitions, and Fraud Detection.** We may be required to disclose or share personal information when required by applicable law, in response to legal proceedings, in response to a request from a competent law enforcement agency, to protect our rights, privacy, safety or property, or the public, or to enforce the terms of any agreement or the terms of the Sites. In the event that Little League or its assets are acquired by, or merged with, another company including through bankruptcy, we may use, disclose, or share your personal information with any of our legal successors. We may use, disclose, or share your personal information and non-personal information in order to investigate, prevent, or take action regarding illegal activities, suspected fraud, situations involving potential threats to the physical safety of any person, violations of this Privacy Policy, or as otherwise required by law.

Retention of Personal Information

We will keep your information as described in this Privacy Policy to the extent necessary to accomplish the purposes for which it was collected. We also prune archival information to eliminate excess data unnecessary for our archival purposes. We may retain your anonymized, depersonalized data after deletion.

Protection of Personal Information

We have implemented appropriate measures designed to protect your personal information from accidental loss and from unauthorized access, use, alteration, and disclosure. Any payment transactions will be encrypted using industry-standard technologies.

The safety and security of your information also depends on you. Where we have given you (or where you have chosen) a password for access to certain parts of our Website, you are responsible for keeping this password confidential. We ask you not to share your password with anyone. We urge you to be careful about giving out information in public areas of the Sites, such as our official social media pages. The information you share in such public areas may be viewed by any user of the Sites.

Although we have implemented appropriate measures to protect your personal information, we cannot guarantee the privacy and security of personal information transmitted to the Sites. Any transmission of personal information is at your own risk. We are not responsible for circumvention of any privacy settings or security measures contained on the Sites.

International Data Transfers

The processing of your personal information as described in this Privacy Policy may require your personal information to be transferred to or stored at data storage locations within the United States that are controlled by Little League International. Personal information regarding individuals who reside in a member state of the European Economic Area ("EEA"), Europe outside of the EEA, the Middle East or Africa is controlled by Little League International through its European and African Region Headquarters located in Kutno, Poland. Personal information regarding individuals who reside in Asia and the Pacific region is controlled by Little League International through its Asia-Pacific Region Headquarters in Hong Kong. Personal information regarding individuals who reside in Canada is controlled by both Little League International and the Little League Canadian Region Headquarters in Ottawa, Ontario, Canada, a separate entity. Personal information regarding individuals who reside in Mexico, South America, Central America, and the Caribbean is controlled by Little League International through its Little League Latin American and Caribbean Region Headquarters in Caparra Heights, Puerto Rico.

We may transfer your personal information to countries outside of the EEA that have different data protection standards to those which apply in the EEA. In such cases, and where appropriate, we have put in place standard contractual clauses approved by the European Commission or will rely on your consent where permitted by law.

Cookies, Pixel Tags, and Similar Technology

What are they? Cookies and pixel tags are pieces of information that a website transfers to an individual's hard drive for record-keeping purposes. Cookies and pixel tags make internet browsing easier for you by saving your passwords, preferences and preferred websites as you browse. The use of cookies and pixel tags are an industry standard – you will find that they are used by most major websites. By showing how and when visitors use the Sites, cookies and pixel tags can also help website developers see which areas are popular and which are not and can help you find information that is most relevant to you based on your search history. The "help" portion of the toolbar on most browsers will tell you how to prevent your browser from accepting new cookies, how to have the browser notify you when you receive new cookies or how to disable cookies altogether. If you reject cookies, you may not be able to participate in certain activities or receive a promotion tailored to you. The Sites do not control and do not guarantee the effectiveness of browser-based tools for managing cookies.

We use cookies, pixel tags, and similar technology on the Sites. As you browse the Sites, cookies, pixel tags, or similar technologies may be placed on your computer so that we can understand what information interests you on our site, in order to continue to provide information in the future. On occasion, we may provide targeted advertising through partners like AdRoll and Facebook to present you with additional information about our program and its offerings based on your previous interaction with the Sites and your online activity across different websites. These techniques do not collect personal information such as your name, email address, postal address, or telephone number, but may collect information regarding your IP address, as well as the type of device, operating system and web browser used to access the Sites, and limited information about your internet browsing history and related online activities. We also work with third party companies to assist us with website analytics such as evaluating the use and operation of our website so that we can continue to enhance the Sites and the information contained within. We do not control the practices of our partners or third party companies with respect to the use of cookies, pixel tags or similar technologies. You can visit NetworkAdvertising.org/Choices or AboutAds.Info/Choices to opt-out of tracking and targeted advertising using cookies or similar technology.

Manage your preferences. Do Not Track (DNT) is a privacy preference that users can set in some web browsers, allowing users to opt out of tracking by websites and online services. At the present time, the World Wide Web Consortium (W3C) has not yet established universal standards for recognizable DNT signals and therefore the Sites may not recognize DNT.

Your Rights and Choices

You have the right to access, transport, update, rectify, or erase your personal information held by us, as well as the right to object to or restrict its processing, transform it into anonymous form, or withdraw from any consent-based uses. You can exercise your rights by contacting us at the contact information provided in this Privacy Policy.

We may decline to process requests that cannot be verified as legitimately made on your behalf, appear vexatious, that jeopardize the privacy of others, or that we are required to process by law or for legitimate business or legal purposes. We may also decline aspects of requests if we believe doing so would undermine our legitimate use of data for security or anti-fraud purposes.

You also have a right to register a complaint to your local data protection authorities if you believe your privacy rights related to your personal information have not been properly observed.

Third-Party Links and Websites

Please note that some information you receive may direct you to a non-Little League website. Please refer to these web sites for specific privacy policies and use of data as we have no control over information that is submitted to, or collected by, these third parties.

Individual Submissions and Promotions

We may offer coupons, special discounts, contests, games, and promotions on behalf of Little League and/or our national partners; or invite you to submit stories, photos, comments, or questions to certain areas of the Sites. On these occasions, we may ask you to voluntarily submit additional information along with your submission so that we can notify you if you are a winner, or to respond to (or ask) questions. Typically, no individual under the age of 13 is permitted to participate or to submit information to any of these promotions, except with parental/guardian consent.

Your California Privacy Rights

This Privacy Policy describes how we may share your information for marketing purposes, as described above. California residents are entitled to request and obtain from us, once per calendar year, information about any of your personal information shared with third parties for their own direct marketing purposes, including the categories of information and the names and addresses of those businesses with which we have shared such information. To request this information and for any other questions about our privacy practices and compliance with California law, please contact us as described below.

Changes to this Privacy Policy

Little League reserves the right to modify this policy from time to time as Little League determines to be appropriate. We will post any changes to this policy on the Little League website. We may contact you with notices concerning our Privacy Policy, but you should check our website periodically to review any changes.

Local Leagues - Include Opt-In to Privacy Policy During Registration

A copy of this privacy policy is available at LittleLeague.org/PrivacyPolicy. We strongly encourage all local Little Leagues to incorporate this policy into the registration process for participant families and volunteers by including a signature on the policy at registration. It is also encouraged that local leagues post the policy on local league websites.

Contact Us

If you have any questions, comments or concerns regarding the Little League International Privacy Policy, please contact us at Privacy@LittleLeague.org or by mail at Little League International, Attn: IT/Data Services, 539 US Highway 15, P.O. Box 3485, Williamsport, PA 17701.

Appendix G
2019 Little League Age Chart

For Baseball Divisions Only

Match month (top line) and box with year of birth. League age indicated at right.

Jan	Feb	Mar	Apr	May	Jun	Jul	Aug	Sep	Oct	Nov	Dec	Age
2015	2015	2015	2015	2015	2015	2015	2015	2014	2014	2014	2014	4
2014	2014	2014	2014	2014	2014	2014	2014	2013	2013	2013	2013	5
2013	2013	2013	2013	2013	2013	2013	2013	2012	2012	2012	2012	6
2012	2012	2012	2012	2012	2012	2012	2012	2011	2011	2011	2011	7
2011	2011	2011	2011	2011	2011	2011	2011	2010	2010	2010	2010	8
2010	2010	2010	2010	2010	2010	2010	2010	2009	2009	2009	2009	9
2009	2009	2009	2009	2009	2009	2009	2009	2008	2008	2008	2008	10
2008	2008	2008	2008	2008	2008	2008	2008	2007	2007	2007	2007	11
2007	2007	2007	2007	2007	2007	2007	2007	2006	2006	2006	2006	12
2006	2006	2006	2006	2006	2006	2006	2006	2005	2005	2005	2005	13
2005	2005	2005	2005	2005	2005	2005	2005	2004	2004	2004	2004	14
2004	2004	2004	2004	2004	2004	2004	2004	2003	2003	2003	2003	15
2003	2003	2003	2003	2003	2003	2003	2003	2002	2002	2002	2002	16

UMPIRE RULE #1

YOUR LITTLE LEAGUE® CAREER NEVER ENDS,

STAY IN THE GAME.

Tips, Tutorials, Training and More!

LittleLeague.org/University/Umpire

LITTLE LEAGUE®
OPERATING POLICIES

LOCAL LEAGUE ADMINISTRATION

Separately, each of the various elements which contribute to the operation of the program affords assistance to those who play Little League. Together they function in teamwork with Little League International, whose primary responsibility is service to more than one (1) million volunteers and nearly 2.4 million participants.

Here is a brief outline of the functions of the component elements:

I. The Local League

The league is the basic unit of organization. It serves the home community and is the core of the volunteer aspect of Little League.

At this level, managers, coaches, umpires, league officers, auxiliary, and other personnel come into close association with the children. It is in the local league perspective that the public sees Little League.

Within the framework of rules and regulations of Little League, the local league is autonomous. It establishes its own administration, elects its Board of Directors, and maintains an organization best suited to meet the needs of Little League in the community.

2. The District and the District Administrator

The field organization, which provides a broad area of administrative service and counsel to local leagues, comprises thousands of competent and experienced volunteer leaders.

Since 1955, Little League has made it possible for leagues to elect a District Administrator as a step towards effecting better service to the league and closer liaison between the league and Little League International.

The District Administrator is responsible to the leagues in the district to acquaint them with information disseminated out of Little League International, assisting them in settling problems, reviewing with them proposed amendments, reporting to them on the business of the Congress, and interpreting adopted changes. The District Administrator is expected to conduct the election in the district, call meetings whenever necessary, assist in the organization and counseling of new leagues, review and investigate the organization; review and investigate problems referred by Little League International, and be well informed on policies, rules, regulations and other pertinent information. Since the District Administrator holds a position of trust and responsibility, that person must be experienced and familiar with all areas and all leagues in the district.

However, the District Administrator never has the authority to suspend or waive any rule or regulation, nor to forfeit any International Tournament game.

ROLE OF LEAGUE PRESIDENT

Apart from all other considerations, sound leadership, couched in knowledge, experience and common sense, is the greatest requirement and most exemplary qualification of the man or woman selected as president of a Little League.

While efficient organizational and administrative abilities are desirable credentials, the search for good leadership must transcend all other attributes in the adult who gives direction to the Little League movement in the local community. Dedication to the goals and purpose of Little League is inherent in the volunteer aspect of those who serve, but all who serve are not equally gifted with the qualities of leadership.

Baseball and softball are the names of the games, but Little League is the name of an elite program and initiative that has given these sports their best dimensions. The stature and integrity of Little League are hard-won hallmarks, accompanied by men and women who have given outstanding leadership at many levels.

A fine tradition of unselfishness and dedicated effort has been passed on annually to thousands of incoming league presidents. Little League is a better and more vital program because of them. Each year as local leagues expand to embrace more participants, the mantle of leadership becomes more demanding and imposes more trust and responsibility upon the league president.

The president learns certain fundamental obligations which have been spelled out in rules and regulations. But the degree of the understanding of the motivations underlying Little League — and the extent of the president's personal leadership in the sensitive area of youth activity — are over-riding qualifications which best gauge a president equal to the responsibility.

The president has many responsibilities in the administration of the league. Each president is elected by, and is accountable to, the local league Board of Directors. Duties of a president are described within the limits of the league constitution which should give each president wide latitude in overseeing the affairs of all elements of the league.

As the chief administrator, the president selects and appoints managers, coaches, umpires, and committees. All appointments are subject to the approval of the league's Board of Directors. They are responsible to the president for the conduct of league affairs, both on and off the field. Importantly, the president is the officer with whom Little League International maintains contact and who represents the league in the council of the District Organization.

The president should be the most informed officer of the league. Each president must know the regulations under which Little League operates and in authorizing the annual application for charter, binds all members of the league to faithfully observe the regulations. Little League reserves the right to require a league to remove any officer who does not carry out the terms of charter application. Serious violation can result in loss of the league's charter.

Beyond the requirements of league administration, the president should personify the best public image in reflection to the community at large. Each president should take an active role in gaining support and winning friends for the league.

The increase of youth activities in a recreation-minded nation challenges Little League to earn the respect and interest of the community. Little League is competitive with many other agencies in this regard. It is in this field that the league president and all other officers must give dignity and stature to Little League representation.

Over the years, Little League has worked out a successful formula for maintaining the autonomous character of local league operation. But it has also established a close-knit liaison with the local league by means of intercommunication between the president and all field levels up to and including Little League International.

It is imperative that the league president maintains updated contact information with Little League International to ensure that important communication is received and shared with appropriate league officers. To register for electronic notifications or verify your email address, visit LittleLeague.org/Register.

It is by means of this free exchange in service and counsel that Little League is a cohesive unit of more than 7,000 leagues, each with an open channel to Little League International. The local league president is one of a great family of league presidents whose aggressive interest in the total program has fashioned — and will continue to fashion — the design of Little League wherever it is played.

LEAGUE OFFICERS

Annually, the regular membership of each Little League is required to meet and elect a Board of Directors. Following the election, the Board of Directors will meet and elect its officers from within the membership of the board. The officers required are: President, Vice President, Secretary, Treasurer, Player Agent, Coaching Coordinator, and Safety Officer. If a league also operates a Intermediate (50-70) Division, Junior League, and/or Senior League, a Vice President or other personnel should be designated to supervise, as is also the case for those leagues operating Little League, Junior League, or Senior League Softball programs. All officers should be members of the league's Board of Directors.

League duties concerning player selection, the transfer of players from Minor Leagues and schedule supervision, should be properly vested in the league's player agent.

Briefly, the duties of league officers and Board of Directors can be summed up as follows:

Board of Directors - The management of the property and affairs of the local league shall be vested in the Board of Directors. The directors shall, upon election, immediately enter upon the performance of their duties and shall continue in office until their successors shall have been duly elected and qualified.

The board membership shall include the officers, including player agent, and a minimum of one manager and one volunteer umpire. (Only volunteer umpires may be elected to the board.) The number of managers and coaches including Minor League representation elected to the board shall not exceed a minority of the total board members. Every board member should have a copy of the Little League Rulebook with Operating Policies for reference to proper operating procedures and policies.

The Board of Directors shall have the power to appoint such standing and special committees as it shall determine by the constitution and to delegate such powers to them as the board shall deem advisable and which it may properly delegate.

The board may adopt such rules and regulations for the conduct of its meetings and the management of the league as it may deem proper.

The board shall have the power by a two-thirds vote of those present at any regular or special meeting to discipline, suspend or remove any director or officer or committee member of the league, subject to provisions of the constitution.

President - Presides at league meetings, and assumes full responsibility for the operation of the local league. The president receives all mail, supplies, and other communications from the Little League International. The president must see to it that league personnel is properly briefed on all phases of rules, regulations, and policies of Little League. The league president is the contact between the local organization and Little League International.

Vice President - Presides in the absence of the president; works with other officers and committee members; is ex-officio member of all committees and carries out such duties and assignments as may be delegated by the president.

Secretary - Maintains a register of members and directors; records the minutes of meetings; is responsible for sending out notice of meetings, issues membership cards and maintains a record of league's activities.

Treasurer - Signs checks co-signed by another officer or director; dispenses league funds as approved by the Board of Directors; reports on the status of league funds; keeps local league books and financial records; prepares budgets and assumes the responsibility for all local league finances.

Player Agent - Conducts annual tryouts, and is in charge of player selection, assists president in checking birth records and eligibility of players; serves as a member of the Board of Directors of the local league and generally supervises and coordinates the transfer of players to or from the Minor Leagues according to provisions of the regulations of Little League.

Safety Officer - Coordinates all safety activities; ensures safety in player training; ensures safe playing conditions; coordinates reporting and prevention of injuries; solicits suggestions for making conditions safer; reports suggestions to Little League International through the league president and prepares the ASAP plan for submission to Little League International.

Umpire-in-Chief (U.I.C.) - Serves as coordinator of and advises the league President on the league umpire program; responsible for recommending umpires to the league President for appointment to the league umpire roster; recruiting and retaining volunteer umpires; establishing a league umpire training program consistent with Little League® guidelines; coordinating and assisting with conducting umpire clinics at league and district level; communicating rule changes to league umpires; scheduling league umpires for regular season games; evaluating league umpires using established guidelines to maintain program integrity; further continual improvement, and prepare league umpires for advancement to tournament levels; communicating with and providing updates to the District Umpire Consultant on the league umpire program, and attending Umpire Training programs at the District, State, Region, and/or Headquarters level.

League Information Officer - Sets up and manages league's official website; sets up online registration and ensures the league rosters are uploaded to Little League; assigns online administrative rights to other local volunteers; encourages creation of team web sites to managers, coaches, and parents; ensures that league news and scores are updated online on a regular basis; collects, posts, and distributes important information on league activities including direct dissemination of fundraising and sponsor activities to Little League, the district, the public, league members, and the media; serves as primary contact person for Little League regarding optimizing use of the Internet for league administration and for distributing information to league members and to Little League International. Provides player, coach and manager records to Little League International in electronic format.

Coaching Coordinator - Represents coaches/managers in league; presents a coach/manager training budget to the board; gains the support and funds necessary to implement a league-wide training program; orders and distributes training materials to players, coaches and managers; coordinates mini-clinics as necessary; serves as the contact person for Little League and its manager-coach education. Receives and distributes coaching information from Little League International and distributes to all coaches and managers.

Sponsor Fundraising Manager - Solicits and secures local sponsorships to support league operations; collects and reviews sponsorship and fundraising opportunities; organizes and implements approved league fundraising activities; coordinates participation in fundraising activities; and maintains records of monies secured through sponsorship and fundraising initiatives.

Concession Manager - Maintains the operation of concession facilities; organizes the purchase of concession products; responsible for the management of the concession sales at league events; schedules volunteers to work the concession booth during league events; collects and reviews concession related offers including coupons, discounts, and bulk-purchasing opportunities; and organizes, tallies and keeps records of concession sales and purchases.

Marketing/Public Relations Manager – Oversees new player recruitment efforts; develops and maintains a league marketing plan focused on player recruitment and retention; oversees efforts to market new divisions of play and initiatives offered by the league; works with local media to promote the interests of Little League, and coordinates efforts to make the local Little League visible in the community year round.

PROCESS TO OBTAIN WAIVERS OF RULES AND REGULATIONS

When a league applies for its annual charter with Little League, it pledges to abide by all the rules and regulations of Little League. However, under special circumstances, it may become necessary to apply for a temporary waiver of a rule or regulation.

It is very important to remember that a league must not take any action contrary to Little League rules and regulations until receiving expressed, written permission through the Charter Committee waiver system. A league wishing to apply for a waiver of a rule or regulation must do so via the following method:

1. The local league Board of Directors votes whether or not to request the waiver.

2. If the local league Board of Directors votes to request the waiver, the president writes a letter, detailing the request. Supporting documents should be attached, and forwarded to the District Administrator.

3. The District Administrator includes his/her written opinion, and forwards all documents to the Regional Director by June 1 of the current year.

4. The Regional Director or Assistant Region Director will present the situation to the Charter Committee for action.

5. The Charter Committee will inform the Regional Director or Assistant Regional Director of its final and binding decision, and the Region will inform the District Administrator.

NOTE 1: Any request for a waiver that does not follow the above steps may be delayed.

NOTE 2: If a waiver request involves more than one league, all leagues involved must submit appropriate documentation.

NOTE 3: All waiver requests to the Charter Committee must be submitted in writing by the league president before the start of the league's regular season or June 1, whichever occurs first. Requests must be submitted to the Regional Office through the District Administrator.

The league, as part of the chartering process, agreed to accept the decision of the Charter Committee as final and binding. Should any new or additional information become available after the Charter Committee's initial decision which the league feels would alter the Committee's decision, the league may submit that information for reconsideration by the above outlined process. The league also agreed, as part of the chartering process, that all Charter Committee decisions will be made in Williamsport but understand that the league may request to personally present their position at a meeting with the Committee in Williamsport. No other person or group has the authority to approve waivers of ANY rules or regulations.

LOCAL LEAGUE DRAFT METHODS

Methods for Existing Leagues

It is recommended that managers not select more than eight players in a given age group. The team roster may be comprised of players of league age 9, 10, 11, and 12 unless modified by the local league according to options established by Little League. The local league may opt to allow only 10, 11, and 12, or 11- and 12-year-olds, to tryout for the Major Division.

Secrecy: Players shall never be told the position in which they were drafted.

Bonus Picks: Each manager requiring eight or more players prior to the draft to complete the roster will be allowed one bonus pick at the completion of round four. If more than one manager is allowed bonus picks under this section, the order of rotation will be identical to that being followed in the draft.

NOTE: All other draft methods for local league Major Divisions, other than the three outlined below, must be approved by the Charter Committee prior to the draft.

Plan A - Conventional Draft Plan

When a thorough tryout program has been completed, the last-place team of the preceding season gets the first choice in every round of the draft, the next to last place team gets the second selection in every round and the remaining teams select in the reverse order of standing.

For the purpose of explanation, let us assume that there are four teams in the league.

First Round:

> Fourth place manager selects the first player
> Third place manager selects the second player
> Second place manager selects the third player
> First place manager selects the fourth player

Second Round:

>   Fourth place manager selects the fifth player
>
>   Third place manager selects the sixth player
>
>   Second place manager selects the seventh player
>
>   First place manager selects the eighth player, etc., until the rosters are completed.

Plan B - Redraft

This draft is actually in two separate parts. The first part includes those players who:

A.   are returning from a Major team in the same division, AND;

B.   have registered for the current season.

This first draft of returning players must be completed before the second part of the draft, and all returning players who qualify under both conditions above must be drafted. Managers are not permitted to waive a draft choice.

The second part of the draft includes all players who are eligible for selection and have attended the required number of tryout sessions.

The draft rotation follows the reverse order of finish from the previous season, with the last place team's manager receiving the first pick, then the second-to-last place team, and so on, or the managers draw numbers to determine who will select the first player. For instance, in a four-team league, the manager of the last place team from the previous season makes the following player selections: 1st choice, 8th, 9th, 16th, 17th, 24th, 25th, etc.; The manager of the team that finished in third place makes the 2nd choice, 7th, 10th, 18th, 23rd, etc.; The manager of the team that finished second in the previous season makes the 3rd choice, 6th, 11th, 14th, 19th, 22nd; The manager of the team that finished in first place gets 4th choice, 5th, 12th, 13th, 20th, 21st, etc., until selections are completed.

NOTE 1: Because there are no players returning to a particular team, and because coaches cannot be named until the draft is completed, Options 2 and 4 (see "Options On Sons, Daughters And Siblings") do NOT apply when using this draft method plan.

NOTE 2: When the second part of this draft method begins, the draft order starts with the team that is due to draft next after the completion of the first round.

Alternate Method for Plan B: Instead of having two separate drafts (one for returning players, and one for new players), a league may elect to conduct a regular draft wherein, if a number of returning Major League players has not been drafted by the time that same number of draft picks remain, those returning players must be the only players eligible from that point forward in the draft. (Example: With nine picks left in the draft, there are nine players who were Major League players in the previous season still not drafted for the current year. Those nine players become the only nine eligible players, and must be drafted.)

Plan C - Blind Draft Method

Step 1: Decide how many Major teams your league will operate for the season. Take the number of eligible 12-year-olds that signed up that opted for Major level play and divide by the number of Major teams.

Step 2: Each manager is assigned a team name (i.e., Rockies, Padres, etc.) and allowed to place their child/children on the roster. No 10-year-olds should be placed on any roster until all other eligible 12- and 11-year-olds are given a roster spot.

Step 3: All eligible 12-year-old names are placed in a non-transparent container; a single name is selected at random and placed on the next team's roster. Each name is drawn and placed on the next team roster until all 12-year-olds have been selected.

NOTE: According to Regulation V - Selection of Players, all candidates who are league age twelve (12) must be drafted to a Little League (Major) Division, Intermediate (50-70) Division (baseball), and/or a Junior League team(s) in accordance with Regulation IV(a).

Step 4: All eligible 11-year-olds that would like to be considered for play at the Major level are placed in the non-transparent container. Each name is drawn out and placed on the next team roster until either all 11-year-old names have been selected, or the team roster is full.

Step 5: All eligible 10-year-olds that would like to be considered for play at the Major level are placed in the non-transparent container. Each name is drawn out and placed on the next team roster until either all 10-year-old names have been selected, or the team roster is full.

Step 6: All eligible 9-year-olds that would like to be considered for play at the Major level are placed in the non-transparent container. Each name is drawn out and placed on the next team roster until either all 9-year-old names have been selected, or the team roster is full.

Methods for Local Leagues in their First Year of Operation

Plan A - Serpentine Draft Plan

The managers draw numbers to determine who will select the first player. In a new four-team league, the manager who draws number one makes the following player selections: 1st choice, 8th, 9th, 16th, 17th, 24th, 25th, etc.; The manager who draws number two makes the 2nd choice, 7th, 10th, 18th, 23rd, etc.; The manager who draws number three, 3rd choice, 6th, 11th, 14th, 19th, 22nd; The manager who draws number four, 4th choice, 5th, 12th, 13th, 20th, 21st, etc., until selections are complete.

Plan B - Team Draft Plan

Another way of balancing the teams in the first year is to use a plan developed with success in some communities. Under this plan, the manager and coaches of all the teams select the best players during the tryouts for the regular league. Normally, they select at least 60 players (four-team league) in the age pattern desired (**Example:** 32 twelve-year-olds, 20 eleven-year olds and eight nine or ten-year-olds.)

Managers and coaches should attempt to divide the players into four teams of equal strength, with the player agent coordinating the activity. When they play several practice games to double-check their judgment, and make any switches of players between teams which seem desirable, the teams are numbered and the managers draw the numbers out of a hat to determine which team each will manage the next season. In this plan, an equitable understanding must be established to permit a manager to acquire a son or daughter for that manager's team by a player trade if this seems desirable.

Plan C - Blind Draft Plan

Step 1: Decide how many Major teams your league will operate for the season. Take the number of eligible 12-year-olds that signed up that opted for Major level play and divide by the number of Major teams.

Step 2: Each manager is assigned a team name (i.e., Rockies, Padres, etc.) and allowed to place their child/children on the roster. No 10-year-olds should be placed on any roster until all other eligible 12- and 11-year-olds are given a roster spot.

Step 3: All eligible 12-year-old names are placed in a nontransparent container; a single name is selected at random and placed on the next team's roster. Each name is drawn and placed on the next team roster until all 12-year olds have been selected.

NOTE: According to Regulation V - Selection of Players, all candidates who are league age twelve (12) must be drafted to a Little League (Major) Division, Intermediate (50-70) Division (baseball), and/or a Junior League team(s) in accordance with Regulation IV(a).

Step 4: All eligible 11-year-olds that would like to be considered for play at the Major level are placed in the non-transparent container. Each name is drawn out and placed on the next team roster until either all 11-year-old names have been selected, or the team roster is full.

Step 5: All eligible 10-year-olds that would like to be considered for play at the Major level are placed in the non-transparent container. Each name is drawn out and placed on the next team roster until either all 10-year-old names have been selected, or the team roster is full.

Step 6: All eligible 9-year-olds that would like to be considered for play at the Major level are placed in the non-transparent container. Each name is drawn out and placed on the next team roster until either all 9-year-old names have been selected, or the team roster is full.

OPTIONS ON SONS, DAUGHTERS, AND SIBLINGS

An option is an agreement between a manager and the player agent covering a special condition. All options must be in writing (except No. 1) and be submitted to the player agent 48 hours prior to the draft. The options are as follows:

1. **Brothers/Sisters in the Draft**

   When there are two or more siblings in the draft, and the first brother or sister is drafted by a manager, that manager automatically has an option to draft the other brother or sister on the next turn. If the manager does not exercise the option, the second sibling is then available to be drafted by any team.

2. **Brothers/Sisters of Players Currently on a Team**

   If desired, a manager shall submit an option in writing on a draftee if the player candidate's brother or sister is a member of that manager's team. If such an option is submitted, the manager MUST draft the sibling within the first three draft selections.

3. **Sons/Daughters of Managers**

   If a manager has sons and/or daughters eligible under Regulation II for the draft, and wishes to draft them, he/she must submit the option in writing. If so stated, the parent/manager is required to exercise the option at or before the close of the specific draft round, depending on the League Age of sons and/or daughters. Parent/manager option takes priority over any other option.

NOTE: These provisions also apply for managers having eligible brothers or sisters in the draft.

4. **Sons/Daughters of Coaches**

   A NEW coach shall not be appointed nor approved until after the draft to avoid "Red Shirting" of players through selective coaching appointments.

   A returning coach, through the manager, may exercise an option in writing to the player agent provided:

   (A) The coach has served as a manager or coach in the league (at any level) for the past two years AND,

   (B) The coach is returning to the same Major League team as last year.

   IMPORTANT: In order for a manager to exercise this option, the coach must qualify under BOTH conditions above.

5. **Draft Rounds**

   If an option is submitted in writing for the son and/or daughter of a manager or coach, such candidate must be drafted in or before the following round:

   BASEBALL

Draft Round	Little League	Intermediate	Junior	Senior
5	9-10	11	12	14, 13
4	11	12	13	15
3	12	13	14	16

   SOFTBALL

Draft Round	Little League	Junior	Senior
5	9-10	12	14, 13
4	11	13	15
3	12	14	16

6. **Special Considerations Which Apply**

   (A) If the manager so chooses, the option on son or daughter may be waived.

   (B) In the event the parent becomes a manager in another league, that parent may not claim the son or daughter.

   (C) Players are eligible only in the league whose boundaries include the parent/manager's home residence (as defined by Little League).

   (D) When a vacancy occurs during the playing season, the player selected to fill the vacancy becomes a permanent member of that team, governed by the same regulations as all members of the team selected in the draft.

   (E) All players, including sons/daughters of managers and coaches at the Minor League level, are subject to the draft.

(F)   Parents of Major League players who become managers or coaches after their children have been selected to a Major team may not automatically claim their sons or daughters, but may trade for them at the proper time, subject to requirements for trading in the next section.

(**NOTE:** THE LITTLE LEAGUE DEFINITION OF RESIDENCE IS LOCATED IN THE "LITTLE LEAGUE RESIDENCY AND SCHOOL ATTENDANCE REQUIREMENTS" SECTION OF THIS RULEBOOKS.)

Alternate Method of Operation - The Regular Season

To aid leagues that are having a difficult time getting enough players for their regular season teams the following option is available:

A pool of players from existing regular season teams can be created with players that are willing to participate in extra games during the regular season when teams face a shortage of rostered players for a regular season game.

Guidelines:

1.   The league's player agent will create and run the pool. The league's player agent will use the pool to assign players to teams that are short of rostered players for a regular season game on a rotating basis from within their respective division.

2.   Managers and/or coaches will not have the right to randomly pick and choose players from the pool.

3.   Players used from the pool will not be allowed to pitch, except during the player's own regular season scheduled game.

4.   Pool players that are called and show up at the game site must play at least nine consecutive defensive outs and bat once.

For details on age alignments for Intermediate (50-70) Division/Junior/Senior League, see Regulation IV of the rulebooks.

LOCAL LEAGUE MAINTENANCE OF ROSTERS

Duration of Title

Each player acquired shall, for the duration of their Major Little League career, be the property of the team and league or division making the acquisition, unless subsequently traded or released. **NOTE:** When local league elects to utilize "Common Pool Draft Method" players shall remain property of the league or division making the acquisition. (**Exception:** If the league's Board of Directors opts to use the Plan B or Plan C draft method for existing leagues, all returning Major Division players must be drafted first, but are not required to be placed on the same team on which they participated previously.)

Regulation II(d) allows the Board of Directors to continue as a player any child whose residence changes after becoming a member of the league. (See the restrictions in the regulation.) However, the best interests of the child should be taken into consideration by the Board in exercising this right.

(**NOTE:** THE LITTLE LEAGUE DEFINITION OF RESIDENCE IS LOCATED IN THE "LITTLE LEAGUE RESIDENCY AND SCHOOL ATTENDANCE REQUIREMENTS" SECTION OF THIS RULEBOOK.)

Trading

Following the draft, managers may, if they desire, trade players until 14 days after the first scheduled game. ALL TRADES SHALL BE MADE THROUGH AND WITH THE APPROVAL OF THE PLAYER AGENT. The following restrictions also apply:

1. Minor League players may not be traded for Major Division players.

2. All trades must be player for player only. (**Example:** Two players from Team A could not be traded for one player on Team B.)

3. Trades involving a player for draft choices are not permitted. (**Example:** A manager cannot trade his/her right to pick the third player overall for an existing player on another team. However, once the draft is complete, a trade may be consummated, providing it meets all other criteria for trading.)

The player agent(s) must monitor any attempts by managers and parents to manipulate the system and thus create an imbalance in the league. ALL TRADES MUST BE FOR JUSTIFIABLE REASONS AND BE APPROVED BY THE LOCAL BOARD.

Replacements

When a player is lost to a team during the playing season for any of the following reasons:

1. He/she moves to another city or state too distant to commute for practice and play;

2. He/she is injured and will not be able to return to play within a reasonable period of time (local league board decision);

3. He/she has for personal reasons decided to terminate his/her association with the team;

4. Any other justifiable reason, reviewed and approved by the Board of Directors;

The manager of the team losing a player shall promptly advise the player agent. The player agent shall advise the president and the board. If loss of player is approved, the president will send a letter of release to the player and the parents stating player is released from the Major League team and the league for a justifiable reason. This action creates a legal opening for a replacement on the team roster.

The manager shall review the available player list with the player agent and shall select a replacement. The replacement becomes a permanent member of the team.

NOTE: Failure by the manager to advise the player agent of a player's continued absence should result in disciplinary action against the manager.

Expansion

Option One: When a league expands by four teams or more teams in one season, it is highly desirable that all of the players be placed in the player pool and the selecting start from "scratch." Many leagues have permitted the established teams to remain intact while giving the new team or teams an opportunity to fill their rosters from new players before the "old" teams select their replacements. When the "old" teams are permitted to retain a nucleus of experienced players, the new teams frequently lose a majority of games by lopsided scores and in too many cases go through a season without winning a single game. It often takes a new team two or three years to come up to league strength in this way, and thus creates an imbalance, an unhappy competitive situation and decreases possibilities for constructive experiences for the participants.

Option Two: If a league has a strong foundation, this expansion plan may seem adequate and less drastic. It may be better than starting from scratch.

When a league expands from four to five or more teams, it would be more beneficial to all concerned if each manager would give up, in a one team expansion, one 12-year-old, and one 11-year-old, and expanding into two teams to give up two 12, and two 11-year-olds. These players will then be placed in a common pool for selection by the new teams. This would give each new team a nucleus of older experienced players. Once this nucleus of eight players is established, the remainder of the teams would be filled through regular bidding or draft.

Option Three: This plan provides the most favorable competitive balance between existing teams at the Major League level over Options One and Two when a local league expands it's Major League to provide additional opportunity for more candidates to participate at the Major League level. Plan Three incorporates many basic features of a plan used successfully in professional baseball. This plan simply has every existing team placing players in a player pool from which the new expansion teams will draft players in a preliminary draft.

The player pool is formed by the following procedure:

1. The team with the fewest returning players will place one player into the pool and in doing so, will establish the key to the number of players all other teams can retain.

   For example, let's assume a division expanding from five teams to six:

   Major Team A has four returning players — contributes one player to expansion pool;
   Major Team B has five players returning — contributes two players to expansion pool;
   Major Team C has five returning players — contributes two players to expansion pool;
   Major Team D has six players returning — contributes three players to expansion pool;
   Major Team E has six returning players — contributes three players to expansion pool;

2. In one-team expansion using this example, the expansion team manager chooses three players in a preliminary draft. All players remaining in the Major League expansion player pool then return to their original teams. (If the expansion is by two teams, each chooses three players, alternating picks.)

3. The regular draft of Minor League players will then begin with the expansion team(s) drafting first in each round. The established teams then draft in reverse order of the finish in last year's schedule.

4. Any trading of players, which may be a necessity, will follow immediately after the draft has been completed. Trading of players can continue until the 14th day after the start of the playing season.

Team Reduction

If the number of teams is to be reduced at the Major League level, the Board of Directors decides which team is to be deleted from the division. All current Major League players affected must be reassigned to a Major League team by one of these two methods:

A.   Through a preliminary draft (reverse order of finish) prior to the regular player draft involving new candidates. Once the preliminary draft is complete, the regular player draft starts over in the reverse order of finish, without regard to the last team to pick; or,

B.   Through a regular draft wherein, if a number of returning Major League players has not been drafted by the time that same number of draft picks remain, those returning players must be the only players eligible from that point forward in the draft. (**Example:** The number of teams is reduced, putting six Major League players back into the draft. At the draft, with three selections left to be made, there are three players from the six returnees who have not yet been drafted. Those three players become the only three eligible players, and must be drafted.)

Divisional Play

When a league charters more than 10 teams in their Major League or when required by action of the Charter Committee, it is necessary to form two divisions (usually an American and National Division). This is accomplished by one of these four methods:

1.   Divide all candidates within the division by odd and even birthdates. For example, candidates with odd birthdates are assigned to the American Division and even birthdates to the National Division. This method could result in an imbalance of candidates and talent during a particular year, and could require members of the same family to participate in separate divisions.

2.   Use the first letter of the last name (surname or family name) to separate candidates between the two divisions. Under this method, the letters A-L would be assigned to one division and M-Z to the other. Like the first method, this could result in an imbalance of candidates and talent. However, it generally results in members of the same family remaining in the same division.

3.   Using a geographical alignment, the players in each division are separated by a boundary line within that of the league itself. Like the first three methods, this could result in an imbalance of candidates and talent.

4.   All teams in both divisions draft from all eligible candidates using the "Common Pool Draft Method." Teams select players alternately between the divisions. This always results in a balance of candidates, and offers a better chance for equal talent distribution between the two divisions.

NOTE: Once a candidate is league age 9 years old or is enrolled for the first time after the candidate attains the league age of 9 and is assigned and/or drafted into a specific division (**Example** - American/National), the candidate cannot transfer to the opposite division(s) during their entire Little League career. This means that a candidate assigned and/or drafted to a Minor or Major League team in the American Division cannot transfer to a National Division team. If the player moves between divisions, they will be deemed ineligible for tournament play. If a league decides to redraft in any form or trade players, this note still applies.

Under any method, players already assigned to Major League teams can be retained by their teams, if the League decides to do so, by application of Regulation II(d) and/or IV(h). Forms for requesting waivers under either of these regulations must be filed annually.

Interleague Play can be requested. However, each division must field its own Tournament Team.

Forms for Divisional Play are available from the Regional Office. Whatever method is used must be approved annually in writing from the Charter Committee before implementation. When leagues receive Charter Committee approval to either operate in divisional format or to operate more than one league under a single management, there can be no transfer of Major Division players between divisions or leagues without written approval of the Charter Committee in Williamsport.

DIVIDING A LEAGUE

It may become necessary to divide the league — thus creating two chartered leagues. Such a division can be accomplished easily and requires no extra fields for play. Under any method, a single Board of Directors can operate both charters, if recommended by the District Administrator and approved by the Charter Committee.

This realignment can be accomplished by one of five methods:

1. Reduce boundaries to include a smaller population. This is the least desirable method, unless some accommodation is made for the population no longer in the league boundaries.

2. Divide the League's service area geographically to provide for two charter areas. This is the most desirable method, particularly if the "new" league is afforded playing fields within its new boundaries.

3. Divide all candidates by odd and even birthdates. For example, candidates with odd birthdates are assigned to the American League and even birthdates to the National League. This method could result in an imbalance of candidates and talent during a particular year and could require members of the same family to participate in separate leagues.

4. Use the first letter of the last name (surname or family name) to separate candidates between the two leagues. For example, candidates with last names beginning with A-L would be assigned to the American League and those with last names beginning with M-Z would be assigned to the National League. Like the previous method, this could result in an imbalance of candidates and talent. However, it generally results in members of the same family remaining in the same league.

5. All teams in both leagues draft from all eligible candidates using the "Common Pool Draft Method." Teams select players alternately between the leagues. This generally results in a balance of candidates, and offers a better chance for equal talent distribution between the two leagues.

   NOTE: Once a candidate is league age 9 years old or is enrolled for the first time after the candidate attains the age of league age 9 and is assigned and/or drafted into a specific league (Example - American/National), the candidate cannot transfer to the opposite league(s) during their entire Little League career. This means that a candidate assigned and/or drafted to a Minor or Major League team in the American League cannot transfer to a National League team. If the player moves between leagues, they will be deemed ineligible for tournament play. If a league(s) decides to redraft in any form or trade players, this note still applies. A sibling of a player already assigned to a specific division is eligible to be drafted to the same division once the player attains league age of 9 or is enrolled by the league for the first time.

Under any method, players already assigned to Major League teams can be retained by their teams, if the League decides to do so, by application of Regulation II(d) and/or IV(h). Forms for requesting waivers under either of these regulations must be filed annually.

Interleague Play can be requested. However, each league/division must field its own Tournament Team(s).

Forms for Dividing a League are available from the Regional Office. Whatever method is used must be approved in writing from the Charter Committee before implementation.

NOTE 1: A league wishing to apply for a waiver of Regulation II(g), or any rule or regulation, must do so via the method prescribed in the "Little League Policies and Principles" chapter of this book, in the "Waivers of Rules and Regulations" section.

NOTE 2: When leagues have received Charter Committee approval to operate multiple leagues under a single management, there can be no transfer of Major Division players between leagues without written approval of the Charter Committee in Williamsport.

LOCAL LEAGUE ELECTION PROCEDURES

These recommended procedures conform to the Sample Constitution. If followed, they will result in fewer accusations of "election rigging" and, possibly, fewer chances of lawsuits.

1.   The first step should actually be taken at least a month before the election.

2.   Establish a Nominating Committee, which should consist of at least three board members and any number of regular members. The Nominating Committee's purpose is to ensure that there will be enough persons interested in being on the Board of Directors to fill all the possible positions. Its purpose is NOT to limit the potential number of nominees. It should also attempt to ensure that there are enough persons interested in individual positions as officers on the board.

3.   Proper written notice stating date, place and time shall be given to all regular members in good standing ten (10) days in advance of the date the election is to be held.

4.   All regular members must have paid their membership dues and have in their possession their membership I.D. Cards plus they must be active and be in good standing to be eligible to vote and/or become a nominee for election to the Board of Directors.

5.   Absentee ballots may be obtained IN PERSON from the Secretary. The ballots should have a number of blank lines equal to the maximum number of persons who could serve on the Board of Directors that year. The absentee voter then fills in the number of names desired IN ORDER OF PREFERENCE. The ballot should then be returned IN PERSON to the Secretary IN A SEALED ENVELOPE to be delivered to the Election Chairman at the meeting, still in the sealed envelope. (**NOTE:** Because Robert's Rules of Order no longer recommends it, proxy voting is to be discouraged in local Little League elections.)

6. When the election portion of the annual meeting takes place, the first order of business is to determine if a quorum is present. Quorum for many leagues is one-third of the total registered regular members, or a number of percentage acceptable to the local league regular membership at a meeting in advance of the annual meeting.

7. Once quorum is established, it is proper to determine how many members are to be elected to the board. The local constitution establishes a number that should be elected but this number can be increased or decreased depending on need by a two-thirds majority of the membership present.

8. After the number of Directors to be elected has been determined, the nominating committee will report and present the established required number of candidates who have been screened and have accepted to serve if elected.

9. After the nominating committee's report is accepted, the nominations shall be opened to the floor and any regular member may nominate another regular member as a candidate for election to the Board of Directors.

10. After the membership present has completed their efforts to nominate additional members, the nomination procedure will be closed by affirmation of the membership.

11. Every regular member will receive one ballot and will list names of eligible candidates in the number to be elected determined previously in the meeting.

12. The appointed Election Chairman, the clerks and tellers will gather and count the ballots. The total number of ballots shall be no more than the number of members present, except if the league has a provision for absentee ballots and which have been properly obtained and returned to the Secretary of the league in a sealed envelope prior to the election.

13. The persons in the number specified to be elected who have the highest number of votes by a majority vote (50 percent +1 or more) shall become the new Board of Directors. The only exception is the number of managers and coaches elected to the board must be a minority. (Regulation I (b))

14. Following the election, the board shall meet as a body and elect the officers of the board from within the membership of the board.

15. The Secretary of the board, as the first official responsibility, shall notify Little League International, the Regional Director and the District Administrator of the election and the identity of the officers so proper communications may commence with the new Board of Directors on or after October 1st, or whenever the fiscal cycle begins for the local league.

THE OFFICIAL SHOULDER PATCH

The Little League Official Shoulder Patch is the only recognized identification which sets a Little Leaguer apart from all other children who play baseball and softball. The patch symbolizes the affiliation with the Little League program and a reminder of the mission of promoting sportsmanship, discipline, teamwork, and physical well-being for the millions of Little Leaguers around the world. The Official Shoulder Patch affixed to the uniform prevents confusion in public identification, especially in news images that reference Little League programs.

Use of the Official Patch is mandatory for all divisions of Little League for both regular season and tournament play.

 Worn centered on the left shoulder sleeve; Patches centered over left chest on sleeveless style.

Patches are worn centered on players' left shoulder sleeves, or centered on the left chest of sleeveless jerseys. The Umpire patch is worn 4" below the left shoulder seem on the left sleeve. The Umpire jacket patch is also placed on the left sleeve, 4" below the shoulder seam.

The Tee Ball Baseball patch, Little League Baseball patch (Minor and Major Divisions), Intermediate (50-70) Division patch, Junior League Baseball patch, Senior Baseball League patch, Tee Ball Softball patch, Little League Softball patch (Minor and Major Divisions), Junior League Softball patch, Senior League Softball patch, Little League Challenger patch, Senior League Challenger patch, and Umpire patches can only be ordered through Little League International (LittleLeagueStore.net or call 800-874-2852).

NOTE: Screen-printing, sublimation, or reproduction of the Patch in any form is not permitted and is a violation of trademark rights. Any abuses should be reported immediately to Little League International at Licencing@LittleLeague.org.

LITTLE LEAGUE POLICIES AND PRINCIPLES
Principles of Conduct

The vitality and growth of any major youth program is dependent upon its integrity and its individual entity. To the extent that the time and energies of its members are diverted to other similar activities, the more limited will be its prospects for continuing success. Failure to maintain an identifiable organization, responsibility for which remains separate and distinct from others, inevitably will result in a loss of public enthusiasm and, ultimately in a process of declining interest and support.

Little League traces its current status as an outstanding youth organization to the unwavering devotion of the many thousands of persons who have unselfishly given their utmost support to the development of leagues in communities throughout the world.

If Little League is to maintain its present stature and develop its fullest potential, the adult participants, both new and old, must recognize their responsibility in observing certain general principles:

Code

1. No officer or board member of a Little League and no District Administrator or other representative of a group of Little Leagues shall, at the same time, hold office or be a member of the Board of any other youth baseball/softball league or function as an official or representative of such a program.

2. No corporate or business entity should raise funds in the name of the league or District without active league participation and decision making.

3. Cooperative solicitation of funds is discouraged. If fundraising with other community organizations, receipts from any general community solicitation should be distributed equitably among participating organizations according to a formula established at the outset and publicly disclosed at the time of the solicitation. In no event should any solicitation be made in the name of Little League in a manner which may create the impression in the minds of the public that the funds received will be devoted to Little League purposes in greater amount than is the actual fact. All funds due to local Little League from any cooperative solicitation shall promptly be turned over to the officers of such leagues without condition or limitation.

4. The loan, sale or any commercial use of Little League records, including lists of players, coaches, umpires or volunteers and/or their addresses by any officer or director of a Little League or by a District Administrator is considered highly inappropriate, is contrary to Little League policy and is strictly prohibited.

5. Little League has, on many occasions, expressed support and commitment to the principle of equal employment opportunity. It is our policy to recruit, hire, train, and promote individuals, as well as to administer any and all personnel actions, without regard to race, color, religion, age, sex, sexual orientation, national origin or ancestry, marital status, status as a disabled or Vietnam Era Veteran, or status as a qualified handicapped individual, in accordance with applicable law. This statement applies to volunteers as well as employees.

In this regard, we have developed a Sexual Harassment Policy for league and District Administrator operation. Consequently, any incident or situation that you believe involves discrimination or harassment of a sexual nature or otherwise should be immediately investigated for corrective action. If necessary, in accordance with the Sexual Harassment Policy, it should be brought to the immediate attention through proper channels to your Regional Director who will contact the Little League International Chief Legal Counsel. Investigation and any corrective action that Little League International determines is appropriate, up to and including dismissal is done so at the organizations discretion.

Little League will not tolerate any unlawful discrimination or harassment and such conduct is prohibited. In this regard, the following Sexual Harassment Policy is for your implementation.

SEXUAL HARASSMENT POLICY

A. **Policy:** It is the policy of Little League International that all of the parties involved in the operation of chartered Little Leagues will provide a League and District Administrator operational environment which is free of all forms of discrimination including incidents of sexual harassment. No individual shall be subjected to verbal or physical sexual behavior. Sexual harassment will be treated as misconduct, and may result in the application of appropriate corrective action up to and including dismissal.

B. **Definition:** Sexual harassment is unwelcome, unsolicited behavior of a sexual nature which creates a hostile environment and/or interferes with an individual's ability to do their duties. Examples of sexual harassment could include but are not limited to, the following:

1. Unwelcome behavior.

2. Repeatedly asking a person for a date.

3. Making suggestive or provocative comments of a sexual nature and/or displaying sexual visuals.

4. Suggestive looks or leering.

5. Creating an intimidating, hostile or offensive operational environment.

6. Making acceptance or rejection of sexual advance

7. Retaliating against any person reporting instances of sexual harassment.

C. **Report Procedures:**

1. Any person who believes they have been sexually harassed shall contact their immediate superior or the official in charge of the Organization, except as noted in C-3.

2. If a complaint of sexual harassment is made directly to a superior, the superior shall contact the official in charge of the Organization before taking action.

3. If the allegation of sexual harassment is made against the person's immediate superior, the complainant shall contact the Organization Head above the alleged harasser or the official in charge of the Organization, or depending on the level of the complaint, the Regional Director.

4. If the complaint of sexual harassment is handled informally, the superior will document their actions and forward, through channels, to the official in charge of the Organization.

5. If a full investigation is requested or required, the complainant shall contact the official in charge of the Organization, and through channels the Regional Director and Little League International Chief Legal Counsel.

6. Any subsequent complaints of a similar nature against an individual, including those involving a different person, shall require a full investigation.

D. **Responsibilities** - Organization Heads and Official Parties shall:

1. Monitor the League and District Administrator operational environment to ensure that it is free of sexual harassment.

2. Ensure incidents of sexual harassment are processed in accordance with this policy.

3. Take immediate action to guard against any adverse impact or reprisals against any person who uses this procedure.

4. Ensure that parties under their position do not engage in any type of sexual harassment.

5. Ensure that confidentiality of reports of sexual harassment is maintained.

6. Consult the official in charge of the Organization for guidance in all sexual harassment matters, and that official, if necessary, will consult for guidance through channels, the Regional Director and Little League International Chief Legal Counsel.

To these general principles of conduct, we trust all other youth baseball and softball programs will subscribe in the conduct of their own activities.

CONFLICT OF INTEREST POLICY

It is considered critical that Members of the Board, Officers of Little League Baseball, Incorporated, Committee Members, Employees, District Administrators, Assistant District Administrators, and all Field Personnel shall not engage in any activity which gives rise to, or could give rise to, an appearance or claim of self-dealing, divided loyalty or conflict of interest by reason of such person's position with Little League International.

In the event such person has reason to believe his or her activities or anticipated activities could give rise to any such claim, he or she shall have a duty to disclose such activities or anticipated activities to the Board of Directors.

In the event any such person may either directly or indirectly be a party to or be in any manner financially interested in any contract or agreement with Little League International for any matter, cause or thing, such contract or agreement shall be made in violation of this Policy and the same shall be null and void.

In addition, any such person violating this Policy will be subject to Article VII of the By-Laws of Little League International, entitled "Disciplining Members, Directors, Officers, and Field Personnel." Article XII provides for disciplinary action including but not restricted to removal or suspension, for any act, conduct or involvement contrary to the rules, regulations, and policies of the corporation or which might tend to bring the Corporation into disrepute, or for any failure to perform properly the duties and responsibilities assigned to each person.

LITTLE LEAGUE CHILD PROTECTION PROGRAM

The entire Little League family, from the Little League International staff to the volunteers, knows that the greatest treasure we have is our children. As adults, we want to ensure that these young people are able to grow up happy, healthy and, above all, safe. Whether they are our children, or the children of others, each of us has a responsibility to protect them. They are our future, and an endless source of joy.

Unfortunately, there are those among us who would seek to do harm to these children, to rob them of their right to feel safe and grow up in a free and healthy environment. These are child abusers, and although it is not an easy or pleasant topic for any of us to think about, the fact remains that child abuse happens. Like many national youth organizations, Little League seeks to attract the most qualified and enthusiastic volunteers to assist our programs. At the same time, we must be aware that this could make us a target for child abusers, since statistics show that the largest number of sexually abused children range in age from 8 to 11 years. Clearly, dealing with child abuse is a major concern for everyone involved in Little League.

Since Little League could not exist without the time and effort that volunteers and parents donate, it is important to communicate directly with the volunteers. For that reason, this statement on the Little League Child Protection Program should be freely copied and distributed to all adults in the local league.

Defining child abuse is the first step in battling it. Child abuse can take several different forms, and it is important for us to make clear right at the start what the prevention goal of the Little League Child Protection Program is.

Definition of Child Sexual Abuse

Child sexual abuse can be defined as "the exploitation of a child by an older child, teen, or adult for the personal gratification of the abusive individual." This form of abuse could involve a range of sexual activities, from touching to non-touching offenses, and may also include acts that are considered non-sexual, but are done for the gratification of the abuser. This might include talking to a child in a sexually explicit way, voyeurism, or exposure of genitalia to a victim and/or victim's exposure of his or her genitalia.

A crucial step in stopping child abuse before it happens is knowing who might be a child abuser, and where child abuse might happen. For better or worse, the answer to each question is simple. Where can it happen? Anywhere. Who could be a child abuser? Anyone. However, we needn't feel that this makes our task impossible.

The National Center for Missing and Exploited Children® (NCMEC), a leading national child protection advocacy group, defines child abuse as "the physical or emotional injury of a child (17 years old or younger) by a person who is responsible for the child's welfare." Although Little League recognizes emotional abuse as a serious offense that should never be tolerated within the organization, the primary objective of this program is more specific: the protection of Little Leaguers from child sexual abuse, as well as the protection of all adults in the organization from being placed in difficult or uncomfortable situations with the children in their care.

Myths and Stereotypes

Child abuse knows no social, economic, or geographic boundaries, but there are a number of statistics at our disposal to help us identify warning signals. What we need to do is separate these facts from the stereotypes that have surrounded child abuse for many years. Let's take a look at some of the fiction and fact.

"Sex abusers are dirty old men." Not true. While sex abusers cut across socioeconomic levels, educational levels and race, the age of sex offenders are, more often than not, in their 30s.

"Strangers are responsible for most of the sexual abuse." Not true again. Fact: 80 to 85 percent of all sexual abuse cases in the US are committed by an individual familiar to the victim. Less than 20 percent of all abusers are strangers.

"Most sex abusers suffer from some form of serious mental illness or psychosis." Not true. The actual figure is more like 10 percent, almost exactly the same as the figure found in the general population of the United States.

"Most sex abusers are homosexuals." Also not true. Most are heterosexual.

"Children usually lie about sexual abuse, anyway." Not true. In fact, children rarely lie about being sexually abused. If they say it, don't ignore it.

"It only happens to girls." Again, not true. While females do comprise the largest number of sexual abuse victims, it is now believed that the number for male victims is much higher than reported.

And this last item on our list points to one of the greatest obstacles in identifying sexual abuse cases: Sexual abuse is shrouded in secrecy. This is because often abusers scare children into silence by saying things like: "This must be our secret-if you tell, something awful will happen."

Child victims are made to feel as though they've brought the abuse upon themselves; they're made to feel guilty. For these reasons, sexual abuse victims seldom disclose the victimization. Children need to understand that it's never their fault, and both children and adults need to know what they can do to keep it from happening.

Education/Prevention of Child Abuse

Education is the most important tool for both our children and our adults. It empowers them to recognize potentially compromising situations, and it places a barrier between abusers and their victims. Here are a few education and prevention suggestions for our Little League volunteers and children.

Meet with them. Since Little League operates with a number of volunteers, our membership changes from year to year. Thus, it is important to hold regular meetings in which both volunteers and parents can talk about child abuse, and ask questions.

Make our position clear. Little League has a clearly defined policy for dealing with child abuse. Make adults and kids aware that Little League will not tolerate child abuse in any form. Suspected abuse must be reported and retaliation for good faith reporting is prohibited.

Stress the role of adults. Children should be encouraged to take an active role in protecting themselves, but ultimately the responsibility for ensuring their safety rests with us, the grown-ups. We are better able to identify potentially uncomfortable situations, for ourselves as well as for them. The welfare of our Little Leaguers is the highest priority in any situation.

Encourage the "Buddy system." It's an old maxim, but it's true: There is safety in numbers. Encourage our kids to move about in groups of two or more children of similar age, whether an adult is present or not. This includes travel, leaving the field, or using the rest room areas. It's far more difficult to victimize a child if they're not alone. Adopt additional reasonable procedures to limit one-on-one interactions between minor athletes and an adult. All interactions between minors and adults should be observable and within an interruptible distance of another adult.

Provide additional information. There are a number of organizations that will gladly assist our efforts to protect our young people, several of which are listed below. Feel free to give these names, numbers and addresses to parents and volunteers, as well as kids.

U.S. Center for SafeSport
1385 South Colorado Blvd., Suite A-706
Denver, CO 80222
SafeSport.org

National Center for Missing and Exploited Children
2101 Wilson Boulevard
Arlington, VA 22201-3052
800-THE-LOST (843-5678)
MissingKids.com
SafetoCompete.org

National Children's Advocacy Center
Visit NationalCAC.org/find-a-cac/ to find a center near you.

Nonprofit Risk Management Center
1001 Connecticut Avenue, NW, Suite 900
Washington, DC 20036
202-785-3891
NonprofitRisk.org

General Guidelines

In addition, the basic safety procedures that Little League follows as a general rule can also be applied specifically to the identification and prevention of child abuse situations. Adhered to properly, these guidelines can enable children and adults to better protect themselves.

Rides — Children dropped off too early or picked up late are targets. Little League parents and volunteers should be encouraged to pick up and drop off on time. And children should be warned about strangers; about not riding with them, about telling someone if they're approached by them.

Access — Controlling access to areas where children are present, such as the dugout or locker rooms, protects them from harm by outsiders. It's not easy to control the access of large outdoor facilities, but visitors could be directed to a central point within the facility. Individuals should not be allowed to wander through the area without the knowledge of the Little League volunteers.

Lighting — Child sexual abuse is more likely to happen in the dark. The lighting of fields, parking lots, and any and all indoor facilities where Little League functions are held should be bright enough so that participants can identify individuals as they approach, and observers can recognize abnormal situations.

Travel — When traveling with the team, make sure that children are sharing rooms with Little Leaguers of the same age. Girls' rooms should not be adjacent to boys' rooms, and rooms should not have adjoining access, either between children or children and adults.

Shower and Toilet Facilities — Most Little Leaguers are capable of using toilet facilities on their own, so there should be no need for an adult to accompany a child into restroom areas. There can sometimes be special circumstances under which a child requires assistance to toilet facilities, for instance within the Tee Ball and Challenger divisions, but there should still be adequate privacy for that child. Again, we can utilize the "buddy system" here.

Rooting Out Child Abuse — A Five-Step Screening Process

Once we know what child abuse is, and where to look for it, we are better able to prevent potential child abusers from entering the ranks of Little League. Another aspect of this prevention is screening all applicants who wish to be managers, coaches, Board of Directors and any other persons, volunteers and/or hired workers who provide regular services to the league and/or have repetitive access to, or contact with, players or teams.

The term "volunteer" in this context refers to every person in the organization coming in contact with the kids: program workers, coaches, bus and carpool drivers, maintenance workers, etc. The goal is to find caring, competent individuals who can provide a safe, positive climate for Little Leaguers.

Little League requires a five-step process for selecting individuals to fill volunteer positions:

1. **Application** - All local leagues are required to use the Little League Official Volunteer Application for all Managers, Coaches, Board of Directors and any other persons, volunteers and/or hired workers who provide regular service to the league and/or have repetitive access to, or contact with players or teams. The Little League Official Volunteer Application is available online at LittleLeague.org. The applicant must also submit a government issued photo ID, usually a driver's license, in order for the league to verify that the information on his/her volunteer application is correct, i.e. spelling of name, address, date of birth, etc.

2. **Background Check** - A background check in compliance with Regulation I(c) 8 and 9 must be conducted on every individual that is required to complete a volunteer application prior to the applicant assuming his/her duties for the current season. The individual is required to consent to a background check on the volunteer application. The local league must conduct a nationwide search that contains the applicable government sex offender registry data and criminal records. Information regarding free background check services is available at LittleLeague.org.

3. **Interview** - The applicant should be made fully aware of the position of Little League regarding child abuse. No person who is a known child-sex offender shall be allowed to participate in any manner in the Little League program.

4. **Reference Checks** - This is important to determine if any information from the references differs from that garnered from the volunteer application and/or during the course of the review.

5. **Exclusion of Certain Individuals** - No local league shall permit any person to participate in any manner, whose background check reveals a conviction for, guilty plea, no contest plea, or admission to any crime involving or against a minor. A local league may prohibit any individual from participating as a volunteer or hired worker, if the league deems the individual unfit or inappropriate to work or volunteer. The local league must conduct a nationwide search that contains the applicable government sex offender registry data and criminal records. If a potential volunteer appears on the National Sex Offender Registry, the league must contact the Security Manager at Little League International prior to appointing the volunteer to participate in any capacity in the league. **NOTE:** The United States Department of Justice National Sex Offender Public Registry is free and available at NSOPR.gov.

In addition, Little League requires all leagues to utilize the national criminal records search available through the Little League website. This additional criminal records check may provide additional important information regarding the criminal records of individuals whose crimes do not require that they be listed on a sex offender registry. If no sex offender registries exist in a province, or country outside the United States the local league must conduct a more extensive search of a country, province or city-wide criminal background check through the appropriate governmental agency unless prohibited by law. Failure to comply with this regulation may result in the suspension or revocation of tournament privileges and/or the local league's charter by action of the Charter or Tournament Committee in Williamsport. If a local league becomes aware of information, by any means whatsoever, that an individual, including, but not limited to, volunteers, players, and hired workers, has been convicted of, pled guilty, pled no contest, or admitted to any crime involving or against a minor, the local league must contact the applicable governmental agency to confirm the accuracy of the information. Upon confirmation of a conviction for, guilty plea, no contest plea, or admission to, a crime against or involving a minor, the local league shall not permit the individual to participate in any manner.

Additionally, the league president should inform the parents of all children who have had contact through the league with the excluded individual of any Public Record information that is the basis of the league's decision to exclude the individual. Public Records are documents received from a governmental body/agency that are available to the general public.

Volunteers are important to the operation of the local leagues. However, to protect the children involved in the local leagues, it is necessary to require the volunteers to complete a volunteer application and consent to a background check. In order to protect the privacy of volunteers, the following procedure has been established:

1. The local league president shall only share any personal non-public record information contained in the volunteer application or attached documents with other league officers in order to make personnel decisions.

2. The local league president should maintain the record of a volunteer for at least two (2) years after the volunteer is no longer in the league. When it comes time to dispose of these records, they should be shredded as they contain sensitive information. All actions concerning these records must comply with any applicable laws.

3. Leagues should also maintain records in the case that the league has taken action or made a decision based upon the information contained in the records. The records should be maintained in a locked and secure area, such as the president's home and not in a club house or similar facility.

Enforcement/Reporting Of Child Abuse

No matter how much education and prevention we put in place to stop child abuse, it can still happen. In the unfortunate instance that a case of child sexual abuse is suspected and/or reported, specific steps should be in place to deal with the situation. Let's take a look at these.

Reporting — Because child abuse reporting laws vary from state to state, a Federal law was recently enacted which established a nationwide standard duty to report suspected child abuse. The "Protecting Young Victims from Sexual Abuse and Safe Sport Act of 2017"mandates that all amateur sports organizations, which participate in an interstate or international amateur athletic competition and whose membership includes any adult who is in regular contact with an amateur athlete who is a minor must report suspected child abuse, including sexual abuse, within 24 hours to law enforcement. An individual who is required, but fails, to report suspected child sexual abuse is subject to criminal penalties. If an individual suspects a case of abuse within their league, they should report it to the appropriate child services organization and/or local law enforcement as well as their league president and District Administrator. Information regarding reporting child abuse can be found at LittleLeague.org. Go to the "Learn More" section and look under Risk Management.

Investigating — An individual and alternate with significant professional background should be chosen by the league from the community to receive and act on abuse allegations. These individuals will act in a confidential manner, and serve as the league's liaison with the local law enforcement community. Little League volunteers should not attempt to investigate suspected abuse on their own.

Suspending/Terminating — When an allegation of abuse is made against a Little League volunteer, it is the duty of the organization to protect the children from any possible further abuse by keeping the alleged abuser away from children in the program. If the allegations are substantiated, the next step is clear: Assuring that the individual will not have any further contact with the children in the league. The Nonprofit Risk Management Center urges Little League organizations to develop policies on suspension and termination of volunteers with a lawyer who can advise about their effects on the rights of the alleged abuser.

Immunity from liability — "Concern is often expressed over the potential for criminal or civil liability if a report of abuse is subsequently found to be unsubstantiated." However, we want adults and Little Leaguers to understand that they shouldn't be afraid to come forward in these cases, even if it isn't required and even if there is a possibility of being wrong. All states provide immunity from liability to those who report suspected child abuse in "good faith." At the same time, there are also rules in place to protect adults who prove to have been inappropriately accused. Little League policies prohibit retaliation of any kind when a good faith report of child abuse is made.

CHILD ABUSE - A FIVE-STEP REVIEW

Let's recap the steps you can take to protect your Little Leaguers:

1. Know what it is, and know where to look. Defining child abuse, and separating the truth from the myths, better enables us all to spot potentially dangerous situations.

2. Educate the Little League parents, volunteers, and children. They need to be supplied with the information necessary to protect everyone. Let the children know that it's never their fault.

3. Follow the safety procedures and guidelines outlined above. Employ basic rules, such as the "buddy system," to limit one-on-one interactions between minors and adults. These basic rules can lessen child abuse from happening in the first place.

4. Screen applicants carefully. An effective five-step screening process can keep potential child abusers out of our Little League programs, and keep our kids safe.

5. Don't be afraid to speak out. Both Little League children and adults need to feel safe to come forward. If an individual honestly feels something is wrong, the laws are in place to protect them.

QUESTIONS AND ANSWERS ABOUT THE CHILD PROTECTION PROGRAM

Q1. What do we, as a league, have to do to comply so that we can be chartered for the next season?

A: Since 2003, the local league has been required to have all board members, managers, coaches, and other volunteers or hired workers who provide regular service to the league and/or who have repetitive access to or contact with players or teams to fill out the Little League Official Volunteer Application. Additionally the league has been and is required to conduct a background check on each of these individuals. **IMPORTANT - A local Little League must conduct a nationwide background check utilizing J.D. Palatine (JDP) or another provider that is comparable to JDP in accessing background check records for sex offender registry data and other criminal records.** Little League Baseball and Softball will require each league to sign an agreement on the charter application that they will comply with Regulation I(b) and I(c) 8 & 9. The leagues are also required to sign a statement on the tournament enrollment form verifying that the process under the regulation has been completed and implemented. Failure to sign the agreement on the charter application will result in the league not being chartered and failure to fulfill the requirement of the regulations will result in the league's status being referred to the Charter/Tournament committee for action to revoke the league's charter and all privileges.

Q2. What type of background check is required by the new regulations?

A: **IMPORTANT - A local Little League must conduct a nationwide background check utilizing JDP or another provider that is comparable to JDP in accessing background check records for sex offender registry data and other criminal records.** This criminal records check may provide additional, important information regarding the criminal records of individuals whose crimes do not require that they be listed on a sex offender registry. The background check provider for United States leagues is JDP, which can be accessed by going to LittleLeague.org/Background. More information can be obtained by going to LittleLeague.org/ChildProtectionProgram. The first 125 checks through JDP are paid for by Little League International and are free to each chartered Little League. If additional checks are necessary, they will cost the league only $.95 per background check conducted.

Q3. What type of offenses are we screening for when we conduct a background check?

A: Local leagues are conducting a nationwide background check that includes sex offender registry data and other criminal records for anyone who has committed any type of offense involving minors. An individual who has been convicted of or plead guilty to charges involving or against a minor, no matter when the offense occurred, must not be permitted to work or volunteer.

Q4. Why is Little League changing the background check minimum requirement?

A: A background check that includes millions of criminal files in addition to national sex offender registry data will provide those individuals making personnel decisions that much more information in determining whether an applicant is acceptable and fit to volunteer, work, or participate in any manner within their local league program.

Q5. Why JDP?

A: Little League has partnered with JDP to provide local Little League programs a criminal background check tool. Through this partnership, each league and District is given 125 free background checks (paid for by Little League International) and any additional checks will only cost $.95 per check. The JDP National Criminal

File database contains more than 450 million records which include criminal records and sex offender registry records across 50 states and the District of Columbia. This program continues to be a great resource and value to local leagues.

Q6. Our league is required by the property owner (city, town, municipality, county, etc.) where we play our games and practices to conduct background checks approved by them on all of our volunteers and/or hired workers before we can use their fields. Are these checks acceptable and do they meet Little League's minimum requirements of Regulation I(c) 8 and 9?

A: No. Most checks required by these entities are local or state only checks which do not meet the Little League requirements. Also, the local league is responsible for conducting and reviewing the background check data and making their own personnel decisions per the regulations. Although the property owner has the right to determine who uses their facility, any decision they make as a property owner may or may not meet the Little League Regulations. **IMPORTANT - A local Little League must conduct a nationwide background check utilizing JDP or another provider that is comparable to JDP in accessing background check records for sex offender registry data and other criminal records.** Background checks must be completed on all Board Members, managers, coaches and other volunteers or hired workers who provide regular service to the league and/or who have repetitive access to players or teams.

Q7. Who in the local league should be responsible to process the background check information?

A: Little League Baseball and Softball recommends the Board of Directors appoint the local league president and two other individuals to handle the background checks. These individuals may be from the board or individuals outside the board. For instance, the Board of Directors may appoint individuals who have significant professional background in this area, such as law enforcement officers or individuals with a legal background.

Q8. What if an individual has previously had a background check?

A: Each league must conduct its own background check on the appropriate individuals annually.

Q9. What will result in termination of a volunteer under these regulations?

A: Any background check that reveals a conviction for, guilty plea, no contest plea, or admission to any crime involving or against a minor must result in immediate termination from the league. Additionally, volunteers who refuse to submit a fully completed Little League Volunteer Application, including their Social Security Number and a government issued photo ID, must be immediately terminated or eliminated from consideration for any position. This includes individuals with many years of service to your league unless the league has used the JDP Background Screening tool (available on the Little League website) in previous seasons. Those returning individuals can use the current Little League "Returning" Volunteer Application which does not require the Social Security Number or Date of Birth as those items are already included and redacted in the JDP program for returning volunteers.

Q10. What if offenses involving or against minors are pending prior to or after appointment to a position in the local league?

A: We suggest the individual not be appointed or should be suspended from his/her current position pending the outcome of the charges.

Q11. What if there are convictions or other offenses NOT involving or against minors?

A: Even though convictions or other offenses may not be against a minor, the local league Board of Directors still may deem these individuals as inappropriate and/or unfit and may prohibit him/her from working as a hired worker or volunteer within the league.

Q12. Who is to be made aware of the information found on the background check?

A: The local league president shall only share personal information contained in the volunteer application, background check or other information obtained through the screening process with other members of the Board of Directors in order to make personnel decisions. If the information obtained through the background check, is public record and causes an individual to not be appointed or to be terminated, Little League Baseball and Softball recommends this information be shared with the parents/guardians of the children who have had contact with the individual previously.

Q13. Where should these records be maintained and for how long?

A: The local league president shall retain each volunteer application, background check information, and any other documents obtained on file and maintain the record of a volunteer for at least two (2) years after the volunteer is no longer in the league. When it comes time to dispose of these records, they should be destroyed as they contain sensitive information. All actions concerning these records must comply with any applicable laws. Leagues should also maintain records in the case that the league has taken action or made a decision based upon the information contained in the records. The records should be maintained in a locked and secure area, such as the league president's home and not a club house or similar facility.

Q14. What is the timetable for completing the screening of each individual?

A: The league must complete the annual screening process prior to the individual assuming his/her duties for the current season. This would include the individual submitting a completed volunteer application and the league completing an appropriate background check. The applicant must also submit a government issued photo ID, usually a driver's license, in order for the league to verify that the information on his/her volunteer application is correct, i.e., spelling of name, address, date of birth, etc.

Q15. What resources are available through Little League Baseball and Softball to assist this process?

A: The current Little League Official Volunteer Application is available at LittleLeague.org/VolApp. **IMPORTANT - A local Little League must conduct a nationwide background check utilizing JDP or another provider that is comparable to JDP in accessing background check records for sex offender registry data and other criminal records.** The first 125 checks conducted through JDP are paid for by Little

League International and are free to each chartered Little League. If additional checks are needed, they will cost the league only $.95 per background check conducted. JDP can be accessed by going to LittleLeague.org/Background.

Q16. What will it cost my league to implement this initiative?

A: The first 125 checks conducted through JDP are paid for by Little League International and are free to each chartered Little League. If additional checks are needed, they will cost the league only $.95 per background check.

Q17. When should local leagues begin to conduct background checks on volunteers and hired workers?

A: In accordance with Little League Regulation I(c) 8 & 9, local leagues must conduct background checks on all volunteers and hired workers prior to the applicant assuming his or her duties for the season. Background checks must be completed on all individuals who are required to complete the "Little League Official Volunteer Application" and who provide a regular service to the league and/or have repetitive access to, or contact with, players and teams. This includes, but is not limited to, managers, coaches, Board of Director members, and other persons or hired workers.

Q18. Does this initiative also apply to those individuals that assist the manager and coaches at practices or games?

A: Yes. Any individual who provides regular service to the league or/and has repetitive access to or contact with players or teams must fill out the Volunteer Application with a Social Security Number, provide a copy of a government issued photo ID, and go through the background check process.

Q19. Who is going to coach the team if a screened manager or coach is no longer able to fulfill his/her duties?

A: Any permanent replacement cannot assume their duties until the volunteer application and background check has been completed. The league may temporarily assign a board member or another screened individual to fill the vacancy until the proper process and appointment has been made.

Q20. Should our league wait until the entire screening process has been completed to submit our Charter Application and Insurance Enrollment Form?

A: No. The appropriate league officers must sign the statement on the form agreeing to adhere to the new regulations requiring the use of the new volunteer application and background screening process as outlined in Regulations I(b) and I(c) 8 & 9. Once this section is completed the balance of the charter application can be completed and submitted to Little League Baseball and Softball.

Q21. As the league president or an official of the local league, how do I explain the need for this initiative?

A: These requirements were implemented in 2002 by Little League and your local league to:

1. protect our children and maintain Little League as a hostile environment for those who would seek to do them harm.

2. protect individuals and leagues from possible loss of personal or league assets because of litigation.

3. take advantage of current technology and laws that have made background check information accessible to your local league. This is an example of the revised mandatory Little League Volunteer Application. A version that can be filled out electronically and printed from your computer is available at LittleLeague.org.

LITTLE LEAGUE PARTICIPANT DISABILITY POLICY

Policy

Little League Baseball, Incorporated ("LLI") aims to promote fair play for all participants through the uniform adherence to LLI's Official Regulations and Playing Rules (the "Rules") concerning performance and play. Accordingly, all local leagues chartered by LLI pledge to abide by the Rules, and all updates thereto.

LLI encourages participation of all children, and acknowledges that some of its participants may require a modification of the Rules due to the participant claiming rights under the Americans with Disabilities Act (the "ADA"). In such instances, LLI will afford participants with a disability as defined by the ADA the opportunity to request modifications of the Rules. LLI is a non-discriminatory organization, and in considering such requests, LLI will ensure compliance with the ADA.

Procedure

The Charter and/or the Tournament Committee (the "Committee") at LLI considers all waiver requests to the Rules. The Committee will consider requests for a waiver to or modification of its Rules for an individual with a disability, upon the written request of the individual, his or her team coach, or his or her legal representative utilizing the procedure for such request as outlined below. LLI and its participating local leagues shall adhere to the Rules until a waiver for the participant is submitted and approved in accordance with this procedure.

A. Length of Waiver Requested

The Committee will consider a waiver request submitted by the participant in the season in which the waiver was received by the Committee. Unless otherwise requested by the participant, the Committee will consider and grant a modification of the Rules for only the season in which the waiver was received. If a participant requests a waiver be approved for longer than a single season, the Committee, in its sole discretion, may extend the waiver request beyond the season in which the request was received, including for the duration of a participant's LLI eligibility. If any waiver is approved by the Committee to extend beyond the season in which received, then the Committee shall identify the length and terms of such approval in the letter resolving the waiver request.

B. Materials Required for Committee's Consideration

In order to initiate review by the Committee, the participant, his/her team coach, or his or her legal representative, must deliver a written request for a waiver to the League President of the local league. The participant's waiver request shall include, at a minimum:

1. The LLI rule in question.

2. An identification of the participant's disability as defined under the ADA and a narrative asserting how the proposed modification of the Rule relates to his or her disability and participation in LLI.

3. Supporting evidence from a licensed physician regarding (a) the participant's disability; (b) duration of the disability; (c) activities limited by disability; and (d) individualized symptoms related to the disability.

4. An executed limited release of confidentiality and waiver of privacy signed by the participant's parent or legal guardian, which will allow the Committee to communicate with the participant's attending physician, health care profession, rehabilitation professional, or the licensed physician who provided the supporting statement outlined above. The release shall be restricted to authorize the Committee to (a) verify the participant's disability in question, and not the participant's broader health history or records; (b) identification of individualized symptoms and effects of the disability as it concerns the participant; and (c) medical professional's opinion concerning the modification of the Rule requested (the "Release"). The Committee will not exercise its rights under the Release until it determines, in its sole discretion, that the additional information to be provided through the Release is necessary to complete the waiver request. Upon such a determination, the Committee or its designee shall notify the participant's parent or legal guardian of its intent to communicate with the participant's attending physician, health care profession, rehabilitation professional, or the licensed physician.

5. If the participant is requesting the use or introduction of equipment into the field of play which is not otherwise permitted by the Rules, then the request shall specifically identify the make, model, and specifications of the equipment or apparatus seeking to be introduced into the field of play for the participant's benefit. All of LLI's specification standards referenced in a Rule are incorporated into the evaluation of the waiver request. Accordingly, equipment submitted by the disabled participant for the waiver request must meet LLI's performance requirements. All equipment used in the field of play must comply with LLI's Rules, until the participant seeking its introduction receives an approved waiver for use in the field of play. The Committee, in its discretion, may require testing of any equipment requested by the participant in the waiver, but not otherwise permitted by the Rules, to ensure compliance with performance standards. LLI will pay for the reasonable costs associated with testing of equipment required by the Committee to assess compliance with LLI's performance standards, as directed by the Committee.

C. Approval Process

Once the waiver materials are assembled on behalf of the participant, the request will be evaluated as follows:

1. The participant, or his or her representative, shall deliver the waiver materials to the President of the local league.

2. The President may add additional facts concerning the request received to the record for consideration by the Committee. Thereafter, the President shall forward the assembled materials to the District Administrator.

3. The District Administrator may add additional facts concerning the request received to the record for consideration by the Committee. Thereafter, the District Administrator shall forward the assembled materials to the Regional Director.

4. The Regional Director will present the waiver materials to the Committee for action.

5. The Committee will take action on the waiver request and inform the Regional Director of its decision. The Regional Director will thereafter inform the District Administrator,who in turn shall inform the President of the local league for dissemination to the participant.

D. Guidelines for Review

In order for the modification of a Rule to be approved, the Committee must first determine that the participant is disabled as defined under the ADA. Accordingly, the Committee is entitled to know that the participant has a covered disability for which a modification of the Rules is requested, and the information identified in Section B of procedure for inclusion with the waiver proposal is necessary to properly evaluate any such request.

The Committee will not grant a waiver when the requested accommodation is unreasonable under the circumstances, provides an unfair competitive advantage for the participant requesting the modification of the Rules, presents a threat to other participants or coaches, or alters the essential nature of the game. The Committee may consult with the participant, his or her representatives, coaches, and local league officials as part of considering the modification of the Rule.

E. Permitted Time for Committee's Decision

Any participant seeking a waiver request under this ADA waiver procedure should submit the request within a reasonable time after registering for participation in his/her local league. In the event the participant becomes disabled and claims rights under the ADA during the season, then the participant shall submit a waiver request outlined in this procedure within a reasonable period of time.

A request shall not be considered fully submitted unless it contains all of the contents. The Committee will strive to render a decision on all waiver requests within a reasonable amount of time, and all such decisions should be rendered no later than three (3) weeks after the request is fully submitted and received by the Committee, unless testing of equipment is directed by the Committee. If the waiver request concerns equipment or apparatus and the Committee directs testing of the equipment, then a review of the waiver request will involve testing the equipment or apparatus to ensure compliance with LLI's performance standards. Accordingly, the timeline for review of such an equipment waiver request will be dependent upon the requisite testing period. No equipment may be utilized by a participant unless the equipment complies with LLI's Rules or until the Committee approves the requested waiver for use of equipment.

LITTLE LEAGUE GENDER IDENTITY POLICY

Policy

Little League Baseball, Incorporated ("LLI") aims to promote fair play for all participants through the uniform adherence to LLI's Official Regulations and Playing Rules (the "Rules") concerning performance and play. Accordingly, all local leagues chartered by LLI pledge to abide by the Rules, and all updates thereto.

LLI encourages participation of all children, and acknowledges that some of its participants may require a modification or waiver of the Rules in order to participate in a manner consistent with their Gender Identity, irrespective of the gender listed on the child's birth certificate. In such instances, LLI will afford children who represent themselves as transgender children and/or children with a Disorder of Sexual Development the opportunity to request a modification or waiver of the Rules.

Definitions

For the purposes of this Policy and Procedure, the following definitions apply:

1. **Transgender Person:** refers to an individual whose Gender Identity does not match their assigned birth gender. Being Transgender does not imply any specific sexual orientation.

2. **Gender Identity:** One's inner concept of self as male or female or both or neither. One's Gender Identity can be the same or different than the gender assigned at birth.

3. **Gender Expression:** Refers to the ways in which people externally communicate their Gender Identity to others through behavior, clothing, haircut, voice, and other forms of presentation.

4. **Disorder of Sexual Development:** Also known as "DSD" or "Intersex" is a general term used to indicate a person born with a reproductive or sexual anatomy and/or chromosome pattern that does not fit the typical definitions of female or male. This may be the result of several different medical conditions involving chromosomal variations, hormonal variations, and/or anatomy that includes both male and female characteristics. DSD is not the same as Transgender, however, the two groups may face similar situations in needing to change gender designations for the purposes of participation in athletic activities.

Procedure

The Charter and/or the Tournament Committee (the "Committee") at LLI considers all waiver requests to the Rules. The Committee will consider requests for a waiver to or modification of its Rules for an individual whose Gender Identity does not match the gender listed on the child's birth certificate, upon the written request of the individual, their parent, or his or her legal representative utilizing the procedure for such request as outlined below. LLI and its participating local leagues shall adhere to the Rules until a waiver for the participant is submitted and approved in accordance with this procedure.

A. Length of Waiver

The Committee will consider a waiver request submitted on behalf of the child in the season in which the waiver was received by the Committee. Unless otherwise requested by the child, the Committee will consider and grant a modification of the Rules for only the season in which the waiver was received. If a child requests a waiver be approved for longer than a single season, the Committee, in its sole discretion, may extend the waiver grant beyond the season in which the request was received, including for the duration of a participant's LLI eligibility. If any waiver is approved by the Committee to extend beyond the season in which received, then the Committee shall identify the length and terms of such approval in the letter resolving the waiver request.

B. Materials Required for Committee's Consideration

In order to initiate review by the Committee, the child, his or her parent, or his or her legal representative, must deliver a written request for a waiver to the President of the local league. The child's waiver request shall include, at a minimum:

1. The child's name and level of play in the Little League program within which they wish to participate.

2. The child's current transcript and school registration information.

3. A written statement from a parent or legal representative of the child attesting to the fact that the child lives consistently in and outside of the home with his/her Gender Identity through their Gender Expression.

4. Written confirmation from a licensed, treating physician/psychologist or other health care provider that the child is receiving appropriate care and/or treatment as either a Transgender Person or person with DSD including when the child began such care and/or treatment.

5. Any other pertinent documentation or information (e.g. revised birth certificate or passport).

C. Approval Process

Prior to participation, an athlete may seek review of his or her eligibility through the procedure set forth below. Once the waiver materials are assembled on behalf of the child, the request will be evaluated as follows:

1. All communications, discussions and documentation submitted as part of this Approval Process shall be kept confidential, unless the child and family elect to make these records open and available.

2. All medical information provided pursuant to this policy shall be treated as confidential, shared only with individuals identified as taking part in this Approval Process and shall be appropriately protect from disclosure.

3. The child, or his or her representative, shall deliver the materials required by subpart B of this Procedure to the President of the local league.

4. The President may add additional facts concerning the request received to the record for consideration by the Committee. Thereafter, the President shall forward the assembled materials to the Regional Director.

5. The Regional Director will present the waiver materials to the Committee for action.

6. The child's request to participate in a manner consistent with his/her gender identity will be scheduled for a review and eligibility before the Committee as expeditiously as reasonably possible. The Committee will inform the Regional

Director of its decision. The Regional Director will thereafter inform the President of the local league for dissemination to the participant.

D. Guidelines for Review

In order for the modification or waiver of a Rule to be approved, the Committee must first determine that the participant is living consistently with his/her Gender Identity. The Committee will rely heavily on the medical and/or psychological caregiver's input.

The Committee may consult with the participant, his or her representatives and the individuals listed above as part of the Approval Process. Should the Committee find that consultation with additional individuals (e.g. school officials, District Administrators, coaches), is necessary for the Committee to make an informed decision, the Committee will first seek a confidentiality waiver from the waiver applicant's legal guardian before any such consultation.

It is important to recognize that some transgender athletes may have undergone hormonal treatments or even surgeries, while others may not. This Policy and Procedure considers inclusion regardless of whether a transgender person has undergone any treatments or surgeries, recognizes that regulating access to LLI programs based on such medical treatment is not necessary, unfair and overly complicated for this age level of competition.

E. Permitted Time for Committee's Decision

Any child seeking a waiver request under this waiver procedure should submit the request prior to the season, but if that is not possible, it should be submitted within a reasonable time after contacting his or her local league. The goal is to complete the process so that if a wavier is granted, the child would have little or no delay in participating fully in the program.

A request shall not be considered fully submitted unless it contains all of the required contents. The Committee will strive to render a decision on all waiver requests within a reasonable amount of time, and all such decisions should be rendered no later than three (3) weeks after the request is fully submitted and received by the Committee.

STANDARDS FOR LIGHTING

Minimum standards are required for all lighting installations. Effective July 1, 1992, unless otherwise noted within these standards, any modification in existing lighting systems after this date must be done so as to result in a lighting system in compliance with current standards. To be in compliance, a system must meet all required, current minimum standards.

To review the current Lighting Standards in their entirety, please visit LittleLeague.org/LightingStandards.

COMMUNICATIONS AND LEAGUE PROMOTIONS

Successful communications in any organization helps cultivate and maintain the best image by not only encouraging better knowledge and understanding of the organization's goals, benefits and operation, but also to effectively keep your players, parents, volunteers, and community informed

In Little League, making sure that the program is known in the community will help earn the respect and support that is essential to successful league operations. To establish the league as an effective force and working agency of the people in the community requires an active avenue of communication, projected to those who serve as well as to reach all levels of community interest. That can come through working with the local news media, updating your own website and social media accounts, and keeping your parents and volunteers informed.

Communicating with Your League

Nearly all correspondence from Little League International, literature, handbooks, newsletters, and a variety of other communications is channeled to the league by way of the league president. It is important for leagues to ensure their officer information is updated in the Little League Data Center.

It is essential that the league president makes this information generally available to league personnel, parents, and in some instances to the public through news media or the league's online outlets.

People who are active in the local program — they range over many categories of volunteer service — should be kept up-to-date on the affairs of the league and the overall program. Their efficiency and contribution to the local program is impeded if they are not informed fully. Resources are available to help support local league operations on Little League University (LittleLeagueU.org).

Local leagues have an open line of communication to Little League International at all times and are urged to make use of it whenever necessary. The president and staff of Little League International welcome comment from local leagues as a means of providing mutually beneficial communication, as well as the Regional staffs.

Communicating with the Media

Little League is the biggest name in youth sports, and the general public and news media will want to know what's going on locally. One of the best ways to be an ambassador for your local league and Little League International is through communicating with the media and your community.

Identifying a person in your league to handle your public relations efforts is a great way to ensure that your league's news and events get to the local news media. Develop a media list of the best contacts at the various news outlets that cover your community, and be sure to send them media alerts prior to events and press releases. Getting the word out through the media about what you're accomplishing can help your league grow. You're encouraged to develop a positive, working relationship with the media. If a member of a news outlet contacts you about a sensitive situation, please contact your District Administrator or the appropriate Little League Regional Office. Sample media releases and templates can be found at LittleLeagueU.org.

News outlets are encouraged and permitted to cover local Little League events (write stories, take photos, and shoot video) regular season games, and tournament action. You're encouraged to help the media as much as you can with their coverage, while ensuring that at no times the media interfere with your game operations. Any time a member of the media wishes to conduct an interview with a Little Leaguer, the player's parent(s) and/or manager or coach must be present throughout the interview. Only working news photographers and videographers with proper news organization credentials are permitted on the field of play, subject to league approval (as noted in Rule 3.15) in any level of Little League Baseball and Softball. Such personnel should never be permitted in dugouts, nor anywhere on fair territory, and at no time should photographers or videographers interfere with game activity or pose a safety risk to players, volunteers, or themselves.

Remember, the words "Little League" should never be used as merely a descriptive term for all youthful athletic programs. Whenever they appear in print, the words "Little League" should always be capitalized or placed in quotes so as to maintain the trademark significance. A public relations director for a local league may wish to inform members of the media that "Little League" and "Little League Baseball" are listed in the Associated Press Stylebook and Libel Manual, and should never be used in reference to non-Little League activities. And, a news outlet can only use photos and video of your Little League activities for editorial purposes. Any promotional or paid usage must be submitted to Little League International for approval.

Communicating Through Online Media

Having a website and keeping it updated with information, important dates, contact information, game schedules and scores, and updates from Little League International is just one way to use online communications.

Another important online tool is social media. Creating a Facebook page or Twitter account for your league or district can help you connect with a broader audience. Keep your social media posts light and fun, with photos from your leagues, stories from the news, game schedules and results, and posts from Little League's social media. When you have urgent messages you need to communicate or events to promote, use social media as a tool to spread the word.

Remember, once it's posted on any website, that statement or image is public. Be careful when you're posting and make sure that you're reflecting your league in the most positive light and that you have permission to use the photo. If your community members start posting or tweeting about a specific issue, encourage them to contact the league via email or attend the next public meeting. Getting into a social media discussion that could become heated should be avoided.

With live-streaming becoming much easier to accomplish, local leagues may be interested in web-casting or live-streaming games through their own local league website, official social media account, or other digital platform. Leagues are permitted to stream/web-cast games through these league-owned platforms granted they follow all Little League policies regarding commercialization and trademarks.

Obtaining Approval to Use Personal Data & Participant/Volunteer Images

Leagues should have parents or guardians sign a model release each season. A generic sample model release can be found here: LittleLeague.org/ModelRelease. This release should give the league permission to photograph, video, or utilize the image or likeness of the player in initiatives that support the growth and promotion of the league and its activities through any advertisements or social media sites. Such use should only grant permission to the league not to any other entity.

The league must also adopt a policy for use of any personal information including images, video, etc., to protect the privacy of the individual participants and their families. The policy must follow Little League International's Privacy Policy (LittleLeague.org/PrivacyPolicy) and associated guidelines. At no time should the league share information with any third parties, unless required by law.

If a league or district chooses to enter into an agreement with a photographer or videographer for a game, tournament, or other league event, Little League International recommends that a formal agreement be arranged between the League and the photographer/videographer, and that all financial aspects of the agreement be fully understood by all parties. It is recommended that model releases be secured from participants before such an agreement is procured.

Game Broadcasting and Streaming

Little League International in South Williamsport, Pa., is the only body that can authorize or disallow the live streaming, webcasting, televising, or radio broadcasting of any game(s) for regular season or tournament play through any outlet that is not fully owned and/or operated by a local league. A contract (provided by Little League International) must originate with the local District Administrator, tournament director, or local Little League president. (See Regulation XV.)

No telecast, broadcast, webcast (recorded or live) of any Little League Baseball or Softball game (in any division) can take place unless the proper contract is completed and approved. This applies to all productions, even if they are unsupported by advertising, sponsorship, or subscriptions. The financial aspect of any telecast, broadcast, webcast (recorded or live) should be fully understood by all parties.

To download a contract for games below the Regional level, visit LittleLeague.org/GameContracts.

For the Regional and World Series tournament levels, all contacts must be originated by the Little League International Communications Department in South Williamsport. Contact Chris Downs, Director of Constituent Communications, 570-326-1921, Ext. 2238; cdowns@LittleLeague.org.

For local leagues, districts, and media personnel, Little League International has guidelines regarding how Little Leaguers should appear in newspapers, on television, in magazines, etc. To download a PDF file of the document, visit LittleLeague.org/Media.

Non-Editorial Media Request

If any business or entity contacts your league about participating in a promotion, commercial, documentary, or anything outside of editorial coverage of your events or games, please note that you must seek approval from Little League International prior to participating in any paid, promotional activity, that identifies your league or shows any Little League logos, patches, or other marks.

WEBSITES

Local League or District Websites

Local leagues and Districts are permitted to host websites that assist with communicating information about their activities in the local community. The local league name, affiliation with Little League, registration, facilities locations, board members, schedules, and other information for parents and volunteers to contact the league should be clearly stated on the website.

Any league or district that wishes to host a website, which includes Little League Trademarks in any manner must submit their website address (www.) or URL (Universal Resource Locator) into the Little League Data Center annually. The URL should be a combination of a league or district's name in conjunction with the words "Little League" or "LL." An example of how a URL should appear: www.HometownLittleLeague.org or www.PA50LittleLeague.org.

Use of the Little League Trademarks, logos, and links to LittleLeague.org are permitted on websites operated by local leagues or districts, however, permission must be granted in advance by contacting Marketing@LittleLeague.org. Under no circumstances may a league, district, or person register a website using the words Little League for any other purpose other than to represent and support their local league or district. This includes websites set-up for the purposes of raising funds such as crowdsourcing websites. If teams within local leagues also host websites, they are required to follow these guidelines and the guidelines for use of Little League Trademarks. Team URLs are not required to be submitted to Little League International. Leagues and teams should not use any commercial entity in their league URL. It is strongly encouraged that local league board members visit the websites of their associated teams to ensure content being distributed is deemed appropriate for children in the Little League program.

Should a league elect not to re-charter or change its affiliation, the league is responsible for transferring any domain name containing Little League to Little League International at the local league's expense.

Leagues are also encouraged to secure model releases as part of the player and volunteer registration process. This allows leagues to host images or video of players participating in league activities.

Little League reserves the right to review any league or district website that uses Little League Trademarks and logos to ensure appropriate permissions from those individuals is granted. It is recommended that you incorporate the Little League Model Release (LittleLeague.org/ModelRelease) as part of the player registration process. Little League reserves the right to require a league to remove content on local league websites, including its social media sites if content is deemed inappropriate.

Official Technology Partners and Provisions for Local League and District Websites and Online Registration Services

Little League has partnered with DICK'S Team Sports HQ powered by Blue Sombrero as the official partner for local league technology services. DICK'S Team Sports HQ works with leagues and districts to provide free websites, free online registration, and many other appropriate technology services that can enhance the administrative functions for local leagues. While leagues are not required to use DICK'S Team Sports HQ, they are strongly encouraged to consider their services.

Additional information on use of websites, online registration, and other technology can be found on LittleLeague.org/Technology.

Local League or District Online Stores (E-Commerce)

Local Leagues may desire to offer apparel, uniforms, and other products to their league membership using an online store to conduct business. This type of activity involves the use of Little League trademarks and must be approved by Little League International.

Therefore, Little League maintains relationships with technology service providers, including DICK'S Team Sports HQ, who may offer this service. Such providers may be found at LittleLeague.org/Technology.

Before utilizing a service, leagues should contact Marketing@LittleLeague.org for more information and guidelines. **NOTE:** For more information regarding use of Little League trademarks in relation to local league fundraising and the solicitation of donations for regular season and tournament, please consult the Little League Operating Policies and LittleLeague.org for additional guidance.

LITTLE LEAGUE TRADEMARKS

Little League Baseball, Incorporated, more commonly referred to as "Little League", is a federally-chartered corporation to which Congress has granted the exclusive right and owner of the following trademarks, service marks and other designations: LITTLE LEAGUE, LITTLE LEAGUER, LITTLE LEAGUE BASEBALL, BIG LEAGUE LITTLE LEAGUE BASEBALL, SENIOR LEAGUE LITTLE LEAGUE BASEBALL, LITTLE LEAGUE SOFTBALL, LITTLE LEAGUE CHALLENGER DIVISION, LL, LLB, International Tournament marks, and the Little League Emblems or logos (e.g. keystone patch; Character, Courage and Loyalty logo; oval baseball and oval softball logos), among others. Collectively these are referred to as the Little League Trademarks, which identify the program, its products, and its services in the United States and other countries including Mexico, Canada, Japan, Australia, among others. Whenever the words Little League appear online or in print, the Little League Trademarks should always be capitalized and refer only to the activities of Little League.

Local League Use of the Words "Little League"

Local leagues receive permission per the annual charter agreement process to use Little League Trademarks in connection with authorized local league activities as described in THE OFFICIAL REGULATIONS, or in the OFFICIAL RULES of the Little League® Rulebook.

This permission, which is effective only while a league remains chartered, includes the right to use Little League Trademarks as part of the local league name, and to use that trademark and the Little League Emblems or logos on uniforms, in press releases issued by the local league, in programs, and at the local league facilities on scoreboards, and other signs. All such uses of Little League Trademarks must include the local league name such as the city, town or other similar reference. The local league may choose to design a logo to represent the league. Such logo may contain the words Little League in conjunction with their local league program. When considering a logo for the local league, please reference Rule 1.11(e) regarding uniform requirements and restrictions.

Limitations of Using the Words "Little League"

Chartered leagues may not use the Little League Trademarks in connection with any other activity or program, or as a part of a composite name covering unrelated programs.

The Little League Trademarks may not, for example, appear on the league website, flyers, commercials, print advertisements, social media posts, or press releases of other sports organizations, commercial enterprises, or businesses. For example, the local league should not grant permission to a local business to advertise its association with the local league whereby the local business directly profits from the use of the name.

Further, the Little League Trademarks may not be used separately or in connection with the name of any other program or activity for the purpose of soliciting funds to be used for activities other than Little League activities. **NOTE:** Special conditions apply for leagues that operate their program in connection with a Parks and Recreation Department. However, all policy requirements regarding trademarks apply.

If you identify a situation where a league or individual is using the trademarks of Little League in a manner you believe violates Little League trademark rights, please contact Licensing@LittleLeague.org.

Soliciting Funds Using the Words "Little League"

The use of the Little League Trademarks by any person, organization, business entity, or league not chartered by Little League or in an unauthorized manner is an infringement of Little League Trademark rights.

It is the policy of Little League International not to endorse any company, commercial product, or service with the exception of those items of approved playing equipment and other materials and entities associated with Little League International. Any use of the Little League Trademarks, unless expressly granted by Little League International, which falsely tends to imply such an endorsement is an infringement.

Additionally, local leagues and Districts that operate under a tax exempt non-profit status must be in compliance with their specific state requirements for charitable solicitations among non-profits. Additional steps may be required of leagues or districts before you are permitted to solicit funds in the name of the league in your local community. Such guidelines also may pertain to games of chance, raffles, crowdfunding, sponsorship, and other contests that are used as fundraisers.

Be sure to check your individual state laws or other requirements regarding fundraising and be sure that you adhering to these guidelines with all activities. Helpful resources can be found by searching LittleLeagueU.org for "state laws fundraising."

Restricted Use of "Little League" By Third Parties

Under no circumstances may local leagues, District Administrators, or other field personnel permit the Little League Trademarks (which includes the words Little League®) to be used on or in connection with any business products or services. The local league does not have the right to permit, transfer, or assign use of Little League Trademarks to any third party entity for any purpose, even if the third party has made a donation to the league. This includes the use of International Tournament marks.

Further, the Little League Trademarks are representative of specific baseball and softball programs chartered with Little League International and should not be used as merely a descriptive term for all youth athletic programs.

Exploitation of the Little League program, a league, a team, or individual players, for the benefit, financially or otherwise, of an individual or a business will not be condoned. Leagues which permit any type of exploitation run the risk of losing their charter.

Licensed and Approved Products/Partners

Little League International encourages all leagues and its members to use the partners of Little League International, including licensed partners, to produce any special goods, products and/or fundraising requests that could benefit the local league.

If producing pins, a Little League vendor must be used*. A list of approved licensed partner and further information can be found here: LittleLeague.org/Licensing. If producing trophies or awards, leagues and districts are encouraged to use an approved licensed partner of Little League.

Such partners are familiar with policies regarding Little League Trademark usage and protection of Little League trademarks. If you have questions regarding the production of trophies, awards or other products, please contact the Little League Licensing Department for more information at Licensing@LittleLeague.org.

There may be a situation in which a league or district cannot use a licensed partner to meet a specific need. In these situations, Little League International may permit a single-use agreement be completed. A single-use agreement, which may be granted on occasion would permit a league or district to use a supplier outside of our licensed partner. Such an agreement must be obtained from the Little League Licensing Department prior to logo use.

A league or district can request the usage of said Little League trademarks in various capacities, however, the understanding is that Little League Trademarks are only dispersed to any other party with the consent of Little League International. It is also understood that the outside supplier may not utilize the marks for financial gain. For more information on obtaining a single-use agreement, please email Licensing@LittleLeague.org. Forms can also be found on LittleLeague.org/Licensing.

*International leagues are encouraged to use a licensed vendor. However, if such vendors cannot meet international requirements, please contact Licensing@LittleLeague.org to obtain a one-time use agreement for country-specific vendors.

Guidelines for Local League Fundraising and Sponsorship

Donors and sponsors of teams at any level of the Little League program should be motivated by the single objective of making a worthwhile community contribution and help make their community a better place in which to live. Sponsorships should be positioned as donations to the local league. Local leagues must recognize that they have a responsibility to the local community to see to it that funds collected in the name of the league are used for league purposes and not for any other purpose. Further, great care must be taken to assure that such funds are not misappropriated or misused.

Sponsorship of local leagues is an important way for local Little Leagues to raise funds for operations. It must be understood, however, that sponsorship donation does not give the sponsoring entity any rights in the operation of the league or any team, nor does it give the local league sponsor the right to use Little League trademarks in any way. For example, such prohibited use includes giving a local business entity the right promote the local league in the advertising, commercials, or public relations in any manner. The local league must conduct its own recognition efforts for any and all promotion of activities related to the local league operations. By way of example, a local car dealership provides a cash and equipment donation to a local league. The local league must do its own press release or announcement to recognize the donation.

The league may not take any sponsorships; advertisements, such as lettering on uniforms, fence signs, program ads, website, etc.; conduct any raffles or contests; or have any affiliation with sponsors, donors, or products that relate to or reference alcohol; tobacco products; e-cigarettes; vaping; marijuana or other controlled substances; firearms; gambling; or adult content. Leagues and Districts should carefully evaluate donations and sponsorships, avoiding those which may, according to local community standards or local league membership, be objectionable or offensive. Additional standards for sponsorship may be set by the local Little League. Little League International reserves the right to restrict a local league or District sponsorship that may be deemed offensive or inappropriate for affiliation with the Little League program.

Little League International also reserves the right to prohibit any local Little League or District from accepting a sponsorship, advertisement, or donation if it deems that the sponsor, advertiser, donor, or its products or services are considered offensive or inappropriate to members of the Little League program or if it violates the provisions of the following statement: Little League does not limit participation in its activities on the basis of disability, race, creed, color, national origin, gender, sexual preference, or religious preference.

While the league or district may implement fundraisers for membership to implement, individuals who do not want to participate, should be given an alternative way to provide fundraising support in order to compensate the league for fundraising donations. No league can deny participation to a player or volunteer in regular season or tournament due to lack of fundraising support.

Local Leagues should also maintain similar guidelines for fundraising during Tournament. Statements noted above apply to local league fundraising at all times throughout the year, including during the International Tournament. Additional information on fundraising guidelines for tournament can be found at LittleLeague.org/TournamentFundraising.

General Fundraising Guidance

Leagues should rely on their District Administrators for guidance on local league fundraising plans. District Administrators are urged to establish communication with their leagues in order to (a) give the leagues the benefits of their experience with proposed fundraising efforts, and (b) to pass on to them the experience of other leagues in similar ventures. Guidance should be provided on fundraising plans and efforts to gather funds from within the boundaries of the local league.

It is customary to formalize an agreement for sponsorship with local businesses. Such an agreement should not put any burden or liability on the league, nor should it grant permission to the business to use any Little League Trademarks. An example of a local league sponsorship agreement can be found at LittleLeague.org/SponsorshipAgreement.

At times, leagues may be asked to indemnify or insure a sponsor for their activities with the league. Leagues should carefully review all provisions of any agreement before signing. Local leagues are not responsible for taking on the liability of the activity of a sponsor, even if that sponsor is supporting a local Little League or is associated with the league through a sponsorship agreement.

On occasion it has come to the attention of Little League International that leagues have been victimized by participating in fundraising plans proposed by outsiders as an easy means to obtain necessary funds. They run a wide gamut but essentially they involve the designation of a company to act as an agent of the local league, authorizing the company to contact businesses or members of the public in behalf of the local league. It involves the solicitation of donations or sponsorships, the sale of goods, of advertising space, of magazines, photographs or consists simply of a solicitation of funds on a straight contribution basis.

The use of a third party company to raise funds, solicit sponsorships, or conduct general marketing or public relations efforts is discouraged and typically results in an inappropriate use of the Little League trademarks or an inappropriate amount of funds being generated for the league. Additionally, no fundraising or sponsorship agreement should require the league to release any data on players, parents or volunteers of the league.

Without authority of any kind, some individuals or third parties are prone to represent themselves as agents of Little League because of the magic of the name to solicit payment in the name of Little League and obtain checks made out to the local Little League. The local league has little control over such situations, and such abuses come to their attention or Little League International after the damage has been done.

The endorsing and cashing, in this manner, of checks made out to Little League may well constitute fraud or forgery.

Make this a subject for league meetings. Request your volunteers notify you of any proposed money-raising plan involving outsiders. Examine the proposal, the need for a signed agreement or contract, and make certain there is no possibility that funds will be collected from within the boundaries of neighboring leagues. Please contact Little League International with any questions at Marketing@LittleLeague.org.

CROWDFUNDING OR OTHER ONLINE FUNDRAISING

This policy is in regard to the use of any form of crowdfunding service or website-based platform for the financial benefit or gain of any level of Little League (i.e., local, district, state, provincial).

Crowdfunding can be defined as, the use of small amounts of capital from a large number of individuals to finance a project, business venture, or to fundraise for a specific cause or charity. Through the use of personal networking, social media platforms, and other internet based resources, funds can be raised to support these different campaigns or efforts from a grassroots level, such as a local Little League.

Per the Little League Operating Policies, charitable funding and contributions can be collected through web-based crowdfunding platforms, so long as standard Little League policies are followed when utilizing this means of charitable fundraising. Current policies state that in no manner should there be any solicitation by a third party or individual in the name of or on behalf of a local league; solicitation of funds is to be done by the league or district itself. Therefore, only the Local League Board of Directors may operate a crowdfunding campaign using the name of the league.

In addition, the use of any Little League registered logos and trademarks must be used in connection with the local league name, and should not be misrepresented or altered in any way, without first contacting Little League International. It's also important to keep in mind as with any league or district fundraiser that any promotion of the effort must be done by the league or district itself and not any outside entity such as local businesses or individual donors. Donations that are collected through this method should not be for any personal or business gain, but strictly to assist youth and to strengthen the community program.

While this may potentially be a way for a league or district to fundraise, it may not always be the most cost effective method of generating funding. When looking into different options related to crowdfunding, please be sure to investigate all the potential drawbacks that may impact the league or district's ability to collect the funds associated with a crowdfunding campaign. Because of the ease of creation of one of these crowdfunding campaigns, local leagues and districts should also closely monitor for individuals fraudulently misrepresenting themselves as a fundraising entity.

Local League or District Online Stores/Fundraising (E-Commerce)

Local Leagues may desire to offer apparel, uniforms and other products to their league membership using an online store to conduct business. This type of activity involves the use of Little League trademarks and must be approved by Little League International.

Such sites are typically not as financially beneficial to leagues as they may appear. Therefore, Little League maintains relationships with technology service providers who may offer this service. Such providers, which includes DICK'S Team Sports HQ, may be found at LittleLeague.org/Technology. Before utilizing a service, Leagues should contact Marketing@LittleLeague.org for more information and guidelines.

NOTE: For more information regarding use of Little League trademarks in relation to local league fundraising and the solicitation of donations, please consult the Little League Policies and Principles section of the Official Playing Rules of Little League and LittleLeague.org for additional guidance.

HIT. FIELD. *INSPIRE.*
RUN. TEACH. LAUGH.
SUPPORT. CELEBRATE.
COACH.

Tips, Tutorials, Training and More!

LittleLeague.org/University/Coaches